WHEN I GROW UP...

The Community Helper Resource Book

Dayle Timmons and Kerry Rogers

Fearon Teacher Aids

Lovingly dedicated

to children who love and want to grow up to be teachers . . .
and to teachers who grow up keeping the joy of a child inside.

Especially to our own children—Wesley, Courtney, Matthew,
Maggie, and Ryan—who continue to grow up before our very
eyes and fill us with love . . . and to our husbands, Jim and Rick,
who keep us young and refuse to ever grow up!

With thanks to each of the following for their continued support and many contributions: Jerry and Barbara Barr, Jackie Crandall, Laura Crooks, Bonnie Davis, Maree Dawkins, Kathy Ford, Kim Forrester, Kathy Grimm, Beverly and Robert Grunwald, Kurt and Kyle Grunwald, Donna Kellam, Jane Marinella, Carey McDonald, Karen McClure, Sandy Mesiano, Suzanne Oaks, Orvilla Rogers, Debbie Schaeffer, Mary Jane Travis, Barbara and Michael Williams, and Ann Winfry.

Executive Editor: Jeri Cipriano
Editor: Susan Eddy
Inside Design: Diann Abbott
Cover and Inside Illustration: Tracy LaRue Hall

FEARON TEACHER AIDS
An Imprint of Modern Curriculum
A Division of Simon & Schuster
299 Jefferson Road, P.O. Box 480
Parsippany, NJ 07054-0480

ISBN: 0-86653-861-5

1 2 3 4 5 6 7 8 9 MAL 01 00 99 98 97 96

CONTENTS

INTRODUCTION

Who?
You!

When?
Now!

What?
Children have endless curiosity and profound imaginations. They have a desire to touch, inquire, and experience all new things. With a little imagination and creativity, you can turn areas of your classroom, such as the home living and writing centers, into something new and different that will support and enhance your themes or curricula. These centers can actually become grocery stores, bakeries, hospitals, or post offices.

Why?
Research tells us that children learn best through play. What better way for children to experience occupations and potential career choices than through dramatic creative play?

There are four important reasons to include community simulations in your classroom activities. The primary reason is to build knowledge and awareness of various community occupations. The second is that these career centers will immediately provide new interest in old familiar areas. The third reason is the opportunity to enhance vocabulary and enrich language skills in a fun way. Suddenly children are using new words because they are necessary and meaningful to their play. And fourth, the centers provide natural opportunities to practice social skills.

How?

Many schools are committed to a thematic, whole-language approach. A career center provides not only an area of interest but also a foundation for individual and group activities throughout the classroom. Here's how to get started.

1. Select a theme from the ten provided or let your imagination be your guide. Go through the list on page 6 and envision the possibilities.
2. Set up the main dramatic play area with supporting props and costumes.
3. Brainstorm activities from those provided to support and enhance the dramatic play area. Keeping your entire room focused on the theme offers continuity as well as a complete study of the topic. Use your imagination to create centers with full-filled experiences that help teach your objectives. The thematic web on page 7 will help you plan a balanced range of activities. The possibilities are endless!

CAREER CENTERS TO CONSIDER

Post Office
Grocery Store/Fruit Stand
Police Station
Hotel/ Motel
Baseball/Basketball/Soccer Park
Hardware Store
Fix-it/Appliance Repair Shop
Airport
Car Wash/Gas Station/Minute Mart
Space Shuttle
Farm
Beach
Art Studio/Gallery
Photography Studio
Movie Theater
Bottling Plant
Office Building
Building Under Construction
Carpentry/Lumber Yard
Florist/Flower Mart
Greenhouse
Dentist Office
Pharmacy/Drug Store
Hospital

School
Bank
Department Store
Mall (different stores)
Shoe Store/Shoe Repair
Election Center
Factory (kinds in your community)
Barber/Hair Styling Salon
Fire Station
Toy Store
Fast Food Restaurant
Ice Cream Parlor
Bakery
Seafood Restaurant
Ethnic Restaurant
Veterinarian's Office
Pet Store
Zoo
Carnival/Fair/Circus
Radio/Television Station
Dance Studio/Fitness Center
Cleaning Service
Day Care Center
Library

THEMATIC WEB

Use this web to help you design a career classroom for an area or occupation not highlighted in this book.

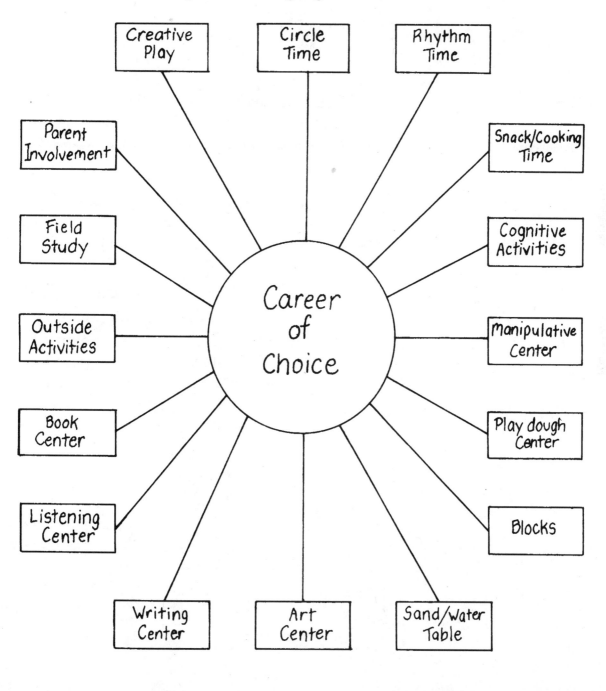

Bakery

Creative Play

Set up your bakery in or near the home living center. You can make use of the dishes, stove, refrigerator, table and chairs, and other items that are part of the kitchen.

Set up the bakery in an area where you can use play dough. Protect the carpet if necessary. See the recipe on page 12 and the ideas in the play dough section that follows. Having play dough available is what brings this center to life!

A bookshelf may be used to display baked goods that are for sale. You may wish to use a puppet theater for the bakery window. Cover the opening with plastic wrap and place play dough pastries in the window. Choose a name for the bakery and invite children design a sign to go over the window.

Plastic Wrap

Tagboard

Place a rocking boat on its side to make a check-out counter or use a box, desk, or small table. Have a cash register and play money available. Supply grocery bags or containers for purchased baked goods. Often, a local super market or bakery is happy to donate these.

Collect pots and pans, mixing bowls, empty spice containers, funnels, measuring spoons and cups, muffin tins, pie plates, cupcake liners, cookie cutters, tongs, cookie sheets, spatula, rolling pin, garlic press, doilies, birthday candles, and anything else that might be used to make doughnuts, cakes, cookies, pastries, bread, pies, and muffins.

Add a pad and pencil to encourage children to take orders and index cards to encourage children to write their own recipes.

Add a sign that says OPEN on one side and CLOSED on the other to hang at the bakery entrance. Use the pattern below or invite children to create their own.

Add simple cake-decorating books and children's cookbooks to the creative play area to encourage children to make bridges from the spoken to the printed word.

Read a version of the story of the gingerbread boy, such as *The Gingerbread Boy* by Paul Galdone or *The Gingerbread Man* by Joyce Evans, to the class. This story is a children's classic because of the repetition of language and plot.

Make your own flannelboard set to illustrate the story of the gingerbread boy or use the commercial set available from Judy/Instructo.

The gingerbread boy is a wonderful story for children to act out. Invite them to divide the room into areas that match the settings in the story. Children may volunteer for each of the parts.

Consider making real gingerbread or gingerbread cookies from scratch or from a mix.

For additional center ideas, look for *Gingerbread Man: A Developmental Unit for Preschool and Kindergarten*, #CD-0842, a "Stick Out Your Neck" book from Carson-Dellosa that contains many teaching ideas correlated to the gingerbread theme.

Play Dough Center

Invite children to help you make your own play dough using the recipe on page 334. Add some special scents. For example, add strawberry to red

play dough, cinnamon to any color, or lemon to yellow play dough. Or you might add a little dry jello to the play dough mixture for smell and color. For example, use cherry with red play dough or lime with green.

- Put out plenty of play dough in several colors. Use complementary colors, such as red, yellow, orange, so that as the play dough inevitably gets blended, children will still have a nice color.

- Provide a set of alphabet cookie cutters with the play dough. Encourage children to use the cookie cutters to write their names, names of other children in the classroom, and words from this unit.

- Make "cookies" with play dough. Add things such as cookie cutters, a rolling pin (a cylinder block makes a fine substitute), and cookie sheets (or flat pieces of cardboard covered with aluminum foil).

- Give children some muffin or mini-muffin liners for a muffin/mini-muffin pan. Have children fill muffin liners with cupcake play dough and use another color play dough for icing. A few straws cut in half, coffee stirrers, or toothpicks make good candles for birthday cakes or cupcakes. Use baker's dough, which hardens, or regular play dough to make cupcakes for display in the bakery window (see recipe on page 334).

- Save disposable pie pans, all sizes, (and ask parents to save them) for this unit. Encourage children to make "cherry," "blueberry," and "plum" pies. Invite them to make small red play dough balls for cherries, blue balls for blueberries, and purple balls for plums and cover the "fruit" with brown or tan

play dough "crusts" rolled out with a rolling pin or long cylinder block.

 Have the children try making doughnuts to harden using baker's dough (see recipe on page 334). Roll play dough into fat ropes and join the ropes into circles or use a doughnut cutter. When the doughnuts harden, use colored glue to decorate the doughnuts or make your own colored glue by adding food coloring or coloring paste to regular white glue. Real candy sprinkles may be added as decorations. Display the hardened doughnuts on cookie sheets in the bakery. Items made for display will look attractive placed on doilies.

 Make "gingerbread cookies" using edible peanut butter play dough. Use the following recipe for every two children in your class. Collect gingerbread cookie cutters of different sizes. They are easy to find around Christmas time. Roll out the play dough with a rolling pin or long cylinder wooden block and cut with gingerbread cookie cutters. Place on cookie sheets. Use raisins to add eyes, noses, mouths, buttons, or whatever details children think appropriate. Eat and enjoy!

Peanut Butter Play Dough

4 tsp. peanut butter	4 tsp. honey
powdered milk	a pinch of ginger

Mix ingredients with hands, adding powdered milk a little at a time until mixture does not stick to your fingers.

Circle Time

 Start with what children know. Ask who cooks at their houses and what their favorite meals are. Invite them to share their own cooking experiences. Ask if they have visited a bakery or ordered a birthday cake. Build on their knowledge to explain the role of the baker.

 Ask children if there is anything they would like to know about the bakery. Put yourself in the learner role and share with children something you would like to learn. Make a list of 3–5 things that you all would like to find out while working on this unit. Discuss with children ways they might find out this information. For example, they might ask a baker, visit a bakery, or look in a book. Be sure to include these opportunities as you plan your unit.

 Use the bakery vocabulary frequently—for example, dough, ingredients, recipe, pastries. Look in magazines and bakery advertisements for pictures that clearly illustrate each word. After children have learned the word for each picture, display the pictures with words written underneath in the writing center.

 Help children list all the things they can think of that are baked at a bakery—for example, fancy cookies, muffins, doughnuts, cinnamon rolls, bread, cakes, pies, birthday cakes, and biscuits. Children may list specific types, such as sugar cookies and chocolate chunk cookies. Look for pictures in magazines or go to a bakery and take photographs to illustrate each item. Glue the picture next to its title.

 Don't forget the baking verbs, such as pouring, mixing, measuring, and baking. Look for suitable illustrations or take photographs of individual children acting them out. Bind the photographs into a class book for the book center. On each page write the appropriate words under the photograph.

Matthew pouring.
Wesley measuring.
Ryan mixing.
Courtney stirring.
Maggie beating.

 Teach children the vocabulary of the baker's tools. Dress in a baker's hat and white apron carrying a large mixing bowl or pot. Use a large cooking pot with a top or a large mixing bowl covered with a dish towel as a "mystery box." Place items in the pot that are used in cooking, such as an apron, measuring spoons, measuring cup, spatula, can opener, egg beater, or muffin tin. Go through your own kitchen drawers and choose items that you use often. Add new items as children master the vocabulary. Discuss with them how each item is used.

 Use the items above and the large cooking pot or covered bowl to reinforce memory skills. Start with three items that children have learned to identify and play "What's missing?" Show the three items to the children and invite them to identify each one. Then ask them to close their eyes while you remove one. Children open their eyes and guess which item is missing. Make the game more difficult by adding more items or by hiding two items instead of one.

 Discuss with children the difference between a chef (who cooks in a restaurant) and a baker (who cooks pastries and bread in a bakery).

Rhythm Time

 There are many songs, chants, and fingerplays in this unit that can be used to enhance reading skills. Write each of the rhymes on chart paper as you introduce them. Use two different color markers for the writing and alternate the colors for each line— for example, red for the first line, blue for the second line, red for the third line and so on. This will help reinforce top-to-bottom and left-to-right progression. Add simple pictures over key words to give children added clues. As you sing or say each rhyme, point to each word with a pointer. A wooden spoon makes a good pointer for this unit. After you have several rhymes around the room, put out some wooden spoons. Invite children to take one and "read the room." You will be amazed at the way in which children take the spoons and, following your example, go around "reading" the rhymes. This activity helps bridge the gap from the spoken to the written word.

 Teach children the nursery rhyme "Pat-a-Cake." A tune for "Pat-a-Cake" can be found on page 33 of *Wee Sing Nursery Rhymes and Lullabies.*

> *Pat-a-cake, pat-a-cake, baker's man,*
> *Bake me a cake as fast as you can;*
>
> *Roll it and pat it and mark it with a B,*
> *Put it in the oven for baby and me.*

 Give each child a spoon. Wooden spoons are great but any kind will do. Encourage children to keep a steady beat for the rhyme by sitting and beating their spoons on the floor. Later invite them to use the spoons and select something to do with baking, such as a pie tin, muffin pan, measuring cup, or pot, on which to keep a steady beat.

 More mature students might enjoy sitting opposite a partner and doing a hand rhyme. To do this, children slap knees with both hands, clap, touch right hands, clap, touch left hands, clap, and repeat to the steady beat. A simpler hand rhyme with a partner is clap, slap both hands with a partner, and repeat.

Once children learn the rhyme, have them try making the Baker Man Cakes in the Snack/Cooking section.

 Teach children the following original fingerplay.

Cookies, cakes, and pies
Are all favorites of mine. (rub tummy with hand)
Lick my fingers 1, 2, 3! (lick 1, 2, 3 fingers)
Tasty treats just for me! (point thumbs at self)

 Make a list of treats that the baker might make for dessert, such as cakes, pies, cupcakes, cookies. Children might list specific examples, such as chocolate chip cookies, but guide them into listing category names. Invite children to draw pictures of their favorite desserts on index cards. Make a graph with category names across the bottom and have children add their index card drawings to the appropriate column. Title the graph "Favorite Desserts." Discuss the results pictured on the graph with your class.

 Teach the following original lyrics to the tune of "I'm a Little Teapot."

I'm a little baker,
Short and fat,
Here is my spoon
And my big white hat.
When I'm all done mixing
I will bake
One delicious chocolate cake!

 Invite children to sing this song in their chef hats (see page 33). They may wish to act out the song by using a spoon.

 Make individual chocolate cakes or cupcakes from a mix with children. Reinforce vocabulary (pouring, mixing), math (measuring), and reading (recipe) as you bake the cakes. Invite children to frost their own chocolate cakes using plastic knives, craft sticks, or tongue depressors to spread the chocolate icing.

Right before serving the cakes, try this cheer.

Give me a C.
"C" (children's response)
Give me an A.
"A"
Give me a K.
"K"
Give me an E.
"E"
What have you got?
"Cake"
Say it again.
"Cake."
One more time!
"CAKE!"
Let's EAT!

 Teach the following lyrics to the tune of "Ten Little Indians."

1 little, 2 little, 3 little cupcakes,
4 little, 5 little, 6 little cupcakes,
7 little, 8 little, 9 little cupcakes,
10 little cupcakes baked.

Make a class book by using the following pattern or have ten children volunteer to draw a single cupcake each. Put one cupcake on each page with the appropriate words. Bind the book accordion-style so children can see the accumulation of cupcakes.

 Teach the class the song "Do You Know the Muffin Man?"

Oh, do you know the muffin man, the muffin man, the muffin man?
Oh, do you know the muffin man
Who lives on Drury Lane?

Oh, yes I know the muffin man, the muffin man, the muffin man.
Oh, yes I know the muffin man
Who lives on Drury Lane.

This song is acted out in the hour-long VHS video *Grandpa's Magical Toys* by Wee Sing. This is an excellent video for children able to enjoy one of this length.

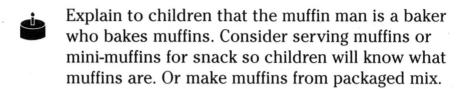 Explain to children that the muffin man is a baker who bakes muffins. Consider serving muffins or mini-muffins for snack so children will know what muffins are. Or make muffins from packaged mix.

Before serving mini-muffins, put some in a transparent container and challenge children to estimate how many muffins are in the container. Children may write their names and estimations on muffin shapes cut from construction paper. When estimations are complete, count out the muffins in front of the children. Discuss the differences between estimates and actual numbers using the vocabulary *more* and *less.*

Write the words *muffin man* on sticky notes. Have students match the words on the sticky notes to the words on the chart song. Count the number of times the phrase "muffin man" is used. Write a list of other "m" words that relate to this unit—for example, mixing, milk, M & M's, mixer, measuring spoons, measuring cups, mix, mash, margarine, meal, marble cake.

Challenge children to "change up" the song "Do You Know the Muffin Man?" by adding other verses, such as "Do you know the cupcake man?" or "doughnut man?" or "pastry man?" This may be facilitated by having the song printed on chart paper. Write the new words on sticky notes to place on top of "muffin man" words on the chart.

 Try teaching this cheer as children are learning to recognize the letters of the alphabet. Encourage children to dress up in baker's hats and aprons.

Give me a M.
"M" (children's response)
Give me a U.
"U"
Give me a F.
"F"
Give me another F.
"F"
Give me an I.
"I"
Give me an N.
"N"
What does it spell?
"Muffin"
Say it again.
"Muffin"
One more time.
"Muffin"
YUM! YUM! (rub tummy)

 Provide the letters for the word M-U-F-F-I-N on flashcards. Children may hold up each letter as you call it out.

Make a reusable class book to practice writing *muffin*. Write each letter on a separate page. Laminate the book and provide a wipe-off marker. Invite children to practice writing the appropriate letter on each page. After all the letters for muffin have been printed, children may wipe off the pages so the book is ready for the next child.

 Teach children this traditional fingerplay.

Three little muffins in the bakery shop! (hold up 3 fingers)
You know the kind with the honey and the nuts on
*   the top? (whisper)*

Along came a child with a penny to pay, (walk with
*   two fingers)*
And bought one muffin and ran away. (run in opposite
*   direction with same two fingers)*
And there were 2 . . .
And there was 1 . . .
And there were no . . .
and said, "WHAT? NO MUFFINS?"

You can start the fingerplay with any number. Try 5
or 10 with more mature students.

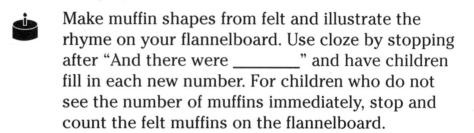

Make muffin shapes from felt and illustrate the
rhyme on your flannelboard. Use cloze by stopping
after "And there were _____" and have children
fill in each new number. For children who do not
see the number of muffins immediately, stop and
count the felt muffins on the flannelboard.

Write the fingerplay on a wall chart and point to
each word as you say it to help children make the
connection between the spoken and written word.
Use a wooden spoon or paper muffin liner attached
to the end of a dowel as a pointer. Leave the pointer
near the chart to encourage children to use it
independently as they say the rhyme.

Write the number words on sticky notes and
encourage children to put the appropriate number
"word" on the corresponding numeral on the chart.
Display a chart with numeral and number words
near this activity so children may "look up" their
answers. For example, 4 - four.

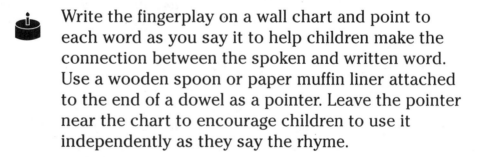

Here is another original rhyme to teach during this
unit.

Mix it, beat it, roll it into balls.
Making muffins for us all.
Place 'em in the muffin tins.

Bake 'em golden brown.
Everyone will love them in our town.

 Read to the class *If You Give a Moose a Muffin* by Laura Joffe Numeroff. This is a circle story that begins and ends with a muffin. Invite volunteers to illustrate the story. Give each one a small paper plate on which to illustrate one thing that happens in the story. Display the paper plates in sequence in a circle, clockwise, with the picture of the muffin at the top to illustrate that the story begins and ends with a muffin.

 Teach the chant and game " Who Stole the Cookies from the Cookie Jar?" The children sit in a circle. Choose one child to start. Keep the steady beat with your hands on your knees.

> *All: Who stole the cookies from the cookie jar?*
> *First child pointing: (Ryan) stole the cookies from the cookie jar.*
> *Ryan: Who me?*
> *All: Yes you.*
> *Ryan: Not me!*
> *All: Then who?*
> *Ryan pointing: Courtney stole the cookies from the cookie jar.*
> *Courtney: Who me?*
> *and so on.*

 Instead of having each child choose a friend to point to in the rhyme, put the names of all the children on cookie-shaped pieces of construction paper in a clear cookie jar and have each child pull out another child's name (to teach name recognition) or a picture of the child (make a supply of class pictures on the copy machine). This circle game is illustrated in the hour-long VHS video *Grandpa's Magical Toys* by Wee Sing.

 Put some ready-made mini-cookies in a clear cookie jar. Invite children to guess how many cookies are in the cookie jar (estimation). Give children pieces of construction paper in the shape of the cookie on which to write their names and how many cookies they think are in the jar. Graph the estimates on the bulletin board using the cookie shapes. After all the children have made a guess, count out the cookies in front of the group. Children may compare their guesses with the actual number of cookies. Use the vocabulary *more* and *less* to help them.

 Make one of the cookie recipes in the Snack/ Cooking section (see page 26).

 Give each child a chocolate chip cookie or M&M-type chocolate chip cookie. You can make these with the class or use a small bag of ready-made cookies (for younger children use mini-cookies). Invite children to guess how many chocolate chips or colored candy pieces will be found on most of the cookies. Write the estimates on sticky notes with the child's name and place the estimates on a cookie jar. Count the actual number of chocolate chips children see on each cookie (you might wish to count only the chips on the top of the cookie). Use the actual cookies in one small bag to make a large graph of the chocolate chip estimates. Discuss with children how their estimates compared to the actual number of chocolate chips. Have the cookies for snack.

 Read to the class *If You Give a Mouse a Cookie* by Laura Joffe Numeroff. This is a circle story that begins and ends with a cookie. Invite volunteers to

illustrate each of the events in the story on round cookie shapes cut from construction paper. Display the illustrations in the order of the story clockwise in a circle with the cookie picture at the top. This will illustrate for children that the story begins and ends with the cookie.

 Teach the children this delightful poem from our oral tradition.

> *I had a nickel and I walked around the block.*
> *I walked right into a bakery shop.*
> *I took two doughnuts right out of the grease;*
> *I handed the lady my five-cent piece.*
> *She looked at the nickel and she looked at me,*
> *And said, "This money is no good to me.*
> *There's a hole in the nickel and it goes right through."*
> *Says I, "There's a hole in the doughnut too!"*

 Emphasize something different in the words each time you read the poem. Stop often and use the cloze technique. Children will soon memorize the words.

 Invite two children to act out the poem. One child may play the bakery owner and the other has the five-cent piece. Use your "pretend" bakery as a backdrop for the scene.

Snack/Cooking Time

 If you have a daily snack time, be sure to use this opportunity to practice counting skills. Encourage children to count out the appropriate number of napkins, cups, and other items and then practice one-to-one correspondence by placing one of each

at every chair. This is a great cooperative group activity. If you give the same snack to all children, consider snacks that are easy to count, such as pretzels, small carrot sticks, mini-boxes of raisins, small cheese crackers, animal crackers. Ask children in turn how many they want and then encourage them to count out the appropriate number. This gives children practice in counting every single day.

 This is a great unit in which to do some cooking. Have children put on their chef hats and aprons and try some simple no-cook recipes. Be sure to reinforce math skills (measuring, identifying shapes), reading skills (reading recipes), vocabulary (identifying each cooking utensil you use, matching words to pictures), and science skills (identifying liquids/solids, dry/wet, hard/soft, hot/cold). Each cooking experience can be a complete lesson.

 Reinforce the idea of washing hands thoroughly before touching food.

 Provide a sequence of pictures with words underneath each picture to demonstrate the steps for the cooking project. Or, for more mature students, write the recipe on chart paper.

 Photograph children performing each step of a recipe. After the cooking is done, glue each picture to a larger card and encourage children to decide on captions. Individual children may sequence the pictures.

No-Cook Recipes

Easy Cookies

1 package of Fig Newtons™ (or any Newton-type cookie)
1 package confectioner's sugar

Cut each cookie into thirds. Pour sugar into a plastic zipper bag. Children may put the cut-up cookies into the bag of sugar and shake to their heart's content. Take cookies out of the sugar and enjoy.

Banana Nut Spread

3 bananas
6 Tbs. peanut butter
graham crackers

Help children mash bananas with a potato masher in a small bowl. Add the peanut butter and continue mashing. Spread on graham crackers. Makes 6 servings. Another option is for children to mix their own individual spread in a plastic bowl or cup. One serving is 1/2 banana and 1 Tbs. peanut butter.

Special Cookies

any type of plain cookies, such as sugar or peanut butter
    cookies
frosting, any flavor
an assortment of decorations, such as sprinkles, raisins,
    chocolate/carob pieces, mini-candy pieces

Give children one plain cookie each. They may spread the frosting with a plastic knife and add decorations as desired.

Baker Man Cakes

rice cakes, any flavor
frosting, any flavor, or cream cheese
an assortment of small decorations, such as sprinkles,
**   raisins, chocolate/carob pieces, mini-candies, peanuts**
tube icing (optional)

Provide children with their own "cake" made by the Baker
himself. Children may spread frosting with a plastic knife
and decorate as desired.

 Share one of your favorite recipes. If you have a stove, toaster oven, microwave, or single cooking unit in your room, consider a recipe that takes advantage of your appliance.

 Read *Thunder Cake* by Patricia Polacco—the delightful story of a Grandmother teaching her grandchild not to fear the loud thunder by gathering the ingredients for a cake before the storm comes. The end of the book provides a recipe for "Thunder Cake" which makes a wonderful rainy-day activity.

Cognitive Activities

 Cut pictures from magazines of pastries, cakes, pies, bread, and other bakery items. Invite children to classify the pictures by placing cookie pictures on a cookie sheet, pie pictures in a pie pan, bread pictures in a bread basket, and so on. After sorting all of the pictures, they may choose their favorite.

 Make cupcakes using the pattern on page 28 and cut between the icing and cake using pinking

shears. Write uppercase letters on the cake portion and lowercase letters on the frosting. Challenge children to put the uppercase letters in sequence and then find the matching lowercase "frosting" to put on top.

cut using
pinking
shears

 Make some round tan cookies from construction paper. Write a number on each cookie and laminate. Invite children to draw the appropriate number of chocolate chips on each cookie with a brown or black wipe-off marker or the appropriate number of M&M's using colored wipe-off markers. Check the work and then have children wipe off the marks for the next child.

 Use the baker's dough recipe on page 334 and alphabet cookie cutters, make a set of hard alphabet "cookies." Make several cookies for each letter. Trace around the cookies with a marker on construction paper to form words from this unit, such as *cookie* and *muffin,* and laminate. Encourage children to locate and place the appropriate letters to make each word. You might also wish to make cards for each child's name.

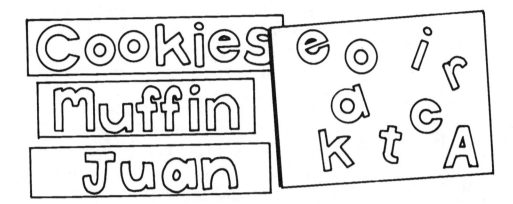

 Count candles on birthday cakes. Make cake shapes on 8–20 pieces of tagboard. Write a number on each card or leave the numbers blank. Encourage children to count the same number onto each card using candles for counters. Thicker candles will not break as easily as small birthday candles. Choose two different color candles for more mature students and challenge them to use the two colors to write addition problems.

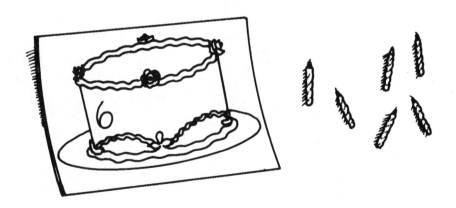

 Collect some small pie tins and write a number on the bottom of each tin. Use red pompoms to make cherry pies, blue pompoms to make blueberry pies, or purple pompoms to make plum pies. Children may count the appropriate number of "fruits" into each pie tin. Tan felt circles may be used for the top crust.

 Use the baker's dough recipe on page 334 to make hard "cookies" in graduated sizes. Look for sets of cookie cutters that have 3–7 graduated sizes, such as hearts, circles, or gingerbread men. Make cookies in graduated sizes and invite children to order the cookies by size. Use the vocabulary words large, small, big, little, first, last, same, different, first, second, third, fourth, fifth, or first, middle, last.

 Use baker's dough to make "cookies" for counting. Use assorted cookie cutters with interesting shapes and different colors of dough for variety. Work with children individually or in small groups. Call out a number and ask children to count that many cookies onto a paper or plastic plate. Or you might ask a child to count a certain number of cookies into your hand. Use other concepts as well, such as, "Please give me all the yellow cookies," "Show me the two largest cookies," or "Please give me the three smallest cookies." To teach other vocabulary, show children two plates and ask, "Which plate has more/less?" or "Which has many/few cookies?"

Manipulative Center

 Encourage children to fill pegboards with pegs. Use various size pegs, depending on the developmental level of the child. Tell children that these are candles on their birthday cake. When the pegboard is full, the child may bring it to you. Invite the child to sing "Happy Birthday to You" and then pretend to blow out the candles.

 Ask children their age and invite them to place the appropriate number of pegs (candles) in the pegboard (birthday cake). Encourage children to fill the pegboard in a two-part pattern, such as red, blue, red, blue, (ABAB), or more complex patterns for more mature students, such as ABB, AABB, AAAB, ABC.

Water/Sand Table

 There are many interesting things to add to your water table during your bakery study. A set of measuring cups, spoons, or funnels are inexpensive and can often be found at flea markets or dollar stores. Parents may also provide items to add to the assortment.

 An egg beater is fun, especially if you add a little liquid soap to the water!

 If you have a real sink area in your room, add a sponge, washing cloth, drying rack, and soap for washing the dishes. Add a little bit of soap to a lot of water in an empty plastic honey-bear squeeze

bottle—children are likely to use an entire bottle washing one sink of dishes! Children may wash all the dishes from the home living area or the pots and pans used for a class cooking project. Be sure to provide water shirts. If you don't have a sink area that you can turn over to the children, place a plastic tub in your water table and have children wash dishes in the tub. Position the drying rack beside the water tub inside the water table. In a pinch, a tub of soapy water on a towel on the floor will do the trick.

Save disposable pie pans to use with sand. Children will enjoy making pies and cakes using pegs or straws for candles. Save microwave muffin containers and other plastic and heavy cardboard microwave disposables as well for children to enjoy.

To provide a different experience, add a little water to the sand. Wet (or even slightly damp) sand can be used in jello molds, muffin tins and pie pans.

Add one bag of dried beans to your sand table. The beans make nice decorations for "cakes." Put a sand strainer or colander in the sand table so the children can separate the beans from the sand.

Place a sheet over the sand in your sand table and add a pan or bowl of flour and a flour sifter. The sheet will keep the sand undisturbed and keep you from having to empty it to enjoy another filler. A plastic pan filled with flour and a sifter could also be enjoyed outside.

Art Center

 Make a baker's oven collage. Cut a piece of construction paper to look like an oven with a cut-out in the center. Cover the cutout with plastic wrap so you can see what's cooking. Fill a page cut the same size with magazine pictures of things a baker might bake. Be sure that when you staple the pages together you can see through to a single picture. Open the oven to see what's cooking!

 Have children make their own white chef's hats following the diagram below. Discuss with children why bakers wear hats (to keep hair from falling in the food). Children may wear their hats in the bakery and while they are cooking.

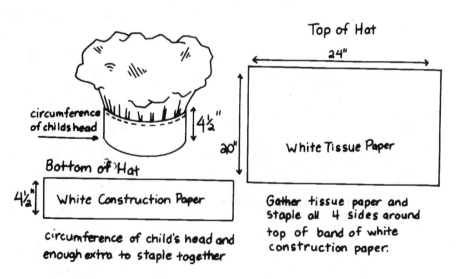

 Make cherry pies at the art table. Collect pie tins. Put some "cherries" in the bottom of each tin (red beads from your stringing beads or look for wooden bead garlands on sale after Christmas). Over the "cherries" add the "topping" (shaving cream or whipped topping). Invite children to put on paint shirts and find the "cherries" with their fingers. Children may count the found cherries and then hide them for the next child. Do this activity outdoors or cover a table with newspaper and place each "pie" on a large cookie sheet or tray.

 Make individual "cakes." Help children cut (on their own or from a pattern) cake shapes from construction paper. Give each child a doily to glue on for a cake plate. Children may use their imagination to add decorations using glitter, sequins, colored glue, small pompoms, and so on. Invite them to add the correct number of birthday candles.

 Children may make their own bakers from white construction paper using the pattern below. Add circle heads cut from pink or brown construction paper and invite children to add facial features, hair, and buttons with markers or crayons. White baker's hats may be cut from construction paper. Encourage each child to make or draw something a baker might make in his bakery and glue it to the baker's hand.

white construction paper

pink / brown construction paper

Writing Center

 Cut sheets of white paper in the shape of a chef's hat, cake, or mixing bowl. Staple several pieces together and invite children to print their names or simply decorate the outside of these booklets. Place them in the writing center and encourage children to draw pictures or write about their experiences using temporary, invented spelling and their own letters to express their thoughts. Children may also copy songs, fingerplays, recipes, or vocabulary words that are written around the room.

 If possible, use a different color sentence strip for each child. On the first strip write, "At the Bakery . . ." For each child, write the sentence "(Child's name) likes to bake _____." Children may complete the sentences and draw pictures on small index cards to illustrate what they would like to bake. Punch a hole in each strip and bind together with a metal ring binder and you have a class book for children to "read."

○ At the Bakery . . .

○ Courtney likes to bake _____.

○ Maggie likes to bake _____.

 Use permanent marker to draw simple pictures from this unit, such as a bowl, chef's hat, spoon, fork, knife, cake, or cookie, on a plastic laminate-topped table. Marker can be erased with hair spray, alcohol, or an abrasive dry powder. Write the word underneath the picture. Provide tracing paper so children can trace over the picture and word or regular white paper so children can copy them.

Use sentence strips to write the words that children will want to know and/or words that children ask you to spell. Keep them in a pocket chart. Invite individual children to illustrate each of the words on white paper or small index cards. Place each illustration beside the appropriate word.

Listening Center

- Tape children singing some of the songs and nursery rhymes in this unit. Provide a teacher- or child-illustrated book to go with each tape.

- Tape yourself reading *If You Give a Moose a Muffin* or *If You Give a Mouse a Cookie*, both by Laura Jove Numeroff, or buy the pre-recorded cassette. Provide the book with the tape.

- Other good stories to tape for listening include *The Baby Blue Cat and the Whole Batch of Cookies* by Ainslie Pryor, *Arthur's Christmas Cookies* by Lillian Hoban, *Jamberry* by Bruce Degen, and *The Cake That Mack Ate* by Rose Robart.

- Children will also enjoy hearing the classic tales of *The Little Red Hen* (available with pre-recorded cassette from Scholastic), *Pancake, Pancake!* by Eric Carle, or *The Gingerbread Man*.

- Collect several empty spice containers (you will need an even number) and cover with self-adhesive plastic so the contents may not be seen. Place things such as rice, a penny, or beans into each pair of containers. Children may shake the spice containers and decide which containers match.

Book Center

- Make an "ABC Bakery Book" with the class. Write letters of the alphabet down the left side of the

paper and challenge children think up words such as the following to go with each of the letters.

awesome apple pie	nutty nutbread
buttery biscuits	outstanding oatmeal cookies
cookies and cakes	perfect pecan pie
delicious doughnuts	quick quiche
excellent eclairs	remarkable raisin rolls
fantastic fudge	super strawberry shortcake
great garlic bread	terrific tarts
homemade honey bread	unusual upside-down cake
incredible icing	very vanilla pound cake
jazzy jelly roll	wonderful whole wheat bread
kwik krispie treats	eXtra good cherry pie.
lemon layer cake	yummy!
marvelous macaroons	zesty zoo crackers.

Write each phrase on a single sentence strip and invite volunteers to illustrate each one on small index cards. Glue illustrations to appropriate sentence strips. Add a sentence strip naming the title, authors, and illustrators. Alphabetize the strips and punch a hole at the left end of each one. Bind with a metal ring binder for a class sentence-strip book.

 Here are some books you may wish to place in your book center. Many of these are also appropriate for reading at circle time. Check your school or community library for other titles.

(ps-1) Degen, Bruce. *Jamberry*. Scholastic, Inc., 1983. Blueberry, strawberry, blackberry, raspberry—a nonsensical story with "berry" words and delightful illustrations. Also available in big-book format.

(ps-1) Henry, B. G. *Jake Baked a Cake*. Scholastic, Inc., 1990. In big-book format with rhyming words in each sentence/phrase. Great pictures of a baker baking a wedding cake.

(ps-1) Numeroff, Laura Joffe. *If You Give a Mouse a Cookie*. HarperCollins, 1985.
Relates the cycle of requests a mouse is likely to make after you give him a cookie. Cassette also available.

(ps-1) Numeroff, Laura Joffe. *If You Give a Moose a Muffin*. HarperCollins, 1991.
Sequel to *If You Give a Mouse a Cookie*. Chaos ensues if you give a moose a muffin and start him on a cycle of urgent requests.

(ps-1) Redhead, Janet Slater. *The Big Block of Chocolate*. Ashton Scholastic, 1988.
A big book of repetitious verse—the story of a chocolate bar put up safely for later, found by different animals, and then eaten by ants and savored thoroughly.

(ps-2) Barkan, Joanne. *Whiskerville Bake Shop*. Putnam, 1990.
Two little mice learn what goes on in a bakery.

(ps-2) Carle, Eric. *Pancake, Pancake!* Scholastic, Inc., 1990.
Jack wants pancakes for breakfast so his mother sends him to cut and grind the wheat into flour, gather the eggs, milk the cow, churn the butter, gather the wood for the fire, and so on—much like *The Little Red Hen*. Also available in big-book format.

(ps-2) Evans, Joyce. *The Gingerbread Man*. Developmental Learning Materials, 1982.
Delightful pictures illustrate this traditional story with a complete teaching guide.

(ps-2) Galdone, Paul. *The Gingerbread Boy*. New York, Clarion Books, 1975.
Well-told version of a classic cumulative tale of the ginger-bread boy that runs away from the oven and is finally eaten by a sly fox after a merry chase.

(ps-2) McQueen, Lucinda. *The Little Red Hen*. Scholastic, Inc., 1985.
Traditional story of the hard-working little red hen who makes bread with no help from her friends. When it comes to eating the bread, however, they all want to help. Also in big-book format. Cassette available.

(ps-2) Pryor, Ainslie. *The Baby Blue Cat and the Whole Bunch of Cookies*. Puffin, 1991.
Baby Blue Cat eats a whole batch of cookies that mother has fixed for all the kittens to eat after playtime and has to find a way to confess.

(ps-3) Berenstain, Stan and Jan. *The Berenstain Bears' Nursery Tales*. Random House, 1973.
Actually three traditional tales: "The Three Bears," "The Little Red Hen," and "The Gingerbread Man."

(K-2) Hoban, Lillian. *Arthur's Christmas Cookies*. HarperCollins, 1972.
Arthur mistakes salt for sugar and ruins the recipe.

(K-2) Kincaid, Lucy. *Little Red Hen*. The Rourke Corporation, Inc., 1983.
A "Now You Can Read. . ." book of the traditional story.

(K-2) Mayer, M. *Marcel the Pastry Chef*. Bantam/Little Rooster.
A hippopotamus tries to be a pastry chef in the king's kitchen, much to the cook's displeasure and the king's delight.

(K-2) Robart, Rose. *The Cake That Mack Ate*. Silver, Burdett and Ginn, 1989.
A delightful cumulative tale about a cake that the dog, Mack, ate.

(K-3) Berson, Harold. *The Boy, the Baker, the Miller and More*. Crown Publishers, 1974.
A circle story, beginning and ending with a piece of bread, and based on an old French folktale. In return for a piece of bread he requests from the baker's wife, a little boy is sent on an endless errand.

(K-3) Brown, Marcia. *The Bun*. Harcourt Brace Jovanovich, 1972.
The little bun rolls through the forest, merrily evading his hungry pursuers, until he is outwitted by the cunning fox. Children will enjoy comparing this story with one of the versions of "The Gingerbread Boy."

(K-3) Cook, Scott. *The Gingerbread Boy*. Alfred A. Knopf, 1987. Traditional story of the gingerbread boy who jumps from the oven and enjoys a merry chase until he is gobbled up by the sly fox. Lovely illustrations.

(K-3) de Paola, Tomie. *Tony's Bread*. Whitebird Books, 1989. Original folk story about Tony, the baker, who makes the best bread in all of northern Italy and marries off his daughter, Serafina, in the bargain.

(K-3) Lillegard, Dee. *I Can Be a Baker*. Childrens Press, 1986. Briefly describes the training and jobs of bakers. Good photographs of bakers at work.

(K-3) Polacco, Patricia. *Thunder Cake*. Scholastic, Inc., 1990. "Thunder cake" refers to stormy Michigan baking weather. The story tells how a Grandmother taught her young grandchild not to be afraid of thunder by preparing a cake before the storm came. Includes a recipe for "My Grandma's Thunder Cake."

Outside

 Make "mud pies." Place a pan of water in the sandbox. Add some pie tins, rocks (or smaller sticks) for decorations, and sticks for stirring.

Field Study

 Often doughnut shops will allow field trips to see the making of doughnuts. Check to see what is available is your area.

 Invite someone who decorates cakes to come in and demonstrate the craft (call a bakery for suggestions or check the yellow pages).

Tour the school cafeteria and have children watch dessert preparation.

Help children prepare something in the room to bake in the cafeteria oven or invite one of the cafeteria workers to your room to make cookies or some other special dessert with the children.

After the field study, invite children to draw something they remember seeing on the field trip. Encourage children to tell you about their pictures. Write down the descriptions and send the pictures and descriptions to the bakery to say thank you.

Take photographs on the field trip and display the pictures to remind students what they saw. Children may dictate captions for the pictures which can be bound into a class book. The book can be used the following year to illustrate words or as preparation for the same field trip.

Parent Connection

Encourage parents to help with the cooking experience by sharing with them some ways in which they can reinforce at home what you are doing in school. Consider the following letter.

Dear Parents,

We are studying about the bakery and the job of the baker. To help your children experience what they might have to do as bakers, we encourage you to try cooking with your child this week. Children might help make cookies or dessert for supper or something for the class snack. Don't try anything too difficult. Keep it simple and be sure to talk about all the things that you use, such as the recipe, measuring cups, spoons, cookie sheet, oven, or whatever. Most of all, enjoy the time together!

Happy cooking!

Post Office

Creative Play

 The writing center is a good place to set up your Post Office. The front of your Post Office may be cut from a large cardboard box, as in the diagram below. Or you may use a tri-fold puppet stage, if you have one. A small flag taped to the top of the Post Office will add authenticity.

 "Wee Deliver" is a kit you can order from the U.S. Postal Service, Office of Literacy, 470 L'Enfant Plaza SW, Washington, DC 20260-3110. The kit comes with a videotape on starting a school-wide post office, a mail bag, cardboard mailbox, rubber stamp, poster, and cardboard cubbies which can be used for sorting mail. This all-inclusive kit is free to schools.

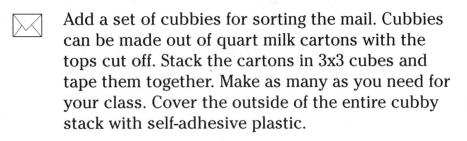 Add a set of cubbies for sorting the mail. Cubbies can be made out of quart milk cartons with the tops cut off. Stack the cartons in 3x3 cubes and tape them together. Make as many as you need for your class. Cover the outside of the entire cubby stack with self-adhesive plastic.

You will also need a table or desk for your post office. Add envelopes (ask parents to send some in or visit a printing shop and ask if they will donate their "mistakes"), pencils or pens, rubber stamps and washable stamp pads, a hole punch, and some plain paper or assorted stationary so children may "write" letters.

Some type of bag for the mail carrier is good. A simple cloth bag or old pocketbook with a shoulder strap will do for dressing up or children may use the bags and hats they make in the art center.

You will need a mailbox. This can be a simple cardboard box painted blue with a slot cut in the top for mail. You might also want one or several mailboxes in which to deliver the mail. Look for a real mailbox that can be placed on a shelf or on a pole anchored in a pot of plaster of Paris. Or you may use simple shoe boxes, empty tissue boxes, quart milk cartons turned on their sides with the tops cut off, the Ellison die mailbox pattern, or mailboxes made from the diagrams on page 46.

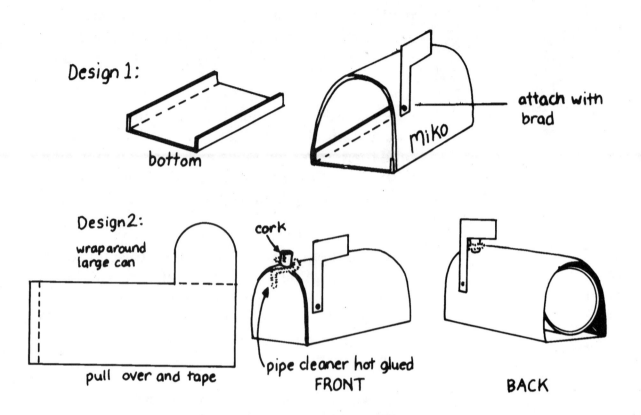

Design 1:

bottom

attach with brad

miko

Design 2:

wrap around large can

pull over and tape

cork

pipe cleaner hot glued
FRONT

BACK

✉ Consider having a mailbox for each child and one for yourself, and a place where children can write notes and draw pictures to mail to each other. You may also deliver mail each evening that you have written to each child. Children will greet each new day anticipating what's inside their mailbox. A teacher note could be a simple "I love you" message, stickers, a "Happygram" commenting on something great the child did the previous day, a question that encourages the child to write back, and so on.

✉ Add a postage or food scale. As children begin to lose interest in the envelopes, add some small packages or boxes wrapped in brown paper. Children may practice wrapping packages with brown paper, tape, and string. You'll never see packages wrapped quite like this but it will provide great fun and practice with small motor skills. Add an address and sticker "stamp" to each package.

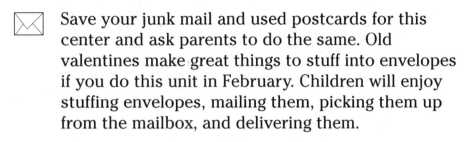 Save your junk mail and used postcards for this center and ask parents to do the same. Old valentines make great things to stuff into envelopes if you do this unit in February. Children will enjoy stuffing envelopes, mailing them, picking them up from the mailbox, and delivering them.

Save stickers and stamps, such as Christmas and Easter Seals, to use as stamps for letters. A jar of pennies and a toy cash register are useful for buying and selling stamps as well.

A wagon makes a nice mail truck. Children can make "U.S. Mail" signs for the wagon.

Write each child's name and complete address on an index card. For less mature students, simply use first names with photocopied pictures of each child. Punch a hole in the upper left-hand corner of each card and hold the "address book" together with a metal ring binder. This will encourage some children to copy their own name and address and the names and addresses of their classmates.

Tell your local post office what you are doing. They will often give you some freebies that can be used in the center, such as stamp posters, coloring books, "Express Mail" envelopes, order forms, and "Priority Mail" stickers. Ask if they have an old discarded postal employee's shirt, hat, or jacket that children can use for dress-up. Ask if you can take some photographs of things in the post office, such as a postal worker, mail box, scale, or stacks of letters and packages. Display these pictures around the center. Some pictures can even be taken when the post office is closed, such as an outdoor mailbox, indoor mail slots, stamp machine, rental postal boxes, or the sign that says post office.

✉ Make an open/closed sign for the post office or use the printed signs below on opposite sides of a piece of tagboard. Punch holes on the top and add yarn so the sign can hang. Put the sign out to let children know if the post office is opened or closed. Close the post office when it gets too messy and things need to be straightened up. Discuss with children why this might be necessary at a real post office (so no mail gets lost).

Circle Time

✉ Find out what children already know about mail carriers. Some children will have seen a mail carrier delivering letters and some will tell about special letters or packages they have received through the mail.

✉ Ask children what they would like to know about mail carriers and the post office. Tell children something you would like to know. By placing yourself in the learner role, you are able to include some of your own objectives in the class list. Make a list of 3–5 things you all wish to learn. Discuss with children how they can find these things out. For example, they might look at books, take a field trip to the post office, or interview a letter carrier. Plan your activities around things children want to know.

✉ This is a good time for children to learn their addresses. Write each child's name and address on an individual envelope. Place the envelopes in a circle on the floor at circle time. Invite children to find them and sit on the spot where they found their envelopes. For less mature students, use first names on the envelopes.

✉ Place addressed envelopes in a mail bag (for less mature students, simply write first names on individual envelopes) and let each child take a turn playing mail carrier and "delivering" the letters by identifying the names and addresses. One child may have a turn each day. While the child is delivering the mail, have the rest of the class sing this song to the tune of "Here We Go Round the Mulberry Bush."

This is the way we deliver the mail,
Deliver the mail, deliver the mail.
This is the way we deliver the mail,
Each and every day.

✉ Read out the address of each child in the class, one at a time, to see if children can identify their own addresses.

✉ Write numbers from 1 to 10 on individual envelopes (more mature students might be able to recognize numbers to 15 or 20). Use the envelopes as flashcards. Flash them in order and then in random order. This same idea can be used for learning the upper or lowercase letters of the alphabet—put alphabet letters on envelopes.

✉ Invite children to name all the different kinds of mail the mail carrier brings, such as postcards, letters, bills, cards, magazines, and packages. Write the types of mail on a piece of chart paper and encourage children to bring in examples to glue on the chart.

✉ Challenge children to name all the ways mail is carried, such as by foot, car, truck, train, ship, and airplane. Write these on a piece of chart paper and invite volunteers to illustrate each on small index cards. Glue the index cards next to the words and display the chart in the writing center.

✉ Look for pictures to illustrate vocabulary, such as mail carrier, envelope, letter, address, return address, postcard, package, stamp, mailbag, uniform, mailbox, mail slot, stamp machine, rubber stamp, and scale. Many picture-language sets have appropriate pictures. You can cut pictures from magazines, or trace or draw your own. Mount the pictures on tagboard to use as flashcards during circle time. After children have memorized the names of all the cards, place the cards in the writing center with the word written under each picture to encourage children to write the words or use them in their writing.

Place the language cards (see previous suggestion) across a chalkboard ledge and ask "w" questions about the pictures. Challenge children to find the picture that answers the question. For example,

What do you put a stamp on? (letter or envelope)
Who brings us packages and letters? (mail carrier)
What does the mail carrier drive? (mail truck)
Where do you go to buy stamps? (post office)

As children get better at this game, encourage them take turns asking questions themselves.

Rhythm Time

 Help children memorize their names and addresses using this idea from *Wee Sing Children's Songs and Fingerplays*. The tune is that of "Rain, Rain, Go Away."

My name is Maria Gonzalez.
This is my address.
135 34th Street,
Chicago, Illinois.

 Teach this original fingerplay.

1 letter, 2 letters, 3 letters, 4,
In this bag there are some more.
Letters for Grandma, Mom and Dad,
When they get them, they'll be glad.

Make a class big book of this rhyme by inviting volunteers to illustrate each of the nine sections indicated by slash marks.

1 letter/2 letters/3 letters/4/
In this bag there are some more/
Letters for Grandma/Mom/and Dad/
When they get them, they'll be glad./

Add the words under each illustration, a cover, and a title page (title, "copyright" date, authors, and illustrators). Bind pages together for a class big book and place in the book center.

Bulletin Board

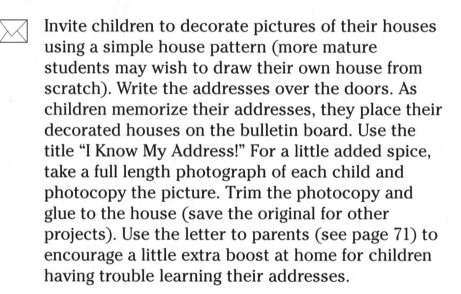

Invite children to decorate pictures of their houses using a simple house pattern (more mature students may wish to draw their own house from scratch). Write the addresses over the doors. As children memorize their addresses, they place their decorated houses on the bulletin board. Use the title "I Know My Address!" For a little added spice, take a full length photograph of each child and photocopy the picture. Trim the photocopy and glue to the house (save the original for other projects). Use the letter to parents (see page 71) to encourage a little extra boost at home for children having trouble learning their addresses.

Send home large simple house patterns cut from tagboard for children to decorate with their families. Suggest that families decorate the houses like their own. Encourage them to write the house numbers on the tagboard houses and to point out to children where they appear on the real houses. Hang these on a bulletin board entitled "Open House" as children memorize their addresses.

Create plain envelopes with each child's name on them. Add a heart, stamp, or sticker if you like. Scatter the envelopes over the bulletin board. Add a large picture of a mailbox, a mail carrier, and a heart border. When children are out of the room or after they go home, place small prizes, such as stickers, an animal cracker, a pencil, a stick of sugarless gum, in the envelopes. The next time children have shown excellent behavior, tell them that they can go "check their mail."

Invite each child to design a postage stamp with markers. Show children several different stamps to give them some ideas (ask your post office for posters or coloring books of stamps). Distribute large square sheets of white paper cut on all sides with pinking shears. Display the designs on a bulletin board entitled "Stamp of Approval."

Snack/Cooking Time

 Make an "envelope" snack using pita bread stuffed with anything you want to make with the class. One suggestion follows.

Individual Egg Salad

1 hard-boiled egg per child
mayonnaise
sweet relish or chopped green olives
grated carrot (optional)
mustard

Give each child one hard-boiled egg and a plastic knife with which to "chop" the egg. Children add a teaspoon of sweet relish or chopped green olives, a teaspoon of mayonnaise, and a squirt of mustard. Salt (do not add salt if you use the olives!), pepper, and shredded carrots are optional. Stuff "envelope" (pita pocket) with a little egg salad and a "letter" of lettuce.

Plan this snack ahead of time.

Envelope Snack

plain envelope
3–5 small crackers, such as animal crackers, or 1 large
cracker, such as a graham cracker, per child

Write each child's name (address optional) on the outside
of a plain envelope. Place crackers in each envelope and
seal. Tell children at snack time that the mail carrier left
them a special treat. Place the envelopes on a ledge and
invite children to find their own names and addresses.

Cognitive Activities

 Try this counting activity. Cover quart milk cartons with the tops cut off with butcher paper (or paint red, white, and blue) and write a number from 1 to 10 on each. Line the cartons up to make individual mailbox cubbies. Children may count the appropriate number of letters (plain envelopes or collected junk mail envelopes) into each cubbie.

Try this math matching game. Collect canceled stamps. Put 1 stamp on a plain envelope, 2 stamps on another, 3 stamps on the third, and so on up to 10 or 20, depending on the ability of your group. Cut pieces of tagboard to fit the envelopes and put a matching number on each card (1, 2, 3). Children may "stuff" the envelopes with number "letters."

✉ Write one uppercase letter on the outside of each of 26 envelopes. Cut pieces of tagboard to fit inside the envelopes and write a lowercase letter (or glue a picture of something that begins with each letter) on the tagboard. Invite children to place each piece of tagboard in the corresponding envelope. Children may also put the envelopes in alphabetical order.

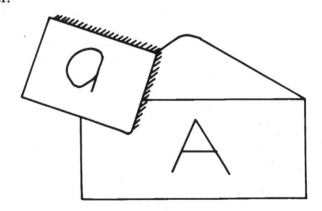

✉ Write each child's name and address on the outside of an envelope. Add a stamp or sticker. Glue a photocopied picture of each child (a school picture will do) to a piece of tagboard or a small index card that will fit inside each envelope. Children may put the picture inside the envelope with the correct name and address

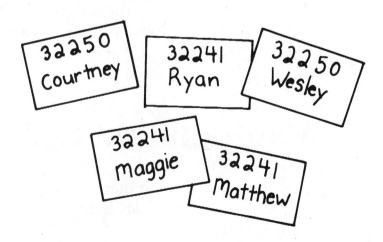

Discuss zip codes with students. The numbers tell which city and state you live in and are used by a computerized machine to sort mail. Write each student's name and zip code on an index card and keep the cards in the post office to encourage students to write their own zip codes and those of other class members. Children may sort the cards by zip code to see how many of their classmates have the same zip code.

Write zip codes on index cards for each student. Invite them to place the appropriate number of self-sticking dots or stars under each of the five numbers.

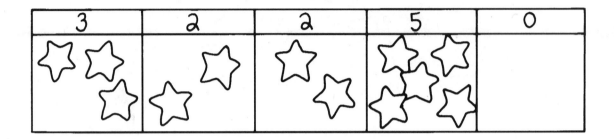

 Practice auditory memory by saying a five-number zip code and having children repeat it. This can be done individually and will give you information on which children are or are not auditory learners. Continue for several days with children who need work on these memory skills.

 Collect canceled stamps. Use small index cards to make sets that are the same or different. On some cards, put two stamps that are just alike and on some cards, put two stamps that are different. Flash the cards to individuals or small groups of children and ask them to respond "same" or "different." Children may also sort the stamps in stacks of same and different.

Manipulative Center

 Put out mail carrier puzzles such as the ones available from Judy/Instructo (J606011 and J606524).

Add figures and cars to the manipulative table (Duplo Family Workers #244830 and Duplo Community Vehicles #281527, available from Childcraft). If you don't have the commercial versions, add any small van and figures. Children will pretend that they are mail trucks and mail carriers. Encourage children to build houses and buildings and deliver mail to each of the houses and buildings.

Place things that would be needed to mail packages on a table. Include small boxes to wrap, brown butcher paper, tape, self-sticking mailing labels or just plain white labels, and markers. Children may wrap and rewrap the boxes.

Play Dough Center

Use play dough of any color to turn this center into a "Stamp Factory." Rubber stamps will make imprints in play dough. Flatten the dough, use a stamp to make an impression, and then use a plastic knife or craft stick to cut around the design to make a square stamp.

Blocks

Put out a floor map that shows community buildings and streets (Drive Around Town Carpet #LC1607 from Lakeshore Learning Materials or Motor Map #HOY-1, Super Roadway Play Mat

#PT-500 from Constructive Playthings) or make one of your own using oil cloth and markers. Children may pretend any wooden car or van is the mail truck. Ask your post office for a small "Priority Mail" sticker to place on the pretend mail truck. Select different destinations, such as the school, grocery store, police station, and invite children to deliver the mail in the mail truck to different destinations.

 Add some envelopes to the block area to encourage pretend mail play.

Sand/Water Table

 Add some mail trucks (simple wooden rectangular blocks can be painted blue and a "Priority Mail" sticker added) to the sand table. Add other wooden blocks to be used as houses. Encourage children to set up a neighborhood and then dig roads so the mail can be delivered.

 Cut some mail truck/van shapes from sponges to put in your water table. Cut some house sponges as well. Children may float the sponges and try to blow the mail truck to different houses to deliver the mail.

Art Center

 Help children make their own mail bags using the diagram on page 61.

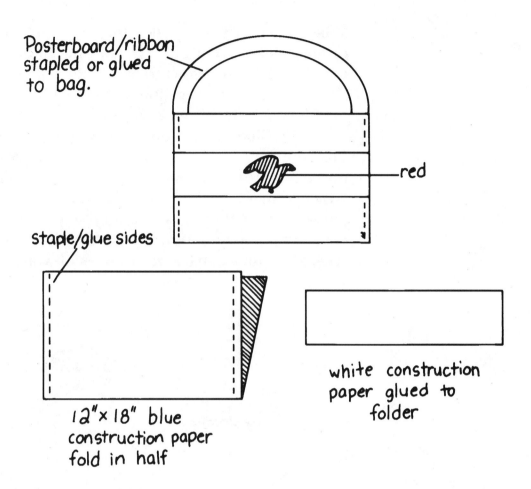

Posterboard/ribbon stapled or glued to bag.

red

staple/glue sides

12" × 18" blue construction paper fold in half

white construction paper glued to folder

✉ Help children make mail carrier visors from blue construction paper using the diagram below.

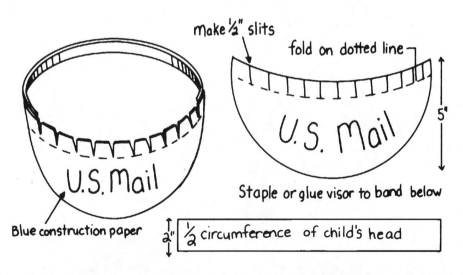

make ½" slits

fold on dotted line

5"

U.S. Mail

U.S. Mail

Staple or glue visor to band below

Blue construction paper

2" ½ circumference of child's head

Make mail carriers. Use the diagram below and cut or help children cut out the pattern. Children may use markers or crayons to add belts and color the shoes. Add buttons (yellow dots available from business supply stores, scraps of paper, or real buttons). Glue on pink or brown circles for heads. Children may add features, such as hair, eyes, noses, mouths, pockets, and badges, with scraps of paper or markers. Add dark blue hats using the pattern and mailbags cut from brown or tan construction paper. Write or have children write "U.S. Mail" on the bags. Rectangles of white paper can be added for letters.

✉ Encourage children to draw pictures and write letters to school workers, such as the principal, cafeteria workers, media specialist, and other teachers. Have them put the "mail" into envelopes and help them write each person's name on the fronts of the envelopes. Children may use their individual mail bags and visors as they go around school delivering the mail.

✉ Save and ask parents to save junk mail, opened envelopes, miscellaneous envelopes, old mismatched stationary and envelopes, postcards, coupons, brochures, or anything else that comes in the mail. Place all of these on the art table and invite children to make post-office collages by gluing pieces of anything they like to pieces of construction paper.

✉ Collect and ask parents to save canceled stamps. Make a collage of all the stamps as children bring them in on a large piece of tagboard. Discuss with the class which is the largest stamp, smallest stamp, favorite stamp, how many stamps have red in them, and so on. Display this collage in the post office.

Book Center

✉ Make a class book using the facts you have learned during this unit. Invite children to help you make a list. For example:

The mail carrier carries a mail bag.
The mail carrier wears a uniform.
The mail carrier delivers mail.

Mail is delivered in a mail truck.
Mail can fly through the air.
Our post office has a flag in front.

After children have made a list, write one of the sentences on each page and invite volunteers to illustrate the pages. Add a cover and title page that includes "copyright" date and authors' and illustrators' names. Add to the book center or send home each day with a different child.

Make a sentence-strip book about mail carriers. Each child may finish the sentence, "Mail carriers _____" (wear blue pants, carry a mail bag, deliver packages, drive a mail truck). Write each sentence on an individual sentence strip. Give children small index cards on which to illustrate their sentences. Glue the cards to the sentence strips, punch a hole in each strip, and bind with a metal ring binder. On the last page, write " _____ can read this book." Children may sign their names when they can "read" the book.

Make an alphabet big book about postal workers. Write the alphabet down the left side of a piece of chart paper and invite children to think of words for each letter related to the post office. This is an especially good activity after a field trip. If children get stuck, consider the following words.

airmail/address
bag (mail)
canceled stamp
delivery
envelope
flag
go (mail trucks)
hat (mail)
ink pad (for stamping letters)
jet (for air delivery)

key (to open mail boxes)
letter
mail/mail carrier
night (workers sort mail at night)
out-of-town
post office/ postcard/ packages
quick delivery (Express Mail)
return address/rented (boxes at post office)/red flag
stamps/stamp pad/scales
trucks (mail)
US Mail
very special people (mail carriers)
wheels (of the mail truck)
x-ray (to see what's inside of packages)
year-round delivery in all kinds of weather
zip code/z-z-z-z (for a sleeping mail carrier at day's end!)

Children may volunteer to illustrate the letters of the alphabet (one picture for each letter).

Alphabetize the pictures and add a cover and title page. Or display in alphabetical order on a bulletin board or clothesline across the room and bind later for the book center.

 Here are some books you may wish to place in your book center. Check your school or community librarian for other titles. Many of these are also appropriate for reading during circle time.

(ps-K) Bond, Michael and Karen. *Paddington Mails a Letter.* Rand McNally and Company, 1986.
Board book about the delightful Paddington Bear. Die-cut slots allow student to push a letter through each page as they follow the route of the mail.

(ps-1) Carle, Eric. *The Secret Birthday Message.* Thomas Y. Crowell, 1972.
Tim's adventure starts as he hunts through a dark cave, an underground tunnel, and other strange places. Bold, colorful illustrations with a simple but suspenseful story. Emphasizes the joy of receiving a letter.

(ps-1) Scarry, Richard. *Richard Scarry's Postman Pig and His Busy Neighbors*. Random House, 1978.
Reviews all the community helpers but centers around Postman Pig as he makes his daily deliveries.

(K-1) Craig, Janet. *Windy Day*. Troll Associates, 1988.
A "First-Start Easy Reader" about a letter that sweeps through the city on a very windy day.

(K-3) Ahlberg, Janet and Allan. *The Jolly Christmas Postman*. Little, Brown, 1991.
This delightful Christmas book can be enjoyed at any time. Pages are envelopes with letters to fairy tale and nursery rhyme characters in each.

(K-3) Ahlberg, Janet and Allan. *The Jolly Postman*. Little, Brown, 1986.
Twelve pages are envelopes containing letters and other written material telling the story of the postman's delivery route one particular day.

(K-3) Hedderwick, Maire. *Katie Morag Delivers the Mail*. Little Brown, 1988.
Little Katie is charged with delivering the mail but a fall in the water obliterates the addresses.

(K-3) Johnson, Jean. *Postal Workers: A to Z*. Walker and Company, 1987.
Uses an alphabet book format to present the work of the postal service in handling our mail. Especially good for more mature children learning the alphabet.

(K-3) Maurey, I. *My Mother the Mail Carrier*. Feminist Press, 1976.
Shows a female mail carrier and describes the job she does.

(K-3) Skurzynski, Gloria. *Here Comes the Mail*. Macmillan Children's Group, Bradbury Press, 1992.
The inner workings of the postal system are revealed as the author traces the path of a little girl's letter from her home in New Mexico to her cousin's home in Utah. Includes tips on how to address an envelope.

(K-3) Ziegler, Sandra. *A Visit to the Post Office*. Childrens Press, 1989.
A class visits the post office to mail their valentines and finds out about the work that is done there.

(K-4) Gibbons, Gail. *The Post Office Book: Mail and How It Moves*. HarperCollins Children's Books, 1986.
Very detailed red, white, and blue drawings follow the journey of a letter.

Outside

 Have a mail carrier relay race. Divide children into teams of 3 or 4. Give each team an envelope. The first child races with the envelope to the "mailbox" (a shoe box will do). The second child races and retrieves the letter (delivery) and gives it to the next child and so on until all the "mail carriers" have finished the "route."

 Play "A Tisket, a Tasket." Children sit in a circle. One child carries a letter in a mail bag/basket/green and yellow basket. The child skips around the outside of the circle while the class sings the following.

A tisket, a tasket,
A green and yellow basket.
I wrote a letter to my love
And on the way I dropped it.
I dropped it, I dropped it,
And on the way I dropped it!

The skipping child drops the letter behind a seated child. The seated child picks up the letter and chases the skipping child, who tries reach the vacant spot before being tagged. The child who picked up the letter takes a turn with the basket.

Field Study

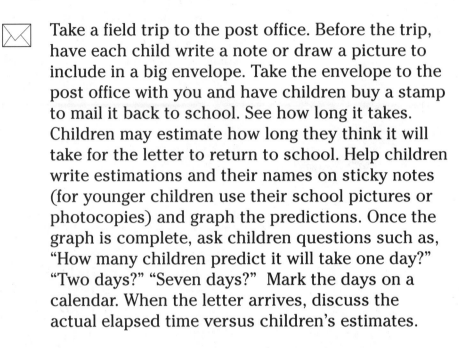

Take a field trip to the post office. Before the trip, have each child write a note or draw a picture to include in a big envelope. Take the envelope to the post office with you and have children buy a stamp to mail it back to school. See how long it takes. Children may estimate how long they think it will take for the letter to return to school. Help children write estimations and their names on sticky notes (for younger children use their school pictures or photocopies) and graph the predictions. Once the graph is complete, ask children questions such as, "How many children predict it will take one day?" "Two days?" "Seven days?" Mark the days on a calendar. When the letter arrives, discuss the actual elapsed time versus children's estimates.

Take photographs on the field trip. Use them to refresh students' memories of what they saw. Invite children to suggest captions for each picture and place them in a book or album for the book center. The book can be used the following year to prepare students for the same field trip.

Consider videotaping your field trip or ask a parent to do it. Show the video soon after you get back from the trip. The children will enjoy seeing it over and over. You can stop the action at strategic places and discuss with children the things they saw or what happened next. Save the video to use as pre-trip viewing for next year's class.

After you come back from the field trip, invite children to draw pictures of something they saw. At center time, children may dictate language experience sentences about their field trip. Enclose the language experience chart and pictures in a big envelope as a thank you to the post office.

✉ Make a sentence-strip class book about what children saw at the post office. On the first strip write, "At the post office . . ." On each of the following strips write "(Child's name) saw _____." Children may dictate one thing they saw for you to fill in. Then give children small index cards so they can illustrate what they saw. Glue the cards to the matching sentences. Make one final page that says "I can read this book." Children may write their names when they can read the entire book. Punch a hole in each strip and bind with a metal ring binder.

✉ Read *A Visit to the Post Office* by Sandra Ziegler — the story of a class trip to the post office. This book is good preparation for the field trip and/or a good review after you return. Compare and contrast what the children saw with what is in the book.

✉ Take a mini-field trip. Stake out the mailbox nearest the school and find out when the mail is delivered. Make arrangements with the mail carrier to greet the class and get a quick "Show and Tell." It will give children a chance to see the mail carrier's uniform and bag, possibly his mail truck, and a chance to ask some questions. If you have a mailbox within walking distance, write a letter from the class and walk children to the mailbox to mail it. Use the estimation and graphing activities from the first field trip suggestion on page 68.

Parent Involvement

 Explain to parents that you have been talking about mail carriers. Encourage them to show their child where their mailbox is at home. You may want to send home the parent letter on page 71. At circle time, open the letters that are sent to the class. Invite children to tell the group how the letter got to class ("Me and my mom wrote the letter. I made those red hearts. I put the letter in the big post office box under the bridge. . . .") Display them in the room. Children will love seeing the letter they sent.

Dear Parents,

We are studying about mail carriers. The children are learning how to mail letters. Please show your child where your mail box is at home. You might even want to mail a letter or picture from you and your child to the class. Your letter can be mailed to:

_____

_____

_____

_____

Please help your child learn your address. Children should know the number and street, city, state and zip code. I will ask children to tell me their addresses each morning and we will continue to practice here at school. When children are able to tell me their complete addresses, they may put their decorated houses on our new bulletin board, "I Know My Address!"

Together we can!

Hospital

Creative Play

✚ Set up a hospital in your classroom. Supply the hospital area with materials such as cots, white sheets, flowers, get well cards, play doctor kits (including stethoscopes, thermometers, blood pressure cuff), empty pill bottles, syringes without needles, lab coats (or men's white shirts), plastic gloves, glasses without lenses, scrub suits, disposable masks, baby dolls (for sick patients), baby bed/crib with white sheets, strips of white material to use for broken bones, eye chart, growth chart, scales, a black doctor's bag (or a large black pocketbook), small pads of white paper and pencils for writing prescriptions, telephone, play watch, child-sized crutches, and a wheel chair. Add a clipboard with a patient's folder in which doctors may write orders.

✚ Make a sign with a red cross for the entrance of your hospital. Children may help you decide on a name for the hospital and make the sign themselves.

✚ You may wish to add a waiting room with chairs, magazines, books, brochures, and pamphlets collected from doctor's offices and pharmacies, a telephone, a reception desk (a table, desk, or box) with a window (puppet theater), appointment book, pencils, and a sign-in sheet.

✚ Set up a pharmacy beside the hospital area. You will need a counter (desk, rocking boat turned on its side, small table, or box). Add a cash register, play money, empty medicine and pill bottles, and small brown bags. The pharmacist will need a lab coat or white man's shirt.

✚ Use a wagon or box painted during art time as an ambulance. Make an ambulance sign and red crosses for the sides of the wagon.

Home Living

✚ Put a telephone in the home living area. Encourage children to use the telephone to call and make doctor's appointments and 911 for emergencies.

✚ Use plastic trays or large cardboard boxtops for bed trays. Encourage children to prepare food for the patients in the "hospital" or at home.

✚ If you do not want to actually set up a hospital, put a baby bed, sick baby doll, or rocking chair in the home living area and have children tend to the sick child there. Add dots with a red marker to a plastic baby doll and pretend the sick baby has the chicken pox .

Circle Time

✚ Many children will be able to share experiences about the doctor's office. Some will have been in the hospital. Invite each child to tell the group about one experience. This will give you an idea of what children already know so you can build on those experiences.

Ask children what things they would like to know about a hospital. Put yourself in the learner situation and share with children something you would like to know. Decide on 3–5 things you and the class would like to learn during the study. Discuss with children how they might find these things out (ask a doctor, ask the school nurse, visit the hospital, look in books). Include these learning goals as you plan your unit.

Look for pictures to use as language cards while you work on this medical profession unit. Ask parents or friends in the medical profession to save trade magazines for you to cut pictures from or go to a doctor's office or hospital and take some photographs. Words you might want to illustrate include doctor, nurse, syringe, stethoscope, lab coat, medicine, band aid/ bandage, doctor's bag, prescription, pharmacist, thermometer, reflex hammer, rubber gloves, scales, tongue depressor, eye chart, ambulance, hospital, pharmacy. After children have learned the names of the pictures, display them in the writing center with the title written below to encourage children to copy words. Or remind them to look at the "Word Wall" for spelling help as they write.

Place the vocabulary pictures you make across a chalkboard ledge. Ask some "w" questions and ask students to find the picture that answers the question. Questions might include:

What takes you to the hospital and has a siren? (ambulance)
Where do go to buy medicine? (pharmacy)
What does the doctor use to listen to your heart? (stethoscope)
Who examines you when you get sick? (doctor)
Who helps the doctor? (nurse)

As the children master this game, invite them to take turns asking the questions.

Show children a real stethoscope. Go around the circle and give children a chance to listen to their hearts beat. Compare a picture of a real heart and a valentine heart shape. Discuss how they are alike and how they are different.

Put some real or toy medical instruments in a black doctor's bag (or old black purse) and play "What's Missing?" Use the doctor's bag as a mystery bag. Pull out each instrument, one at a time, as children name the instrument. Put the instruments back in the bag and pull out all but one. Challenge children to remember which one is missing (still in the bag). Start with about three instruments but increase the difficulty of the game as children are ready by adding more instruments and by having more than one instrument left in the bag.

Bring in a first aid kit from home or borrow the school kit. Remove each item from the kit and discuss with children when and why each would be used.

Rhythm Time

✚ Teach your class the delightful traditional rhyme "Monkeys on the Bed."

You can teach this rhyme starting with any number.

Five little monkeys jumping on the bed (hold up 5 fingers)
One fell off and bumped his head (hit side of head
  with hand)
Momma called the doctor and the doctor said
  (hold pretend phone up to ear)
"That's what you get for jumping on the bed!"
  (shake index finger)

Four little monkeys . . .
Three . . .
Two . . .
One . . .

Read Eileen Christelow's *Five Little Monkeys Jumping on the Bed* which illustrates this traditional rhyme. It is a good poem with which to use verbal cloze. Stop after "Momma called the doctor and the doctor said" and have children finish the last sentence.

Try having children say the poem while clapping a steady beat. Girls may clap one verse and boys the next.

Children love to act out this rhyme. Invite ten (or any number) volunteers to jump up and down on the first line. Choose one child to fall down and bump his or her head. All the children may shake their fingers and say, "That's what you get for jumping on the bed."

Write the poem on chart paper. Point to each word with a pointer (tongue depressor) as you read the poem with the children. Leave some tongue depressors nearby to encourage children to read the rhyme on their own.

Make a reproduction of this book with illustrations done by your students. Draw a bed on each of six tagboard pages and invite children to draw jumping monkeys on plain white paper. Cut out each of the jumping monkeys and place the appropriate number of monkeys on each page. Less mature students may use a monkey rubber stamp or they can make fingerprint monkeys on each bed. Add the appropriate words to the bottom of each page. Make a cover and a title page and bind the book together. This makes a great accordion book for your book center.

Teach children "Just a Spoonful of Sugar" from Mary Poppins. Discuss with children what this song means (that medicine often tastes yukky and a spoonful of sugar would help the taste). Write the song on chart paper. Use a spoon as a pointer and point to each word as you sing the song. Leave a spoon out beside the chart to encourage children to point to the words as they sing on their own. To help with name recognition, write each child's name with permanent marker on a wooden spoon. Children may find their own spoon to use for pointing.

✚ Children will enjoy the 25-minute video *What I Want to Be!* (Kidsongs View-Master Video Warner Brothers Records, Inc., 1987) which includes many songs about occupations and the delightful song, "So You Want to Be a Doctor," which leads into a song about bones.

Snack/Cooking Time

✚ Discuss healthy snacks with the class. Write a note to parents (see page 99) and encourage parents to send in only healthy snacks for snack time. Invite children to show their snacks each day. Have them draw pictures of healthy snacks on plain white paper plates (label each picture) or make a large collage of healthy snacks using pictures cut from magazines.

✚ Ask one parent to send in ingredients for a healthy snack each day during the unit. One possibility is small carrots, celery, cauliflower florets, and slices of cucumber with ranch dressing for dip. Or children may make the healthy dip on page 79. Children may help prepare snack by washing the vegetables and cutting them into strips with plastic knives.

Healthy Dip

1 cup lowfat yogurt
1 cup lowfat sour cream
1 Tbsp. onion, chopped finely or 1 tsp. onion powder
1 Tbsp. parsley
1 tsp. dill weed

Combine yogurt and sour cream. Add spices. Onion is optional. Use with any fresh vegetable.

Cognitive Activities

✚ Explain to children that a nurse often measures and weighs them each time they visit the doctor's office. Measure each child from head to toe by lying them down on the floor and measuring with a length of string or yarn (or use adding machine tape and let children decorate their lengths of tape). Compare the lengths. Which is the longest? The shortest? Are there any the same length? Order the strings from shortest to longest.

✚ Save empty plastic prescription bottles without child-proof tops (most pharmacies will give these to you for free). Put a number on each pill bottle from 1 to 10 or 20, depending on the maturity of the group. Use beans for pills and let the "pharmacist" put the appropriate number of pills in each bottle.

✚ Make 5–20 faces of children. Laminate for durability. On each face, place a number. Children may use a red wipe-off marker to place the appropriate number of chicken pox "dots" on each face. If you want the game to be self-checking, place the appropriate number of red self-stick dots on the back of each face.

Make black doctor bag shapes from construction paper. Write a letter on each bag. Draw or find pictures that illustrate medical words starting with each letter. Children may place the appropriate pictures in each bag.

✚ Use plastic prescription bottles and dried lima beans or cut prescription bottles and pills from construction paper. Write uppercase letters on the bottles and lowercase letters on the pills. Use permanent marker to write on lima beans. Children may place the correct pill in each bottle.

✚ Collect 5–20 metal band-aid boxes with flip-tops (ask parents to save these for you). On the front or top of each box, write a number. Unwrap band-aids and stick each one to a piece of tagboard to make them sturdier. Collect different types and sizes of band-aids. Children may place the appropriate number of band-aids in each box.

✚ Collect get well cards or buy ten from a card shop. Laminate each card and let children use wipe-off markers to circle all the "Mm's" with one color, all the "Tt's" with another color, and so on.

✚ Create matching pairs of tongue depressors. For example, children may match tongue depressors of the same color, a color to the color word, same shapes, uppercase letter to lowercase letter, numeral to set, numeral to number word, and so on. Make several different sets to use while studying this unit.

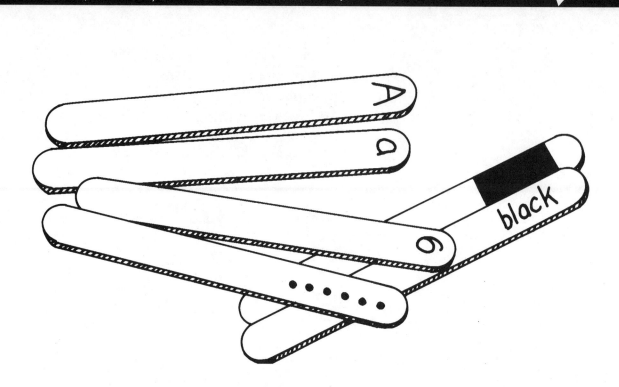

✚ Make flower arrangements for the sick. Collect empty half-pint milk cartons. Cover each carton with construction paper. You may wish to pre-cut construction paper in a strip that goes around the four sides, laminate, and staple to the carton for durability. On each carton write a letter of the alphabet. Make flowers with craft-stick stems. In the center of each flower, glue a picture that starts with one of the initial consonant sounds that you are working with. Child may put the flowers in the appropriate vase. Make about three flowers for each vase. You may wish to add small aquarium rocks, play dough, or florist clay to the bottom of each milk carton to provide a stable base for the flowers but this is not necessary. Less mature children may match colors. Make cartons in red, blue, green, yellow, orange, purple, black, and white and flowers to match.

Manipulative Center

✚ Put out some puzzles such as these from Judy/Instructo: Doctor #J6060010, 16 pieces; Nurse #J606522, 13 pieces; Shape Ambulance #J041018, 9 pieces; Great Big White Ambulance Floor Puzzle #J036071, 19 pieces.

✚ Playmobile has a hospital room set available with characters and supplies that would be fun for students during this unit (Playmobile Hospital Room #PLM-3495 from Constructive Playthings).

✚ The game "Operation" can be purchased at most toy stores. More mature students will especially enjoy this game, as it strengthens fine motor skills by requiring children to pick up small plastic items with tweezers.

Play Dough Center

✚ Add tongue depressors to the play dough area. Children will think of many ways to use them.

✚ Add heart-shaped cookie cutters to the play dough. Put out some plastic knives, tongue depressors, or craft sticks. Encourage children to do some "heart surgery."

✚ Put out some empty pill bottles. Invite children to make some "pills" for the bottles.

Blocks

✚ Encourage children to build a hospital with blocks. Put out some white tagboard and red markers for children to make red crosses and "Hospital" signs for the block buildings.

✚ Use some wooden blocks to make an ambulance. Tape the blocks together and paint white (or leave them as they are). Add black construction paper wheels and a red tape cross. Ask children for other suggestions.

Water/Sand Table

✚ Look for interesting medical things that can be added to your water table. Large syringes without needles and eye droppers are fun. Bedside cups and water pitchers from a hospital stay are also fun for pouring and measuring.

✚ Fill your sand table with dried beans. Put some empty plastic pill bottles in the table and let the children fill the bottles with "pills." Put numbers on the bottles for more mature students and they can fill bottles with the appropriate number of pills.

Art Center

✚ Purchase several medicine droppers (most pharmacies sell these—they are very inexpensive). Discuss with children ways in which medicine droppers are used, such as to put drops of medicine in the ear when you have an earache. Demonstrate this on a baby doll but stress that *only an adult can put drops in eyes or ears*. Cover the work area with newspaper. Water down several different colors of tempera or use about 12 drops of food coloring to 1/4 cup water. Place each color in a small baby food jar. Children may suction paint into the medicine dropper and then squeeze it onto paper. Use absorbent paper, such as coffee filters, white paper towels, or thick paper dinner napkins. Children may fold the paper, crumple it into a ball, or simply lay the paper flat and put drops of different colors on the paper. Folding the paper will create a design. Crumpling will give an abstract effect which usually has some white spaces left and laying it flat will produce an abstract of color. Cut a frame from construction paper or use overhead-transparency frames to mount the colorful pictures. Use the art in the hospital as a way to brighten the day for "sick" children. You can tape the pictures on the ceiling or the coffee filters can hang from the ceiling. You might even wish to tape the pictures around the top of the wall to provide a colorful border for the hospital room.

✚ Cotton swabs can be used as paintbrushes. Explain to children that cotton swabs are usually used for cleaning ears by demonstrating on a baby doll. Stress that *only an adult can use cotton swabs in the ears.* Place several colors of tempera paint in small baby food jars or in a muffin tin and invite children to paint pictures of their choice. When cotton swabs begin to unravel, replace them with new ones.

✚ White is the color of the medical profession. Put white paint at the easel or invite the children to use white fingerpaint on dark-colored paper.

✚ Invite children to practice making faces on white drawing paper. After the face is drawn, give children red markers or a cotton swab with red paint and let them put red chicken pox dots on their faces. Display the sick children faces with the get well cards that follow.

✚ Encourage children to design get well cards for someone who is sick. Fold pieces of construction paper in half and have children draw pictures for the fronts. They may pick a message, such as "Get

Well" or "Hope you feel better soon," for the insides or make up messages of their own. Take or mail the cards to the pediatric wing of a local hospital.

✚ Children may make doctor's or nurse's headpieces according to the diagrams below.

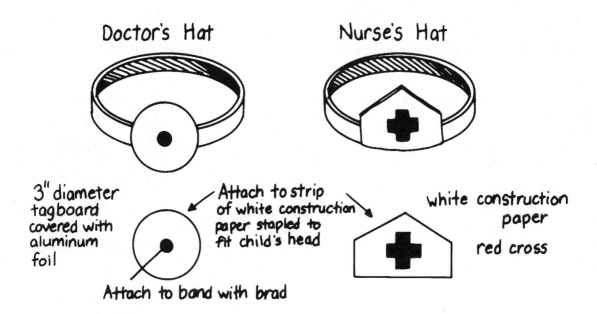

Doctor's Hat

Nurse's Hat

3" diameter tagboard covered with aluminum foil

Attach to strip of white construction paper stapled to fit child's head

Attach to band with brad

white construction paper
red cross

✚ Make a doctor's bag from construction paper according to the diagram on page 88. Inside the bag children may create a collage of real items, such as cotton balls, cotton swabs, tongue depressors, and band-aids, or you may enlarge the diagram on a photocopier and glue it inside the bag for children to color.

Dr. Maggie

fold on dotted line

Black construction paper 12"x24"

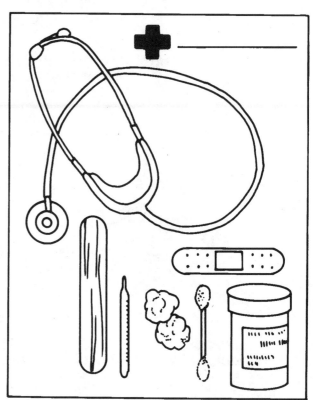

Each child may make a doctor and/or a nurse using the diagram on page 89. Cut the body from white construction paper. Glue on a pink or brown circle for the head. Use a marker to add facial features, color the shoes, and so on. Add a red cross to the nurse's uniform and a black bag for the doctor. Encourage children to add other features and accessories as well.

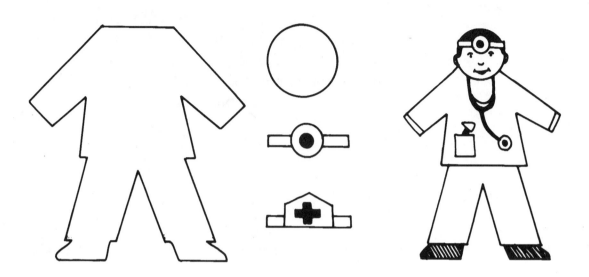

➕ Show children some of the "designer" band-aids currently on the market. Invite children to design their own on construction paper. Children may choose the color of construction paper, cut it into a band-aid shape, and use markers to make their own designs. Display on the bulletin board with the title "Band-Aids Stuck on Me!"

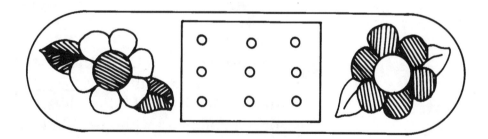

➕ Share with students Shel Silverstein's humorous poem "Band-aids" from *Where the Sidewalk Ends,* which talks about band-aids all over the body even though there are no cuts or sores. Invite children to draw full-length self-portraits. When portraits are complete, give students some band-aids (or use the band-aid Ellison die) and invite them to put band-aids on some of the places mentioned in the poem. Display on a bulletin board with the designer band-aids.

Writing Center

✚ Use a Styrofoam meat tray, piece of cardboard, or large plastic lid to cut out a cross pattern that may be used as a stencil. Explain to children that a red cross is the international sign for medical help. Invite children to make red crosses using red markers and the stencils.

✚ Use a pocket chart and write some of the words that children may want to use in their writing, such as doctor, nurse, chicken pox, and stethoscope, on sentence strips. Invite children to use small index cards and illustrate the words. Place the index card drawings beside each of the words in the pocket chart.

✚ Ask each child to finish the sentence, "Doctor, doctor, I broke (hurt) my _____!" (arm, head, foot). Then have children illustrate what they broke or hurt on plain white drawing paper. A real band-aid can be added to the broken body part for effect. Bind the pictures together into a book for the book center. Add a cover and title page listing authors and illustrators.

Listening Center

➕ Record yourself telling stories, such as Ludwig Bemelman's *Madeline*, Lynne Cherry's *Who's Sick in Bed*, Eileen Christelow's *Five Little Monkeys Jumping on the Bed*, or Charlip and Supree's *Mother Mother I Feel Sick Send for the Doctor Quick Quick Quick*. *The Berenstain Bears Go to the Doctor* can be purchased with an audio cassette for the listening center.

➕ Look for prescription or pill bottles you can't see through with child-proof tops. Place things such as rice, beans, pennies, and buttons into pairs of bottles. Children may shake the bottles and try to locate the pairs that have the same sound.

Book Center

➕ Use a large refrigerator box to make a hospital reading nook. Cut a door and some windows in the box. Take the box outside and have children paint it white. After it is dry, children may paint red crosses on the box. Bring the box inside, place a few pillows in it, and invite children to use it as a cozy individual reading area.

➕ Contact your local hospital (most have a Public Relations Department) about the possibility of borrowing a scrub suit, nurse's hat, or lab coat to wear for your first story time. Most hospitals are more than willing to help. This is a good introduction for the unit. Children are often afraid of people in the medical profession and it is reassuring to have a familiar face behind the mask.

✚ Make an ABC book with the class using facts they have learned about the hospital. Start by making a list of words associated with the hospital for each letter of the alphabet. Invite volunteers to illustrate one word for each letter. Pre-write the words on drawing paper for your volunteers. When all the illustrations are complete, alphabetize the pages and invite one child to make a cover. Add a title page with illustrators' names and bind together for a class book. Here are some word possibilities.

ambulance
band-aid/bed/bandage
card (get well)
doctor
emergency room/ examination
flowers (for sick patients)
growth chart
hospital/ healthy food
ICU/instruments
junk food
kiss (from mom to make it well!)
lab coat
medicine/ mask
nurse
office (doctor's)/orderly
pills/prescription
quiet
receptionist/red cross
shot/stethoscope/sick/stitches
tongue depressor
uniform (nurse's)
vaccination/vitamins
white/waiting room
x-ray
YUCK! (the taste of medicine)
z-z-z-z (sleeping patient)

Here are some books you may wish to have in your book center. Check your school or community library for other titles. Many of these are also appropriate for reading to the class at circle time.

(ps-K) Berry, Joy W. *Teach Me About the Doctor.* Childrens Press, 1988.
Typical physical at the doctor's office. Simple colored drawings.

(ps-K) Kuklin, Susan. *When I See My Doctor.* Bradbury Press, 1988.
Four-year-old Thomas describes his trip to the doctor for a physical. Color photographs of a real visit.

(ps-K) Linn, Margot. *A Trip to the Doctor.* Harper and Row, 1988.
Questions with picture-answer options. Lift flap for answers.

(ps-K) Mayer, Mercer. *Doctor Critter.* Paperwing Press, 1987.
Board book with Mercer's delightful illustrations.

(ps-K) McCue, Lisa (illustrator). *Corduroy Goes to the Doctor.* Viking Penguin, Inc., 1987.
Simple, reassuring board book about Corduroy's visit to the doctor.

(ps-K) Rockwell, Anne and Harlow. *Sick in Bed.* Macmillan Children's Group, 1982.
Little boy describes feelings when sick in bed with a sore throat.

(ps-1) Allen, Julia. *My First Doctor Visit.* Aro Publishing Company, 1987.
Very simple book of a child's visit to the doctor's office.

(ps-1) Cherry, Lynne. *Who's Sick in Bed?* Dutton Children's Book, 1988.
Rhyming text and illustrations introduce a variety of animals with different ailments. Good book for story time.

(ps-1) Rockwell, Harlow. *My Doctor.* Macmillan Children's Group/ Greenwillow, 1975.
Describes a young child's visit to the doctor's office. Clear, simple individual illustrations of doctor's instruments.

(ps-1) Strong, Stacie. *Going to the Doctor.* Simon and Schuster Books for Young Readers, 1991.
A pop-up book with delightful pictures explaining what doctors do and the instruments they use.

(ps-2) Carlstrom, Nancy White. *Barney Is Best.* HarperCollins, 1994.
A trip to the hospital can be scary but it's no so bad if you have a special friend along.

(ps-2) Rogers, Fred. *Going to the Doctor.* Putnam Publishing Group, 1986.
Photographs describe what a child would see and do on a doctor's visit.

(ps-2) Rogers, Fred. *Going to the Hospital.* Putnam Publishing Group, 1988.
Photographs describe what a child would see and do as a hospital patient.

(ps-2) Sommers, Tish. *Big Bird Goes to the Doctor.* Western Publishing Company, 1986.
Part of the "Sesame Street Growing-up Books" series that presents stories about challenges children face growing up.

(ps-2) Venus, Pamela (illustrator). *This Weekend I Had the Measles.* The Wright Group/ Ginn and Company, 1987.
This is a wordless book about a young child miserable with the measles. The book also includes excellent suggestions for discussion.

(ps-2) Wolde, Gunilla. *Betsy and the Doctor.* Random House, 1978.
Part of a series of "Betsy Books." Betsy falls at nursery school and has to be taken to the hospital for stitches.

(ps-3) Berenstain, Stan and Jan. *Berenstain Bears Go to the Doctor.* Random House, 1981.
Dr. Grizzly gives the bears a regular check-up. Also available with a cassette.

(ps-3) Christelow, Eileen. *Five Little Monkeys Jumping on the Bed.* Clarion, 1989.
Illustrates the traditional rhyme of the same name. Delightful illustrations.

(K-2) Bemelmans, Ludwig. *Madeline*. Penguin Books, Ltd., 1978.
Caldecott Honor book and childhood classic. Madeline gets appendicitis and has to go the hospital. Rhyming text. Also available on 30-minute color videocassette through Hi-Tops Video.

(K-2) Charlip, Remy and Burton Supree. *Mother Mother I Feel Sick Send for the Doctor Quick Quick Quick*. Four Winds, 1982.
Delightful story written in rhyme with bold colors and shadow play about a child who gets a stomach ache and the doctor who discovers all kind of things in his tummy. Children might enjoy following up this book by drawing a silhouette picture of themselves and what the doctor might find in their tummy!

(K-2) Davison, Martine. *Kevin and the School Nurse*. Random Books for Young Readers, 1992.
Developed for the AMA about Kevin's visit to the school nurse after feeling weak from not having eaten all day. Kevin finds out about the four major food groups.

(K-2) Davison, Martine. *Maggie and the Emergency Room*. Random Book for Young Readers, 1992.
Developed for the AMA about Maggie falling off her bike. Her mom takes her to be examined, x-rayed, and stitched in the emergency room.

(K-2) Davison, Martine. *Rita Goes to the Hospital*. Random House for Young Readers, 1992.
Developed for the AMA about Rita's visit to the hospital to get her tonsils out.

(K-2) Davison, Martine. *Robby Visits the Doctor*. Random House for Young Readers, 1992.
Developed for the AMA about Robby waking up with an earache. He feels better after a doctor's visit and several doses of medicine.

(K-2) Greene, Carla. *I Want to be a Doctor*. Childrens Press, 1958.
When twins Jim and Jane go to the doctor's office for a camp physical, Jim listens to Jane's heart through the stethoscope and decides to be a doctor when he grows up.

(K-2) Steal, D. *Freddie and the Doctor.* Dell Publishing, 1992.
Freddie has had the same doctor for a long time. Shows the doctor doing lots of things.

(K-2) Steal, D. *Freddie's Accident.* Dell Publishing, 1992.
Freddie runs in front of a car and has to go the hospital. Shows many of the hospital workers helping.

(K-2) Wando, M. *My Daddy is a Nurse.* Addison Wesley, 1981.
Looks at the job of a nurse.

(K-3) Behrens, June. *I Can be A Nurse.* Childrens Press, 1986.
Color pictures, mostly photographs about nursing.

(K-3) *The Giant Book of the Human Body.* Children's Books, 1992.
Big board book that explains the body systems: blood system, digestive system, skeleton, muscles, nervous system. Provides large diagrams with a touch of humor.

(K-3) Dresler, Joan. *Your Doctor, My Doctor.* Walker and Company, 1987.
Good pictures, lots of words.

(K-3) Greene, Carla. *Doctors and Nurses: What Do They Do?* Harper and Row, 1963.
An "I Can Read" book. Simple illustrations and text explaining the jobs of the doctor and nurse.

(K-3) Hankin, Rebecca. *I Can Be a Doctor.* Childrens Press, 1985.
Color pictures, mostly photographs.

(K-3) Reit, Seymour. *Jenny's in the Hospital.* Western Publishing Company, 1984.
Story of how Jenny broke her arm and her stay in the hospital. Good book for story time.

(K-4) DeSantis, Kenny and Patricia A. Agre. *A Doctor's Tools.* Dodd, Mead and Company, 1985.
Good photographs with explanations of things like stethoscope, otoscope, eye chart, tongue depressor, thermometer, scales. Not a read-aloud but good to flip like flashcards to identify tools or to use as a reference.

Outside

✚ Make an ambulance from a box or use a wagon. Have the children make red crosses for the ambulance. Encourage children to play "Rescue 911." Help them recreate scenes of broken arms, bike accidents, and so on and have the "ambulance" come to the rescue. Be sure to make siren sounds!

Field Study

✚ Many community hospitals offer field trips. A trip will help take the fear out of the real-life experience. Take photographs of the hospital or have a parent videotape the trip. Show the photographs or video the next day and invite children to comment on things they remember. Use the photographs and/or video as a pre-activity for the same field trip the following year.

✚ After you return from the hospital, ask children to make a list of all the different people they saw working in the hospital, such as a doctor, nurse, surgeon, receptionist, X-ray technician, pharmacist, and physical therapist. If you visited a large hospital with a gift shop, restaurants, and so on, children may also name some of those people. Once the list is complete, discuss with children what each of these people do.

✚ An alternative to a field trip is *Sesame Street Home Video Visits the Hospital* (Children's Television Workshop, Random House Home Video, 1990). This

30-minute video is the story of Big Bird's short stay at the hospital after he gets sick. The video can also be used prior to a field trip to prepare children for what they will see and/or as a review after the trip.

+ Arrange a field trip to a pediatrician's office or invite a doctor to come and visit the class. Ask the doctor to bring some instruments to show children, such as a black bag, crutches, or stethoscope.

+ Arrange for the school nurse to come talk to the class or go to the school clinic and invite the nurse to tell about what he or she does. The nurse may weigh and measure the class or take someone's temperature. You might enjoy reading *Kevin and the School Nurse* by Martine Davison, which tells about Kevin's visit to the school nurse. Or ask the nurse to read it!

+ Invite children to draw pictures of things they remember seeing on the field trip. Encourage them to use temporary, invented spelling and their own letters to label the pictures.

+ Ask children to tell you their favorite things about the field trip. Write the sentences on chart paper. Make a copy of the sentences with some of the children's pictures and send as a thank you to the hospital or doctors office.

Parent Involvement

+ Try to get parents interested in providing healthy snacks for their children. Consider using the parent letter on page 99.

Dear Parents,

We are studying about different medical professions. As part of this unit, we will be talking about things to eat that help keep us healthy. This week, please send in a "healthy" snack for each day. The children will have an opportunity to stand up each day and show the rest of the class something healthy they have brought. Some suggestions are celery and peanut butter, raisins, pieces of fresh fruit (apple, banana, tangerine, grapes), carrots, whole grain muffins, or raw veggies with dip.

Eat healthy!

Grocery Store

Creative Play

● Set up the "Grocery Store" next to the housekeeping area so children can "buy" groceries and then go "home" and cook. Organize the home living area in a way that encourages children to put the appropriate groceries in the refrigerator/freezer, canned goods on the shelf, and so on.

● If you have any parents or friends who work in a grocery store, ask for some donated items, such as banners, posters, price markers, paper bags, or sale tags, for your store. Many grocery stores are happy to give you banners after they have finished with them.

● Ask parents to help you save empty grocery containers (see page 133) that can be used to stock the shelves such as peanut butter jars, milk, syrup, catsup, mayonnaise, and 2-liter soft drink bottles (plastic); cereal, instant potato, powdered sugar, and powdered milk boxes; cans, and fruit or vegetable cans—unopened or with no sharp edges. With use, some of the boxes will get torn and smashed. Cut out the labels to use for other projects and replace the boxes with new "stock." Add any plastic fruit and vegetables you have.

● Borrow shelves from another part of the room to use for stocking groceries. Many grocery stores will

let you borrow empty plastic milk crates that can be turned on their sides and used as shelves.

You will want a check-out counter, such as a table, box, or wooden rocking boat turned on its side. The check-out counter will need a toy cash register, play money, and brown bags which can be used over and over. Play money may also be borrowed from a game such as "Monopoly," made with money rubber stamps, or purchased.

A small toy grocery cart, miniature grocery basket, or any type of basket may be used for collecting groceries while shopping. Some grocery stores will let you borrow a few grocery baskets and return them later. There are grocery carts and baskets available commercially, such as the shopping cart (#4444) or the grocery basket set (#4484) by Little Tikes.

A stock person's apron, hat, and shirt adds authenticity but any type butcher's apron will do.

Use the vocabulary words you are teaching, such as cashier, customer, coupons, stock, grocery cart, cash register, aisles, check-out counter, dairy, bakery, produce, as you participate in the grocery store. Do lots of role-playing with children—model the cashier, the customer, the bagger, the stock person, the manager, and so on. Continue until children are using the vocabulary and taking on the roles independently.

Add a scale to weigh fruits and vegetables. An old broken scale that can no longer be used by a grocery store works well but a food, postage, or balance scale will also do.

© 1996 Fearon Teacher Aids

Grocery Store • 101

You will have to "close" the grocery store periodically to restock the shelves—use this as an opportunity to talk about the jobs of stock persons. Make a sign that says OPEN on one side and CLOSED on the other to indicate when you are closed to restock. Children may write their own sign or you may use the example below. Glue to opposite sides of a piece of tagboard, punch holes on both ends, and add yarn so the sign may be hung.

Closed

Invite children to sort items in the grocery store by groups, such as fruits, vegetables, milk, or cereals. Discuss what each group has in common. Provide pieces of posterboard and markers and encourage children to make signs for groups of foods, such as, "Meats," "Cans," "Bread," "Fruit," or whatever children decide to call each group. They may wish to write prices or labels for different items or sections. Children may decide what to write, using "invented" spelling and letters.

Sort the grocery containers on the shelf into like kinds, such as cans, boxes, and plastic containers.

Put each type into a line or "train" and encourage children to predict which they think will be the longest or shortest. Discuss the result. Count how many are in each line.

Sit in the grocery store with more mature students and try activities such as the following.

Who can find something that begins with the letter B?
Find something that rhymes with silk.
Find three vegetables/fruits/meats.
If I wanted a snack or dessert, what would you choose
*   for me to eat?*
Find two things that are made from milk.
Find a food that has the same beginning sound as
*   your name.*
Find the foods you would need to make a ham sandwich.
Find the foods you would need to make vegetable soup or
*   fruit salad.*
Find three foods that have to go in the refrigerator
*   or freezer.*
Find foods to cook for breakfast.

While sitting in the grocery store with students, have them line up the groceries using a pattern, such as ABAB (can, box, can, box), or a more complex pattern, such as AAB (can, can, box). Children may think up other patterns.

Circle Time

Almost every child in your group will have had some experiences with grocery shopping. Invite each child to tell something he or she remembers about the grocery store to give you an idea of what children already know. Ask children if there are things they would like to know about the grocery

store. Make a list of these things and be sure to include them in your study.

For more mature students, write the letters of the alphabet down the left side of a piece of chart paper. Challenge children to suggest things that can be bought at the grocery store for each of the letters. For example:

A apple, avocado, apple juice, applesauce
B beets, banana, butter, beans
C cabbage, croutons, cucumbers, cauliflower
D diet soda, doughnuts, devil's food cake, dog food

After your classroom grocery store is set up, give students each a flashcard letter of the alphabet and invite them go to the store and find something that starts with that letter. Children then come back to the circle and share their selection.

Place five real or fake foods in a grocery bag and play "What's missing?" Bring out each one for children to identify. Return all five to the bag. Pull out four and invite children to guess which one you left in the bag. For more mature students, place more than five items in the bag and have them guess the one still in the bag. Or challenge them to guess the two, three, or four that are still in the bag.

Play a memory game sitting in a circle—"I went to the grocery store and I bought . . . ." The first child names one thing that can be bought in a grocery store. The second child repeats what the first child said and names something new. The third child repeats the first two items in order and then something new and so on. Students who are more sure of the alphabet may give their answers in alphabetical order. The first child gives an answer starting with

"A," the second child something starting with "B," and so on.

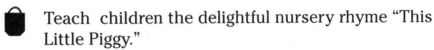 Invite children to make a list of all the grocery stores they can think of, such as ShopRite, Food Lion, A&P, Piggly Wiggly. Write all grocery store names on a piece of chart paper. As the week goes by, look for the grocery store logos (environmental print) in the newspaper or at the stores to glue beside each of the printed grocery store names (or go by and take a photograph of each store's logo/sign). Put this chart in the writing center to encourage children to use these words in their writing.

Rhythm Time

Teach children the delightful nursery rhyme "This Little Piggy."

> *This little piggy went to market.*
> *This little piggy stayed home.*
> *This little piggy had roast beef.*
> *This little piggy had none.*
> *This little piggy went "wee-wee-wee" all the way home.*

Discuss with children what the word *market* means, (another word for grocery store).

Hold up one finger for each of the little piggies and then on "wee-wee-wee" tickle the child nearest you. This is an especially beloved rhyme of very young children.

Each line of this nursery rhyme is beautifully illustrated in Magnetic Way's *Into Children's Literature: Nursery Rhymes.*

This Little Piggy, a board book by Moira Kemp, contains wonderful illustrations and is a great book to read at circle time.

Encourage children to memorize the nursery rhyme. Reward children with a little treat, such as a pig sticker or pig face drawn on the back of a child's hand, when the child can recite the entire rhyme.

Write the nursery rhyme on chart paper. Add simple pictures over key words. As children memorize the rhyme, they will be able to point out words, bridging the gap between the written and spoken word.

Encourage children to act out the rhyme. Make pig noses from individual pink Styrofoam egg carton compartments tied around the head with pink yarn. Add pig ears (ears on a strip of pink paper or sentence strip stapled to fit the child's head). Or make a pig mask from pink tagboard for children to hold in front of their face on a stick.

The Wright Group also has an adaptation of *This Little Piggy*. In this book, each little piggy is eating a different food and the book ends with "But this little piggy has nothing . . . because he didn't say 'Please'." You may wish to make a class big book in a similar style. Invite each child to fill in the sentence, "Child's name (or "This little piggy) had _____ to eat" and then illustrate what was described.

Make "Pigs in a Blanket" for snack. Cut hot dogs in half or use cocktail sausages. Roll each piece of meat in a flattened crescent-shaped biscuit,

available in the refrigerated section of the grocery store. Discuss with children why this snack is called "Pigs in a Blanket."

 Teach this original rhyme to the class.

G is for grapes we buy at the store.
R is for raisins—I always want more.
O is for onions that make me cry.
C is for cake, my favorite to buy.
E is for eggs we put in our cart.
R is for raspberries bought at the mart.
Y is for yummy food that we eat.
Grocery shopping with (mom or dad) just can't be beat!

Cut the letters GROCERY from felt. Put the appropriate letter up for each line of the rhyme.

Have children illustrate the rhyme. Write each line on the bottom of a piece of white drawing paper and invite volunteers to illustrate each line. Put the pages in order and bind together to make a class big book or tape together for an accordion book.

"Change-up" the rhyme. Write the rhyme on chart paper. Using sticky notes, invite children to change the words. For example, instead of grapes, children may suggest another "g" word to go in its place, such as gingerbread. You might try brainstorming all the words the class can think of for each letter

and then selecting the one children like best. After they have "changed-up" each of the foods, ask the class to read the revised rhyme. This new rhyme can also be illustrated and made into a big book.

Try these original verses to the tune of "The Farmer in the Dell" about workers in a grocery store.

> *The baker bakes the cakes.*
> *The baker bakes the cakes.*
> *We adore the grocery store!*
> *The baker bakes the cakes.*

Similarly, try these.

> *The butcher cuts the meat.*
> *The cashier scans the food.*
> *The bagger bags the goods.*
> *The stocker stocks the shelves.*

Challenge children to think of other verses.

Teach this original rhyme to the class:

> *A trip to the grocery store—mommy (or daddy) and me,*
> *A long list of things, as you can see.*
> *Eggs, milk, and tuna to put in our cart.*
> *Mommy (daddy) finds them all 'cause she's (he's) so smart.*
> *We find all the food, then the cashier we pay.*
> *The bagger bags our goods and says, "Good day!"*

Write the rhyme on chart paper, pointing to each word as you say it. Then invite children to help you make up actions for each of the lines.

Invite children to practice making a grocery list on a chalkboard or marker board. Suggest that they draw a picture beside each word on this shopping list. Encourage children to use invented, temporary spelling or to copy words that you have around the room to make their list.

Have available blank grocery lists and pencils that
children can use to practice writing lists.
Reproduce the list below or just provide lots of
blank paper.

My Grocery List

The Corner Grocery Store and Other Singable Songs
by Raffi comes as an album or a cassette. The cover
has a wonderful picture of a corner grocery store
and the title song is certainly worth a listen.

Snack/Cooking Time

Buy vegetables or fruits on a field trip to the grocery store for one of the following recipes.

Very Vegetable Soup

1–2 potatoes	3 carrots
1 tomato	2–4 mushrooms
1 medium onion	2–3 stalks of celery
1 small cauliflower	1 small cabbage
1 can of corn	handful of peas or beans
1 large can vegetable juice	

Visit the grocery store the day before the field trip to make sure all the vegetables on your list are available. Invite children to rinse the fresh vegetables and then use plastic knives to chop them into chunks. You may have to cut some of the vegetables into strips for children to chop. Don't worry if chunks are uneven. It may be necessary to cut chunks of potato and carrot into smaller pieces to cook faster. Place all the vegetables in a crockpot. Pour vegetable juice over the vegetables and add enough water to cover the vegetables. Turn on the pot at the end of the day and the soup should be ready the next morning. If you have a microwave available, microwave the potatoes, carrots, and fresh beans or peas for a few minutes before adding other ingredients Using a stove, microwave, or individual eye will cook the soup very quickly—in time for a late afternoon snack. Be sure to let soup cool for a few minutes or add an ice cube to each bowl before serving.

Put the recipe on chart paper for children to use as they add the vegetables to the soup (pictures drawn by you or the children or pictures cut from magazines for each ingredient will give children an

extra hint). Words and pictures help bridge the gap from the spoken to the written word.

Read one of the versions of *Stone Soup* (see page 128) to the class. Although the versions of this French folk tale are different, they both involve making soup with a magic stone. You can make your own stone soup by using the previous soup recipe or by following the steps in each of the books and adding a small, well-washed stone or bouillon cube to represent the stone.

Keep a few vegetables to use for printing with tempera paint. Cut a soup bowl from construction or wallpaper (see below) to put on a larger sheet of construction paper. Use the vegetables for printing over the bowl. For example, use the flat side of half a potato to make prints using white paint; half a carrot to print circles using orange paint; a mushroom cut in half lengthwise to print in brown paint; a celery stalk dipped in green paint to make half circles; and so on. Write "I had vegetable soup today!" on the bowl. If you don't have time for the art project, send a sentence strip home that says "I ate vegetable soup today" to encourage parents to ask about the experience.

RECIPES

Veggie Tray

cauliflower	carrots or mini-carrots
celery	broccoli
cucumbers	cherry tomatoes

Invite children to each choose one vegetable they like to buy at the grocery store. Upon your return, invite children to wash their vegetables and cut them into bite-size chunks using a plastic knife. Encourage children to try each vegetable at snack time. Try dipping the veggies in ranch dressing.

Fabulous Fruit Salad

2 cans pineapple tidbits or chunks
1 green and 1 red apple
1 pear
2 bananas
1 peach or nectarine
2 tangerines or tangelos
handful of green and red seedless grapes
exotic fruit, such as kiwi or carabola, if available
handful of berries, such as strawberries

Make a visit to the grocery story the day before your field trip to see which fruits are in season before you make your list. After returning, make sure that children wash hands before starting. Start by emptying the cans of pineapple into a large bowl. Do not drain—pineapple juice will keep the other fruit from turning brown. Children may rinse and chop the other fruit and add it to the bowl. You may have to cut the apple into wedges before children chop it into chunks. Don't worry that the chunks are uneven—the children won't care! Mix well, coating the fruit with pineapple juice. Chill or serve immediately.

Have children draw pictures of their favorite fruits on small sticky notes. Make a blank graph with all the fruits across the bottom on a piece of chart paper. Invite children to put their pictures in the column of the fruit they like best. Discuss the graphing results with children.

Write the name of each piece of fruit on an index card using the same color ink as the fruit (red for *apple,* yellow for *banana,*) to give children a visual clue to the word. Display the index cards in the writing center to encourage children to use the words in their writing.

Cognitive Activities

Bring in grocery ads, flyers, and coupons (available in grocery stores, through the mail and in special newspaper sections). Invite children to cut out three to six pictures to make up grocery lists. They may glue their pictures to a piece of brown paper cut into a grocery bag shape or to the outside of a real grocery bag. Children may go to the your classroom grocery store to find the items.

Ask parents to send in two small, identical cans of fruit or vegetables. The cans should show a picture of the contents on the label. Use the cans for these activities.

Children may match cans that are alike.

Children may match cans to pictures (a can of green beans to picture flashcard of green beans).

Children may match cans to plastic fruit and vegetables (can of sliced pineapple to plastic pineapple).

Children may sort cans by color, size, fruit vs. vegetable, or any other way the group can think of.

Write the numbers 1 to 10 on the front of 10 grocery bags (one number per bag) and have children count the appropriate number of cans to put into each bag.

Put cans on the shelf of the grocery store to use for "shopping." When you are finished with the cans, donate them to a needy family, homeless shelter, soup kitchen, or food pantry.

Use empty cans for the above activities. Be sure there are no rough edges. When you are finished with the empty cans, save the labels to use for other projects.

Mount sets of labels from fruit, vegetable, pet food, and soup cans on index cards and laminate for durability. Invite children first to match "like" labels. Once students can do this, place the labels face down so children may play "Concentration." Children turn up two cards. If they match, player keeps the set and continues until a non-matching pair is turned up. The child with the most matching pairs wins.

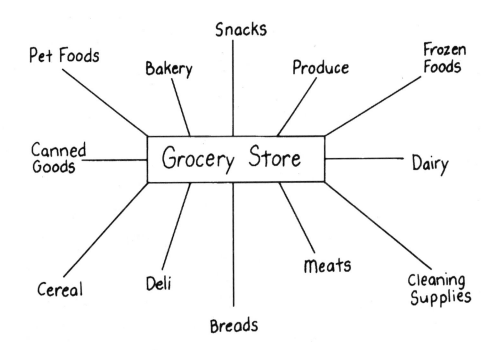 Make a web on a large sheet of chart paper (see below) using names of grocery store areas suggested by children, such as dairy, produce, meats, deli, bakery. Use fronts of boxes, labels from cans, and other items you have been saving to glue to the appropriate section. This will be an on-going process as children bring in new things to add. Children may have to add new sections for the grocery store as they realize that things they bring in do not fit one of the categories—use this as a learning process.

Snacks

Pet Foods

Bakery

Produce

Frozen Foods

Canned Goods ─── Grocery Store ─── Dairy

Cereal

Deli

Meats

Cleaning Supplies

Breads

Invite children to sort money by denomination and practice identifying the coins. Look for money rubber stamps that can be used to make an assortment of games and activities. Real money tends to get lost but there are several types of plastic money available that feel and look much like the real thing. More mature students can count out coins to match the amounts on coupons.

Count strawberries. Put out ten or twenty berry baskets. In the bottom of each basket put a number (1 to 10 or 20). Use red wooden beads from your stringing beads or red pompoms as strawberries. Children may count the appropriate number of "strawberries" into each basket. For more fine motor practice, challenge children to use tongs to pick up the strawberries to put in the baskets.

Count grapes. Write a number from 1 to 10 or 20 on the bottom of several Styrofoam meat trays. Use green or purple wooden beads from your stringing beads or green or purple pompoms as grapes. Children may count the appropriate number of "grapes" onto each tray.

Collect plastic milk jug tops of different colors. Place them in a large transparent container and invite children to sort them by color or use them as counters. Make number flashcards shaped like milk cartons and have children count the appropriate number of milk jug tops for each number.

Put foods such as rice, dried beans, dried peas, or water into pairs of film canisters. Challenge children to shake the canisters and find the two that match. Some students will try to open the canisters (inquiring minds want to know!) so be sure to introduce this activity in groups.

Cut Ellison dies, such as milk/juice carton, green onion, peeled banana, banana, broccoli, potatoes, radish, tomato, dairy group, corn, eggs, fish, fruit and vegetable group, grapes, grain group, meat group, orange, pumpkin, strawberry. Use the cut-outs to make patterns on long strips of paper. Glue the first two or three shapes in place to start the pattern and invite children to glue shapes to continue the pattern to the end of the strip.

Manipulative Center

Put out puzzles of the grocery store, such as grocer #J606083, 17 pieces, and cashier #J066007, 11 pieces (available from Judy/Instructo). Look for other puzzles of foods, such as fruits or vegetables.

Magnetic Way has an entire supermarket to set up with moveable pieces and a teacher's guide. Set up different areas of the supermarket and put out the large magnetic board for students to manipulate.

Place plastic bottles with their tops that you have collected in a large milk crate. Invite children to take off all the tops and put them in a pile. The task is to match the tops to their containers.

Play Dough Center

Have children practice packaging grapes. Provide green or purple play dough, small Styrofoam meat

trays, and plastic wrap. Children may make grapes by rolling the play dough into small balls. They then place the "grapes" on the Styrofoam tray and when it is full, cover the package with plastic wrap. Introduce this activity by showing children a picture of packaged grapes or a real package of grapes from the grocery store. If you use real grapes, children may count out a specific number for snack.

 Introduce this activity by showing children a picture of strawberries or bring in a basket of real strawberries from the grocery store. Provide red play dough and berry baskets. Encourage children to fill the berry baskets with "strawberries" made by rolling play dough into balls. Use the real strawberries for snack. Children may decide whether or not they like strawberries and graph the results using a yes/no "T" graph. Each child records an answer to the question "Do you like strawberries?" by placing a clothespin on the appropriate side of the graph.

Introduce this activity by showing children a picture of eggs in their carton or bring in a dozen eggs in a carton from the grocery store. Put out several empty egg cartons and white play dough. Children may roll the play dough into eggs and fill the egg cartons. While you are making the eggs, talk about a *dozen*. Invite children to count the eggs when the egg carton is filled with play dough eggs. Use the real eggs to make boiled eggs, egg salad, or scrambled eggs for snack later.

Encourage children to make "food" with whatever color play dough you have out. Make a list with children of all the foods of that color they might wish to make with the play dough. Place the list, with simple drawings, in the play dough area. For instance, if you have put out green and yellow play dough, children might make pears, green apples, peas, string beans, or bananas.

Put a few unopened cans of fruits or vegetables in various sizes at the play dough table. Children may make prints in the play dough with the bottom of the cans. You can then talk about circles, count the number of prints that are made, see if the child can completely cover a can with play dough, and so on. Look for other grocery items that will make patterns in the play dough, such as berry baskets, milk jug tops, or dog biscuits.

Blocks

Place some large brown grocery bags in the block area. Invite children to fill the bags with different

types of blocks—they will enjoy simply filling the bags and carrying them around. Some students may be able to count the number of blocks they can carry in a bag. Cardboard brick blocks are good for this activity but any type of blocks will do.

Place unopened cans in the block area to use for building and stacking. Try to find cans with rounded bottoms made for stacking. Make a design with the cans and invite children to copy the design.

Sand/Water Table

Add interesting plastic containers that can be found in the grocery store to the water table this week, such as plastic squeeze bottles (mustard, liquid detergent, catsup bottles, shampoo bottles, honey bear bottles). Children also like plastic bottles with tops. You will find children enjoy these free containers as much as any commercial water toys.

Take your water table outside on a warm day. Use some squirt bottles and have children write numbers, letters, words, or designs by squirting water on the hot cement. Have a contest to see who can squirt water the farthest.

Save empty containers, such as margarine tubs, plastic peanut butter jars, 2-liter soft drink containers, and small individual water and soft drink containers, for the sand table. Children will enjoy filling them up and putting the tops on.

Collect different sizes of plastic jars with screw-on lids, such as peanut butter jars, for the sand table. Use a permanent marker to mark a line on the sides of the jars. Invite children to practice filling the jars up to the marks. Some students may be able to decide how many tablespoons/cups/scoops it takes to fill the jars to the marks.

Save the scoops from coffee, dry drink mixes, and dry laundry detergent for the sand table.

Cut 2-liter soft drink bottles in two right above the label. The top of the bottle can be used as a funnel and the bottom like a sand pail. Children will enjoy these in the water and sand table.

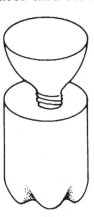

For a change of pace, invite parents to send in one large bag of dried beans of their choice and fill your water table with dried beans. Add some empty cans or scoops. You'll be surprised how fast the table will fill up.

For another change of pace, add rice to the table. Ask parents to send in a box or bag of white rice and add some empty grocery containers for hours of fun.

Art

Invite children to make grocery store collages by cutting pictures from magazines of things they would like to buy at the grocery store and gluing the pictures to a grocery bag.

Children may make "theme" collages in small groups or individually using pictures cut from magazines or coupons. Consider some of the following themes: fruits, vegetables, meats, canned foods, junk food, things we drink, foods of a certain color, breakfast/lunch/supper foods, pet foods, breads and grains, or snacks.

For very young students, provide coupons, glue sticks, and a large sheet of paper for a class collage. Children may glue the coupons to the paper.

Make grocery carts. On a sheet of light-colored construction paper, have each child use the bottom of a plastic berry basket to make a print. Or you may draw rectangles and have children make lines first down and then lines across. Add black construction paper circles for wheels or make wheels using a cork as a stamp in black paint. On separate pieces of paper, invite children to illustrate things they would buy at the grocery store. Cut around these drawings for children to glue to the top of their grocery baskets when dry. To substitute a language experience, ask children to dictate what they would buy and simply add the words. Label the picture "(Child's name's) Shopping Trip."

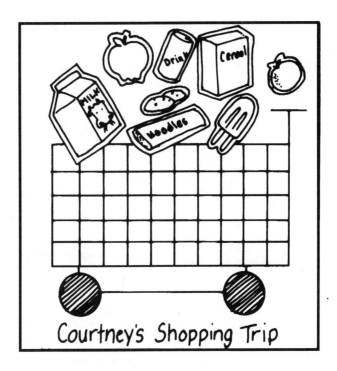

Courtney's Shopping Trip

Make a large grocery store mural. On top of a large piece of bulletin board paper, invite children to paint the name of the grocery store. Cut large rectangular pieces of white butcher paper and ask children to decide on a vegetable or fruit they would like to print. Bring in some real fruit (apple, pear, orange, kiwi, pineapple, strawberry) and vegetables (mushroom, squash, corn, large green bean). Slice the fruit or vegetable so that when children print, they can see the actual shape of the fruit or vegetable. Use an appropriate color of tempera paint and encourage children to print one type of fruit or vegetable on each rectangular piece of paper. When all the printing is done, glue each of the rectangular pieces of paper on the larger bulletin board paper. Under each type of food item, print the name of the fruit or vegetable or have students print them.

Ask children to decide on a name for the grocery
store and design a sign to hang in the store area.
You may wish to write the letters for the name of
the store in pencil and have a child paint over the
letters. Or you can turn the sign into a mural by
having children illustrate one thing they would buy
at the grocery store, cutting these out, and gluing
them on the sign in collage form. Children may
have even better ideas for a sign.

Writing Center

Have children cut pictures from magazines
showing food labels that could be bought at the
grocery store. Look for labels that have pictures of
the food. Glue the pictures to index cards and put
these in the writing center to encourage children to
copy some of the words on the labels. Allow
children the opportunity to go over to the grocery
store area and write words from the labels.
Children will love knowing that they are "reading"
this environmental print.

Collect coupons. Give each child a coupon, a marker, and a letter of the alphabet. Children may use the marker to mark the letter every time they see it on the coupon. Choose another letter and another color marker and repeat the activity. Less mature students might start with the first letter of their names.

Create a writing journal for each child by stapling sheets of white paper together. Cut brown paper bags to cover the journals. The grocery store logo on the front of the bag makes a nice cover. Encourage children to write and draw in their journals this week using temporary, invented spelling and their own letters, and the environmental print around the room.

Collect pictures to illustrate vocabulary from the grocery store. Cut pictures from magazines, look at language sets, draw your own pictures, or invite volunteers to illustrate words (write words on sentence strips and have children illustrate them on small index cards). Place the word under each picture and display in the writing center.

Use permanent marker to draw some simple food pictures from this unit, such as apple, orange, broccoli, brown grocery bag, on a plastic laminate table. Write the word under each picture. Provide some white tracing paper, drawing paper, markers, and crayons so children can trace the picture and word or draw it from the model. Permanent marker can be removed with alcohol or hair spray.

Listening Center

Record yourself (or send book and blank cassette home for a parent to record) reading one of the fiction books, such as *Don't Forget the Bacon, The Shopping Basket, Stone Soup,* or *The Supermarket Mice.* Place the cassette and book at the listening center for children to enjoy.

Book Center

Make a class big book using the environmental print in your grocery store. Make a page for each letter of the alphabet from construction paper. Invite children to identify something in the grocery store that starts with each letter. Cut the front from the box or the paper label from around the can and glue to each letter page. Try to choose brands and names with pictures that children can easily identify. Display the pages in alphabetical order. Later you may wish to use the pages as flashcards. Say for each sheet, "A is for _____" and have children fill in the word. When children can identify each of the labels, alphabetize the pages for a class big book.

On the following pages are some books you may wish to have in your book center. Check your school or community library for other titles. Many of these are also appropriate for reading to the class at circle time.

(ps-K) Bryant, Donna. *One Day at the Supermarket.* Ideals Publishing Company, 1989.
Child's-eye view of the supermarket from the grocery-cart seat.

(ps-K) Hucklesby, Hope. *This Little Piggy.* The Wright Group, 1990.
Variation on the traditional nursery rhyme featuring each little piggy with a different food.

(ps-K) Kemp, Moira, illustrator. *This Little Piggy.* Dutton/Lodestar Children's Books, 1991.
Board book illustrating each line of the nursery rhyme with delightful illustrations.

(ps-K) Kent, Lorna. *The Shopping List.* The Wright Group/Ginn and Company, 1987.
A little girl goes shopping with her dad and the baby and tries to be helpful. This wordless book is one of six in a series called "More and More" that give children the opportunity to predict what comes next. Discussion questions at the end.

(ps-1) DeLafe, Ida. *ABC Pigs Go to Market.* Garrard Publishing Company, 1977.
Mother Pig goes to the grocery store with her three little piglets and puts things in her grocery cart in alphabetical order. After reading this book, invite children to make their own "ABC Grocery" big book.

(ps-1) Fann, Charlie. *The Supermarket.* The Wright Group/Ginn and Company, 1989.
Dad and his three children go grocery shopping—illustrated with humor that will be familiar to any parent or child. The repetitions make this predictable book easy to "read." Also good for children to use as the basis for a class big book, each child contributing a picture.

(ps-1) Berenstain, Stan and Jan. *The Berenstain Bears at the Super-Duper Market.* Random House, 1991.
"First Time Book" in rhyme featuring the famous Berenstain Bear family on a trip to the grocery store.

(ps-1) Gordon, M. *The Supermarket Mice.* Dutton, 1984
Happy in their home until a large cat takes up residence, the supermarket mice quickly learn to deal with him by feeding him.

(ps-2) Grossman, Bill. *Tommy at the Grocery Store.*
HarperCollins Children's Books, 1991.
Tommy is mistaken for items in a grocery store until his
mother comes to the rescue. Written in humorous rhyme.

(ps-2) Rockwell, Anne and Harlow. *The Supermarket.*
Macmillan Publishing Company, Inc., 1979.
Trip to the supermarket.

(ps-2) Schotter, Roni. *A Fruit and Vegetable Man.* Joy Street
Books, 1993.
Warm story about the simple joys of doing something you
love and sharing it with someone new.

(K-2) Burningham. John. *The Shopping Basket.* Crowell, 1980.
On his way home from a quick trip to the store, Steven
encounters several marauding animals ready to relieve him
of the groceries in his basket.

(K-2) Hutchins, Pat. *Don't Forget the Bacon.* Greenwillow
Books, 1976.
Delightful rhyming read-aloud about a little boy who goes to
the store for his mother and tries hard to remember her
instructions.

(K-2) McGovern, Ann. *Stone Soup.* Scholastic, 1986.
When a greedy old lady claims she has no food to give him, a
hungry young man proceeds to make soup with a stone and
water. Delightful rendition of the old French folk tale with
colorful illustrations. Available with an 8-minute cassette
from Scholastic.

(K-3) Berson, Harold. *The Rats Who Lived in the Delicatessen.*
Crown Publishers, 1976.
A rat lives happily in a delicatessen until he lets other rats
come and live there. A good story to read when discussing
the word deli/delicatessen.

(K-3) Brown, Marcia. *Stone Soup.* Charles Scribner's Sons,
1947.
This Caldecott Honor Book is the story of three hungry
soldiers who come to a town where all the food has been
hidden. They set out to make a soup of water and stones.
Also available on book and cassette from Live Oak Media.

Outside

- Take grocery carts outside for children to play with. Add some groceries and create a supermarket race.

- Invite children to fill clear 2-liter bottles with colored water. Children will enjoy simply loading them into a wagon and carrying them around the playground. You might also want to have a relay race by putting the same number of bottles in two stacks at one end of the playground. The first child from each team pulls the wagon across the playground, puts all the bottles into the wagon, brings them back, and sits at the end of the line. The next child takes the load down, unloads, comes back, and sits at the end of the line. Repeat until all on one team are seated. To make the game more cooperative, have all the children on each team help with the loading and unloading. The first team to have all players seated is the winner.

- Collect a set of empty matching plastic bottles that could be bought at the grocery store, such as individual water containers. Set the bottles up outside to use as bowling pins (try adding some sand to the bottles). A soccer ball works well as a bowling ball. Use cones or sticks to set a perimeter for the "bowling alley" so other children will not walk through the game in progress. Invite children to bowl in pairs. One rolls or kicks the ball and one resets the bottles. Partners change places after 5 minutes.

Field Study

Plan a field trip to a local grocery store. Many major chains will plan a tour for you. You can visit the bakery, meat department, and so on, or plan your own field trip to pick up vegetables for vegetable soup or fruits for fruit salad (see pages 110-112). Have each child choose one ingredient to buy (have pictures of foods and how much you want on small index cards) or divide the class into small groups, led by an adult, and have each group purchase one item for the project. Groups should all go through the entire process of selecting an item and going through check-out.

When setting up your field trip, don't be afraid to inquire about things you would like the children to see and do. For instance, can a child be chosen to scan the items you buy at the check-out? Might another child bag the groceries under the supervision of the grocery staff? Might you see a cake being decorated or go back into the bakery to see the large mixing bowl? May children go into the meat locker and see the butcher cut some meat? May children go into the freezer or see boxes mashed for recycling? Some of these things are not permitted for safety reasons but different stores have different guidelines. You may even give managers ideas for things they never thought would be interesting to children.

Take photographs on your field trip. Mount them on posterboard and have children suggest captions for the pictures. Hang the picture board at students' eye level. Take pictures you can use next year as vocabulary or to prepare students for the same field trip.

🛍️ Videotape the field trip or ask a parent to do it. Review the tape after returning to school.

🛍️ When you return from the field trip, make a sentence strip for each child that says, "(Child's name) saw _____." Fill in each sentence with whatever each child remembers seeing. Give children index cards and invite them to illustrate the things they saw. Glue the illustrated cards to the sentence strips. Add a first sentence strip to the sequence, "At the grocery store . . ." These can be put on a chart for the children to read or made into a sentence-strip book by punching a hole and binding with a ring binder. On the last page, write "I can read this book." Children able to read the book may sign their name or glue their photograph to the page (a photocopy of a photograph works well).

Make a thank you banner to send to the grocery store. Write "Thank you, (Name of Store)!" on a computer banner or write the letters in pencil and have children paint over your letters. Encourage child to dictate something they remember about the grocery store for you to write down. Send the banner to the store.

Parent Involvement

Write to parents explaining that children will be learning about jobs people do in the supermarket, and the food and other items available there. You may want to send home the parent letter on the facing page.

Dear Parents,

We are going to be setting up our own grocery store in the classroom. Please save empty boxes and jars (no glass) that we can stock our shelves with, cans with the tops cut out (no sharp edges), empty milk and orange juice jugs, empty detergent boxes, and so on. Just send them in and we will do the rest.

When you go to the grocery store this week, be sure to take your child with you. Take a few minutes to identify all of the different fruits and vegetables in the fresh produce section, identify the parts of the grocery store (bakery, produce section, deli, meat department and so on). Discuss with your child how the grocery store is arranged with "like" things together. Encourage your child to put some things in the grocery cart.

When you get home, invite your child to help you put the things in their proper place—on the shelf, in the refrigerator, in the freezer. Enjoy your mini-field trip!

Happy shopping!

© 1996 Fearon Teacher Aids

Fire Station

National Fire Prevention Week is in October each year. Contact your local fire department about activities planned for that month You can also contact the National Fire Protection Association for useful educational information.

National Fire Protection Association
Public Education Department–MB
1 Batterymarch Park
P.O. Box 9101
Quincy, MA 02269-9101
617-984-7285

Creative Play

 This center works well next to the home living center. In a corner of your room, add things that will encourage children to simulate being firefighters, such as raincoats, boots, gloves, hats (see page 156 or use one of the red plastic fire hats available in toy stores), flashlight, pieces of a garden hose or rope (see page 157 for homemade hoses), walkie-talkies, fire truck (made from a wagon or painted box), a bell, and pails. If you know a firefighter, ask what things he might be able to donate for children to use.

 Add some cots or sleeping bags to the area so children can role-play sleeping in the fire station,

hearing the bell, jumping out of bed and getting dressed to go to the emergency.

Look in flea markets and garage sales for a stuffed Dalmatian puppy to add to the fire station.

Home Living

Make a paper fire extinguisher to mount on the wall in the home living center or ask the fire department about an empty extinguisher for the children to use.

Add telephones (toy or real ones that no longer work) to the home living area. Put a "911 Emergency" sticker on each telephone. Encourage children to pretend there is a fire and have them practice calling 911 to report it.

Explain to children that often firefighters actually live at the fire station part of the time. Encourage them to pretend to cook meals for each other. Make use of the home living stove, refrigerator, and sink for preparing food.

Make "fake fire" to use in the home living center. This can be made from construction paper or use shredded tissue paper or crumpled cellophane in red, yellow, and orange. Children may pretend a fire is starting, call 911, have firefighters come to put out the fire, and so on.

Place a class telephone book by the telephones. Write each child's name and telephone number on an index card and add a photograph or

photocopied picture of each child. Also add a card for "911 Emergencies." Punch a hole in each card and bind them all together with a ring binder. For a fancier telephone book, cut pages in a telephone shape from colored tagboard or construction paper, laminate, and bind. Encourage children to use the telephone book to practice dialing or punching in numbers.

Circle Time

 Start by finding out what children already know about firefighters. There may be a child in your group who has been involved in some type of kitchen fire or who knows someone who has had a house fire or had a firefighter come to their house. Help children dictate a list of the things they know about firefighters so you will know what foundation they already have.

Ask children what they would like to know about firefighters. Put yourself in the learner's role and share with children something that you would like to know. Decide on 3-5 things you would all like to find out about and write the questions on chart paper. Discuss with children how they might find out the things they want to know (look in books, take a field trip, ask a firefighter, call the fire station, and so on). Plan your unit around things children want to know.

Come to circle time wearing a fire hat and using a "fire hose" as a pointer to help read a big book or sing a song about firefighters. Leave the fire hose pointer near the books for students to use for independent "reading" during center time.

Use play telephones or any old telephone that no longer works. Practice calling in a fire alarm with children by dialing 911. Have children practice saying their full names, addresses, and telephone numbers (some systems will have this information when the call is made). Be sure children understand that they should not hang up until told to do so.

Tape segments of "Rescue 911" or other television programs where children use the telephone to call in a fire. Be sure to use segments with positive outcomes that will not frighten young children. Discuss with them how the child on film used the telephone to get the fire department and other options, such as getting out of the house as fast as you can, running to get a neighbor's help, not returning to a burning house, and so on.

To promote vocabulary, look for picture cards illustrating things associated with firefighters or

make your own vocabulary cards by cutting pictures from magazines or drawing your own. You might also ask permission to take photographs at a fire department. Pictures you might want are firefighter, fire truck, ladder, fire hose, ax, oxygen tank, walkie-talkie, fire alarm, fire station, smoke, fire, fire hydrant, fire extinguisher, flashlight, firefighter's boots, coat, gloves, and hat/helmet. During circle time, use the pictures like flashcards.

 When children have mastered the picture cards, place them on a chalk ledge where children can see them and ask "w" questions like the following.

> *What does the firefighter wear on his head?* (hat/helmet)
> *What does the firefighter use to break open doors in a fire?* (ax)
> *What does the firefighter drive?* (fire truck)
> *Who fights fires?* (firefighter)
> *Where do the firefighters stay when they are waiting for a fire?* (fire station)

Children may guess which picture you are describing. Continue until you have used all the vocabulary cards. Picture cards with the words written underneath may be used later in the writing center.

 Use walkie-talkies for a lesson if you have them at your school. Divide the class in half and have an adult with a walkie-talkie take each group to a different location. Invite each child to take a turn talking to the other group. Bring children back together and discuss ways that firefighters might use walkie-talkies.

 Teach children that smoke rises and so they should lie on the floor and crawl if they are caught in a fire. Have children practice crawling around the room,

pretending they are in a smoke-filled environment. Place two chairs three feet apart to represent the door of escape.

● Teach children that a hot door indicates fire on the other side. Practice by having children crawl to all the doors in the room. Tell them whether the door is hot or cold (or place red dots for hot doors and blue dots for cold doors) and encourage them to react appropriately. If the door is hot, children do not open the door but must find another way out. If the door is cold, it is okay to open.

● Discuss with children reasons why they should never play with matches or a cigarette lighter, such as that they might get burned or start a fire. Over one-third of burns to children ages three to eight result from playing with matches and lighters. Ask children what they would do if they found matches or a lighter. Answers might include throw them away or give them to an adult.

● Discuss with children what to do in case of a clothing fire—stop, drop, and roll. That is, children should stop, freeze like a statue (running fans the flames), drop or fall to the ground, and roll—turning over and over—until the fire is out.

● Have children point out where in the room the fire alarm is located, how it sounds, and why it goes off. If possible, demonstrate how a home fire alarm works by pushing the test button and setting it off. Encourage children to go home and find out where the alarms are in their homes. Make sure that the children know what to do if they hear the sound.

Discuss appropriate behavior during a fire drill (lining up quietly and quickly, staying in line facing away from the building until the signal is given to return). Discuss with children why they do each of these things. Write "Fire Drill Rules" with children's help to post in the room.

Give children hypothetical situations such as the following and discuss what they would do.

> *What would you do if you heard a smoke alarm ringing in your house?*
>
> *If a friend wanted to start a fire "just for fun," what would you do?*
>
> *What would you do if your best friend found a can of gasoline in the garage and wanted to play with it?*
>
> *What would you do if you smelled gas in your house?*
>
> *What would you do if you woke up and smelled smoke?*
>
> *What would you do if you saw smoke coming from the house next door?*
>
> *What would you do if your friend wanted to light a candle in a tent?*
>
> *What would you do if you found a pack of matches or a lighter?*
>
> *What would you do if you woke up and saw fire in your bedroom?*
>
> *What would you do if your clothes caught on fire?*
>
> *What would you do if a friend's clothes caught on fire?*

Make some number flashcards using fire truck and firefighter shapes (cut from the Ellison, drawn from red construction paper or tagboard, or use fire engine-shaped notepads #SE-193 from Shapes, Etc.) Put one number from 1 to 10 (or higher if appropriate) on each flashcard. For more mature students, flash a card and ask, "What number comes next?" or "What number comes before this one?" Try holding up the number and using cloze, having children fill in this chant with the correct number: "Driving to the fire in engine number 3." (As they get proficient, you'll pick up a rhythm). These same ideas can be used at circle time for alphabet flashcards.

Rhythm Time

 Sing to the tune "Ten Little Indians"

One little, two little, three little firefighters,
Four little, five little, six little firefighters,
Seven little, eight little, nine little firefighters,
Ten little fi-re-fight-ers.

Here are some other suggestions for the song.

Hold up one finger for each number as you say the rhyme. The finger puppet pattern can also be used during this activity—hold up one finger for each number.

Some students may be able to sing the song backwards.

Make a class big book to illustrate the song. Use firefighters (cut from the Ellison, shape-cut firefighter notepads, firefighters drawn by individual children, or firefighter patterns cut from red construction paper). Place a numeral on each firefighter. Page 1 will have one firefighter with a 1 on him. Page 2 will have two firefighters with 1 and 2 on them, and so on. There should be one page for each number with the words to that line of the song written at the bottom. With this book you can teach number sequence, concepts of greater than and less than, numeral identification, and matching numerals to number words.

1 little,   2 little,   3 little firefighters,

"Change up" the words to the song by replacing *firefighters* with *fire trucks*. Make an accordion-style book. Put one fire truck on each page until you have ten trucks in a row. Use fire trucks drawn by the children or use individual sheets of fire truck-shaped note pads (Mini-Fire Truck # SE-758 from Shapes, Etc.). Place numerals 1–10 on the trucks in sequence. Write the words to the song at the bottoms of the appropriate pages. Once this book is complete, you can cover up a numeral and have students tell you what it should be. You may wish to stick a piece of Velcro where each number should be and place 10 Velcro-backed circles in a pocket at the back of the book. Students may stick the numbers in appropriate places. This is a great book for reinforcing number sequence, before and after, matching number words to numerals, and numeral identification. Children can make similar individual books to take home.

1 little, 2 little, 3 little fire trucks, 4 little,

 Sing these original words to the tune of "Mary Had a Little Lamb."

Firefighters have big black boots,
Big black boots, big black boots.
Firefighters have big black boots
To help them fight the fire.

Try these other verses.

Firefighters have heavy axes . . .
Firefighters drive big red trucks . . .
Firefighters have long water hoses . . .
Firefighters have tall, tall ladders . . .
Firefighters have spotted Dalmatians . . .

After children have learned the song, write it on chart paper and point to the words as you sing with a pointer stick made by adding "fire" (strips of red, yellow and orange tissue paper) to the end of a dowel or pencil. Or you might hot glue a picture of a Dalmatian puppy to the end of a dowel. Pointing will reinforce the left-to-right movement used in reading. Keep the pointer nearby to encourage

children to use it as they read the chart independently. Use small illustrations over key words to help students "read" the words. This will help build the bridge between oral and written language.

Invite students to illustrate each verse of the song on sheets of construction paper. Put the pictures in a big book with the words to each verse on the bottom of the page.

Write the word *firefighter* on as many sticky notes as there are verses. Have students match the sticky note to the same word on the chart. You can extend this activity by counting how many times the word *firefighter* was used.

Cut a firefighter shape from red felt for your flannelboard. Cut felt pieces, such as black boots, gray ax, red fire truck, gray hose, brown ladder, to illustrate each of the verses. Put the pieces up as you sing each verse.

 Teach this original fingerplay adapted from a traditional rhyme. Hold up all 10 fingers, putting one finger down with each number.

Firefighter, firefighter, number 10,
Down the pole go women and men.
Firefighter, firefighter, number 9,
Jumps on the fire truck from behind.
Firefighter, firefighter, number 8,
Puts out the fire inside the gate.
Firefighter, firefighter, number 7,
Hit his head and looked to heaven.
Firefighter, firefighter, number 6,
Down goes the door as he kicks.
Firefighter, firefighter, number 5,
Saves a child who's still alive.
Firefighter, firefighter, number 4

Feels it's cold and opens the door.
Firefighter, firefighter, number 3,
Rescues a kitty cat up in the tree
Firefighter, firefighter, number 2,
Takes off his boots and finds his shoe.
Firefighter, firefighter, number 1,
Tired and sooty but a job well done.

Here are some other things to do with the rhyme.

Make finger puppets (see page 142—10 per child or 10 to use as a teacher tool). Hold up all firefighter fingers. Lower one finger as you say each verse.

Write the fingerplay on chart paper to help children make the bridge between the spoken and written word. Use a pointer stick on each word as you read the rhyme with the class. Draw small pictures over some of the key words to help children "read" the rhyme. Pointing to each word will illustrate the left-to-right tracking used in reading.

Write numerals 1–10 on ten sticky notes. Have students place sticky numbers on the matching numerals of the charted poem. For more mature students, write out the number words and have students match word to numeral. You may wish to color code the numerals and number words at first to make the connection clearer.

Invite children to keep a steady beat by hitting their thighs with both hands as they say the rhyme.

Invite volunteers to illustrate each two lines of the rhyme with paintings or drawings. Hang the drawings on the bulletin board in sequence. After children have enjoyed the drawings for a while, place them into a bound big book to enjoy in the book center.

Discuss rhyming words. Encourage children to find pairs of rhymes in each verse, such as five and alive.

 Teach these original words to the tune "I'm a Little Teapot."

I'm a firefighter strong and brave (clench fists and bend arms up to show muscles)
It's my job to go out and save (use thumb to point to self)
When the bell rings, (pretend to ring bell)
It's off I go. (clap hands together with one hand going away from body)
Out that fire. (pretend to use hose to out fire)
I won't take no! (shake index finger)

 Use the tune of "A-Hunting We Will Go" to teach these original words.

A-fire fighting we go,
A-fire fighting we go,
We will put it out, you know,
A-fire fighting we go.

Parade around the room with fire hats and hoses (see pages 156-157).

 Try this original chant.

Down the pole
Ready to roll
In engine number _____.

Children hold up a number and stand up when it is their turn or you may use flashcards and have children read the numbers you flash.

 Children will enjoy the 25-minute VHS video, *What I Want to Be!* (Kidsongs View-Master Video) which includes a series of songs about occupations including being a (woman) firefighter!

 Teach children the words to the song, "There'll Be a Hot Time in the Old Town Tonight" —based on the

Great Chicago Fire of October of 1871. At that time, Chicago was mostly wooden structures and fires kept flaring up all over the city. Finally on October 8, a fire broke out at the O'Leary barn and was spread by winds. Firefighters' efforts to control the blaze were hampered when the city's water works burned. This lighthearted popular folk song is illustrated in Robert Quackenbush's *There'll Be a Hot Time in the Old Town Tonight: The Great Chicago Fire of 1871*. The musical notation is included. Ask children if they think that fire could happen today.

Cognitive Activities

 Cut ten or twenty Dalmatian patterns from white tagboard. Write a number on the collar of each dog and laminate. Children may use black or brown wipe-off markers to make the appropriate number of spots on the Dalmatians. Or they may use black beans or checkers to count the appropriate number onto each dog.

Cut pictures of hot (fire, iron, stove, pot boiling on stove, sun, people dressed in swimsuits or sweating from exercise, food with steam rising) and cold items (popsicle, ice cube, ice cream cone, refrigerator, freezer, people dressed for cold weather, iced drink, snow) from magazines and glue the pictures to individual index cards. Sort the pictures into stacks of "hot" and "cold."

Write numerals 1 to 10 or 20 down the left side of a sheet of paper. Children may use a rubber stamp (firetruck SE-439 from Shapes Etc.) or fire-colored (red, yellow, and/or orange) bingo dabbers to stamp the appropriate number of marks beside each numeral.

Cut an old hose into varied lengths. Place the hose pieces in a wagon or milk crate and invite children to order the pieces from shortest to longest or vice versa.

Use Ellison dies or make your own simple patterns for firefighters and fire trucks. Write uppercase letters on the firefighters and lowercase letters on the fire trucks (or pictures that start with each of the letters). Invite children to alphabetize the letters and match each firefighter with his fire truck. More mature students may match pictures of rhyming words.

 Cut 26 simple fire truck patterns from red tagboard. Cut 52 circles from construction paper for wheels. On each wheel write a letter of the alphabet, using all the upper and lowercase letters. Children may find the matching upper and lowercase wheels and attach them to a fire truck. More mature students may match initial letter sounds with pictures beginning with that letter.

 Cut Dalmatian patterns from white tagboard and add black spots. Write a color word on each dog. Make collars from different colors of tagboard or construction paper. Use half of a self-adhesive Velcro dot on the back of each collar and on each dog's neck. Children may match the collars to the dogs with the correct color word.

Snack/Cooking Time

🔥 Try to find a dog-shaped cookie cutter and make dog cookies from rolled cookie dough. Children may use plastic knives, craft sticks, or tongue depressors to spread vanilla icing on each cookie. To make a Dalmatian, children may add raisins or chocolate chip "spots."

🔥 Make ladder snacks. Use celery cut into sticks, carrot sticks and/or stick pretzels to make the ladders. Give each child all three and let them design their own ladders. They can eat their way to the top!

Ladder Snacks

celery, carrot, and/or pretzel sticks
peanut butter or softened cream cheese (optional)

Give children one of the stick choices to make ladders or give them all three choices and invite them to design their own ladders. Peanut butter or cream cheese will hold the structure together.

 Use peanut butter play dough to make firefighter's water hoses. Make long hoses and short hoses, fat hoses and skinny hoses. The best part is that the child can eat the results!

Peanut Butter Play Dough

4 Tablespoons peanut butter
4 Tablespoons honey
powdered milk

Mix ingredients with your hands, adding powdered milk a little at a time until mixture does not stick to your fingers.

Manipulative Center

 Put out puzzles of firefighters, such as firefighter J066003, 11 pieces; firefighter J606015, 13 pieces; shape fire engine J041016, 6 pieces; great big red fire engine floor puzzle J036010, 18 pieces; firefighters floor puzzle J036003, 15 pieces—

available from Judy/Instructo, or fire truck LR-2168, 22 pieces, (crepe foam rubber) available from Lauri.

Use manipulatives, and interlocking building toys to make ladders and to build fire stations.

Put a small fire truck and/or firefighter at the manipulative table (Duplo Family Workers 244830 and Duplo Community Vehicles 281527, available from Childcraft, or Mega Blocks™ firefighter set). If you don't have the commercial versions, add any small red truck and some small figures. Children will pretend they are fire trucks and firefighters.

Play Dough Center

See page 334 for a recipe for homemade play dough that's as good as the commercial brands and lots cheaper! Red is a great "fire" color.

Make fire truck ladders with play dough. Roll "ropes" for the sides of the ladder and then add toothpicks, coffee stirrers, or straws cut into pieces for rungs. Try adding tongue depressors, coffee stirrers, straws of various sizes, or craft sticks to the play dough area and watch children come up with their own way to make ladders for the firefighters.

Encourage children to make fire hoses by rolling "ropes" or "snakes." Make them long, short, thin and thick. Show children how to coil the hoses. Use a garlic press and blue play dough to make water coming out of the hoses.

Children love riding fire trucks with good wheel treads through play dough and looking at the patterns left by the tires.

Use red and yellow play dough to make fire. Show children how mixing the two colors will make orange. Roll all three colors into a ball and flatten by using a rolling pin or cylinder-shaped block. Use a pizza cutter, plastic knife, craft stick, or tongue depressor to form jagged flame outlines.

Make a fire truck with play dough. Flatten red play dough with a rolling pin or cylinder-shaped block. Use a plastic knife or a pizza cutter to cut out a rectangular fire truck. Roll two balls from another color play dough. Slightly flatten the play dough balls with the palms of the hands and add "wheels" to the fire truck. You may wish to add a ladder made from play dough and/or a fire hose by rolling a "rope" and coiling it into place on the fire truck.

Put out white play dough and a dog-shaped cookie cutter. Encourage children to make Dalmatians. Use a straw to punch holes for spots.

Blocks

Encourage children to construct buildings with blocks and pretend they are on fire. Add a fire truck, such as Big Fire Truck #6683 by Little Tikes, to put out the fires. Use red, yellow, and orange strips of tissue paper or construction paper for fake fire.

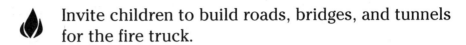 Invite children to build roads, bridges, and tunnels for the fire truck.

Place a vinyl floor map of a town on the floor. There are several commercial versions (Drive Around Town Carpet #LC1607, a washable carpet from Lakeshore Learning Materials or Motor Map #HOY-1 Super Roadway Play Mat #PT-500, both from Constructive Playthings) or you and the children can draw your own map. Add "fake" fire on one of the town buildings. Using a toy or cut paper fire truck (or even a red block) encourage children to find the shortest route to the fire. Encourage siren sounds and role-playing.

Art Center

Put "fire" colors at the paint easel this week (red and yellow) and encourage children to paint fire.

Invite children to fingerpaint with red and yellow. They will discover that red and yellow combine to make orange. See the recipe for homemade finger-paint on page 334.

Invite children to make firefighter's hats from red construction paper using the diagram on page 156. You may wish to cut the inside of the hat and have each child cut the outside for themselves. Fold on the dotted line. Add a yellow badge to the front with the child's name.

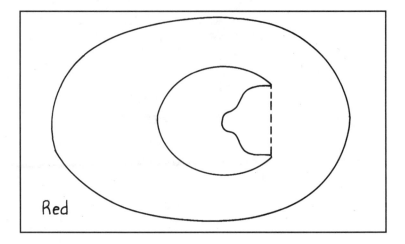

Red

 Cut simple fire truck shapes (or children may cut their own) from red construction paper (or children may fingerpaint paper red, trace a fire truck stencil, and cut it out). Use the fire truck diagram below. Invite children to draw faces in the windows. Add two black circles for wheels or have children cut their own by rounding the corners of two squares cut from black construction paper. Children may make toothpick ladders in any arrangement they desire. It may be necessary for you to draw the ladder with glue and have children place toothpicks on the glue. Break or cut toothpicks in half for rungs.

Extend the previous activity by making the art into a book. Place a number on each child's truck, for example "Engine #1." Instead of drawing a firefighter's face, substitute a photo of each child behind the driver's seat. School pictures photocopy very well and you can enlarge or shrink them to the appropriate size. Each child should be represented on one page. Write an easy-reading text, such as, "Chenly drives fire engine #9." Bind the pages in numerical order into a book (or mix the order to challenge more advanced students). Bind the book in the traditional format or in accordion style so when the book is open, it looks like a fleet of fire trucks going to a fire.

Matthew drives Engine #1.

Courtney drives Engine #2.

 Invite children to make fire hoses to use in role-play from gray, white, or brown construction paper according to the following instructions.

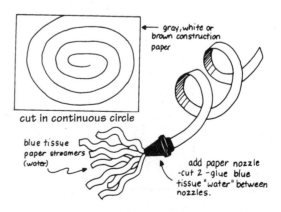

gray, white or brown construction paper

cut in continuous circle

blue tissue paper streamers (water)

add paper nozzle -cut 2 -glue blue tissue "water" between nozzles.

🔥 Make a fire ax using brown, black, or gray construction paper and a painted paper towel tube according to the following instructions. You may wish to make a belt with the ax attached so children will not use it as a weapon.

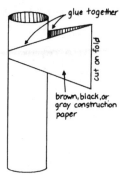

🔥 Put out pictures of firefighters and invite children to make firefighters using the following ideas. Children may cut uniforms and hats from red construction paper and circle heads from any shade of pink or brown. Encourage them to add facial features and hair. Black magic markers can be used to color the boots, add buttons to the coat, and so on. Encourage children to add other details.

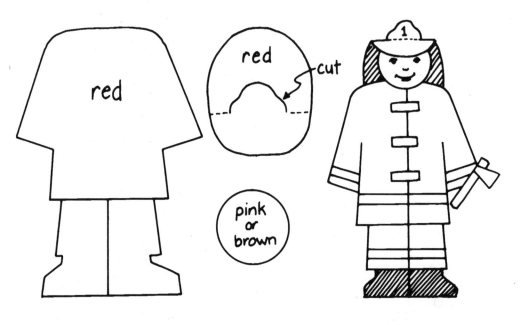

🔥 Paint paper red and cut it into the shape of a fire hydrant. Add white Dalmatian cut-outs. Have students paint black spots on the dogs.

🔥 Read Walt Disney's *One Hundred and One Dalmatians: A Counting Book* to the class. Children may also enjoy the 60-minute video or some of the books (such as the Little Golden Books) based on the Disney movie. Invite children to draw or paint and cut out several Dalmatian puppies. Be sure they understand that you will need 99 puppies all together. Place the puppy cut-outs on a bulletin board in groups of 10. Add two larger Dalmatians for the mom and dad. Aha! 101! Encourage children to use a pointer to count the dogs.

🔥 Show children a piece of charred wood, such as a log partially burned in a fireplace. Have children use pieces of charcoal to draw trees (left-over pieces of charcoal can be used outside to draw on the sidewalk). Use colored chalk in red, yellow, and orange to add fire after the trees are drawn. Discuss

forest fires and how they start. Look for "Smokey the Bear" posters to display. See page 171 for additional information about Smokey.

 Make a fire truck from a large mattress box. Cut a hole in the top so children can climb inside. Bend half of the cut portion up. Take the box outside so children can paint it red. Add wheels and a ladder to the side with black paint when the red paint has dried. Include any other details the children think of, such as head and tail lights. These can be painted on or you may use circles of foil. A Frisbee makes a good steering wheel.

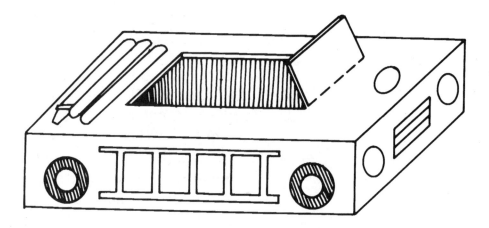

Extend this activity by taking a photograph of each child dressed in a firefighter hat and pretending to drive the fire truck. Glue each picture to a larger piece of tagboard to make a book, using the format from *Brown Bear, Brown Bear.*

Carlos, Carlos, who do you see?
I see Francisca looking at me.

Francisca, Francisca, who do you see?
I see . . . .
I see all the firefighters looking at me (picture of fire truck with all the children in and around it).

For the title page, take a picture of yourself in the fire truck!

 Make individual fire trucks from shoe boxes or milk cartons. Shoe boxes may be painted red and milk cartons may be covered with red construction paper. Add wheels, windows, firefighters, ladders, and other details—children may use their imaginations.

Writing Center

 Show children how to draw ladders.

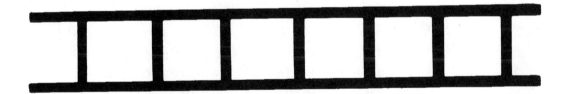

 Use a wall chart and write some of the vocabulary words that the children might want to use in their writing this week, such as boots, hose, firefighter's hat, fire hydrant, fire, ladder, on sentence strips. Invite volunteers to illustrate each word. Place the pictures beside the matching words and leave in the writing center.

Use the same picture vocabulary cards that were made for circle time. Place the word under each picture and display in the writing center. Students may copy and illustrate these words in journals pre-cut in the shape of a fire truck.

Use permanent marker to draw some simple pictures from this unit, such as boots, fire truck, ladder, on a plastic laminate table. Write the word under each picture. Provide white tracing paper, drawing paper, markers, and crayons so children can trace the picture and word or draw it from the model. Marker can be removed with alcohol or hair spray.

Practice writing numbers 911.

Encourage children to practice copying (writing) their own names, telephone numbers, and addresses as they would tell them to the operator if they were to dial 911.

Make special pencils for this unit. Cut a 3" x 2" (7.5 cm x 5 cm) oval from white construction paper and make a picture of a firefighter on this paper. Punch two holes (just large enough to fit a pencil through snugly) at the top and bottom of the oval. Slide the pencil through the holes. It's a firefighter sliding down his pole!

Design your own worksheet similar to the one illustrated to help the firefighter get to the fire. Extra roads may be added for more mature students. These can be laminated for repeated use with a washable marker.

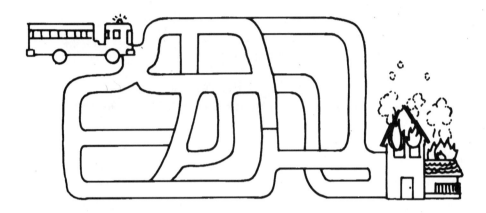

Listening Center

Tape yourself reading stories such as Margaret Rey's *Curious George at the Fire Station* or Margaret Wise Brown's *The Little Fireman* for the listening center.

Tape children singing one of the songs or fingerplays about fire fighters. Provide a written version with illustrations provided by you or the children to read along with the tape.

Book Center

 Make an ABC Firefighter's class book. Invite children to decide on a relevant word for each letter of the alphabet. Read Jean Johnson's *Firefighters: A to Z*. Here are a few words in case you get stuck.

ax, alarm
boots, burn
coat
Dalmatian, (fire) drill
eating (at the firehouse), engine
fire, forest fires, firefighter
gloves, gurney
hose, hydrant, hot
ignite
jump
kerosene
lightning, lights
matches
nozzle, 911
oxygen mask/tank
protection, pole, paramedics
never quit
ready to go, red
safety, siren, smoke, station
truck, teamwork, telephone
uniform
victory
water, walkie-talkie
x-tra effort
yawn after a hard day's work
z-z-z-z back to sleep

Invite volunteers to illustrate each letter. Add text, such as "A is for ax," on each page. Alphabetize pages and bind for the book center.

 Here are some books you may want in your book center. Check your school or community library for other titles. Many of these are also appropriate for reading to the class at circle time.

(ps-K) Bracken, Carolyn. *Fast Rolling Fire Trucks*. Grosset and Dunlap, 1992.
Board book shaped like a fire truck with real wheels.

(ps-K) Mayer, Andy and Jim Becker. *Look and Listen Fire Truck*. Scholastic, Inc., 1993.
Delightful board book with pushbutton to make fire truck sound.

(ps-1) Brown, Margaret Wise. *The Little Fireman*. HarperCollins Children's Books, 1993.
First published in 1952. Great big tall fireman and little fireman, whose firehouses are right next door, each find a fire the right size for them to fight.

(ps-K) *Firehouse*. Little Simon/Simon & Schuster, Inc., 1983.
Simple board book in the shape of a fire station. Clear color illustrations.

(ps-1) Chlad, Dorothy. *When There Is a Fire . . . Go Outside*. Childrens Press, 1982.
Simple explanation of what to do if there is a fire at home.

(ps-1) Cox, Mike and Kris and Stan Hushbeck. *Fire Drill*. Aro Publishing Company, 1979.
Simple story of a fire drill at school.

(ps-1) Horowitz, Jordan. *Working Hard with the Busy Fire Truck*. Scholastic/Tonka Corporation, 1993.
Tom and Sam (a woman), firefighters in a small community, battle blazes in the country and the city.

(ps-1) Kundhardt, Edith. *I Want to be a Fire Fighter*. Grosset and Dunlap, 1989.
Dad is a firefighter. Includes pictures at the fire station and safety tips. Great photographs.

(ps-1) Rockwell, Anne. *Fire Engines*. Dutton Children's Books, 1986.
Describes parts of a fire engine and how firefighters use them to fight fires.

(ps-2) Lenski, Lois. *The Little Fire Engine*. Henry Z. Walck, Inc., 1960.
Fireman Small and his fire engine answer a call, rescue a little girl, and save a burning house.

(ps-2) Quackenbush, Robert. *There'll Be a Hot Time in the Old Town Tonight: The Great Chicago Fire of 1871*. J. B. Lippincott, 1974.
Illustrations accompany the verses of the folk song describing the Chicago fire. Includes music and information on fire safety.

(K-2) Johnson, Jean. *Firefighters: A to Z*. Walker and Company, 1985.
Black and white photographs. Lots of words but good for children learning the alphabet.

(K-3) Leonard, Marcia. *Jeffrey Lee, Future Fireman*. Silver, Burdett and Ginn, 1990.
Jeffrey takes a tour of the firehouse with his class and dreams of the time when he can be a firefighter. At various points in the text, the reader is asked to explain what's happening

(K-3) Elliott, Dan. *A Visit to Sesame Street Firehouse*. Random Books for Young Readers, 1983.
A fire chief shows the Sesame Street characters how firefighters fight fires and the equipment at the firehouse.

(K-3) Hankin, Rebecca. *I Can Be a Firefighter*. Childrens Press, 1985.
Excellent color photography of a firefighter's life.

(K-3) Hannum, Dotti. *A Visit to the Fire Station*. Childrens Press, 1985.
Describes a visit to the fire station and the equipment and methods used by firefighters in their work with tips on fire safety.

(K-3) Maass, Robert. *Fire Fighters*. Scholastic, Inc. 1989.
Describes what it means to be a firefighter, including life at the fire house, practice drills, service to the community and fire emergencies. Great photographs and abundant text.

(K-3) Rey, Margaret. *Curious George at the Fire Station*. Houghton Mifflin, 1985.
One in a series of Curious George books describing a visit to the fire station.

(K-3) Slater, Teddy. *The Big Book of Real Fire Trucks and Fire Fighting.* Grosset and Dunlap, 1987.
Beautifully illustrated big book of all different types of fire trucks, clothes and equipment used by firefighters, pictures and an explanation of the different jobs of firefighters at a fire, and pictures of a typical night at the fire house.

(K-3) Stephen, R. J. *Fire Engines: Picture Library.* Franklin Watts, 1986.
Glossary of terms. Color photographs of equipment, tools and the work of firefighters.

(K-4) Barrett, Norman. *Picture World of Fire Engines.* Franklin Watts, 1990.
Describes the vehicles, equipment, and clothing used by firefighters.

(K-4) Gibbons, Gail. *Fire! Fire!* Thomas Y. Crowell, 1984.
Detailed book in the fine Gail Gibbons style with colored drawings.

(K-4) Marston, Hope Irvin. *Fire Truck.* Dodd, Mead and Company, 1984.
Black and white photography of fire trucks. Lots of reading.

(1-4) Peterson, Johanna. *Career with a Fire Department.* Lerner Publishing Company, 1975.
Good reference book with excellent photographs and good job descriptions, such as fire marshal, fire inspectors, training instructor, dispatcher, chief, fire captain, arson inspector.

(1-4) Brockel, Ray. *Fire Fighters.* Childrens Press, 1981.
Discusses the work, uniform, and tools of the fire fighters and describes a variety of fire trucks. Great photographs.

Outside

 When you go outside, spend a few minutes leading a "Firefighter's Workout." Do exercises such as jumping jacks and knee bends. Ask children why they think a firefighter needs to be in good shape. Invite a different child be the captain each day and lead the workout.

💧 Set up an obstacle course outside for the "firefighters." Ask children why they think a fire-fighter should practice on an obstacle course. Lay down a ladder for the children to walk or run through as one of the "training exercises."

💧 Place two garden hoses (or pieces of hose) about 12 inches apart. Explain to children that firefighters have to be in very good shape to fight a fire. Encourage them to practice leaping over the hoses. Widen the space as they master shorter distances.

💧 Discuss with children "Stop, Drop and Roll"— a technique used to extinguish clothing fires. Tape balloons to children's clothes and have them stop, drop, and roll in the grass until all the balloons burst. Some children will be scared to hear the balloons pop and they certainly should not be required to play, but others will have a great time. Explain to children that they should not run if their clothes catch on fire—that will only make the fire worse.

💧 Pretend the ladder on the sliding board is a ladder leading to a fire on the second floor of a building. Using a very short jump rope as a hose, encourage children to climb up and douse the flames with water, then quickly slide down to safety.

💧 If your playground happens to have a fireman's pole, be sure to point it out to children and explain that it is like the pole in some firefighter's sleeping quarters. See if children can decide why firefighters use a pole instead of stairs.

💧 Use a wagon as a fire truck. Put one child in the truck ringing the bell or making siren sounds. Put

another inside holding the fire hose (jump rope). A third child is the driver who pulls the wagon. Tricycles and bikes can be other emergency vehicles on their way to a fire. Great outside drama!

On a hot day, pull out a real garden hose. Put up wooden blocks for houses and encourage children to "put out the fires." Or you can draw houses and fire on the sidewalk with colored chalk and let the "firefighters" wash the fire away. Children will get wet but on a hot day, they will dry quickly. You may also wish to use squirt bottles, such as the ones that contain dishwashing liquid. Children may fill these with water to put out "fires."

Have children form an assembly line to pass a bucket for dousing a fire, as they did in the days before fire hoses. Line children up and give the first in line a large bucket. The first child fills the bucket, which is passed from one child to another until they reach the "fire" (last child in line) with the bucket of water. After that child has doused the fire, he or she goes to the beginning of the line and the action begins again.

Field Study

For an "in-school" field trip, take children on a tour to look for "fire-type" signs, such as fire extinguishers, emergency exit signs, 911 on a secretary's telephone, fire alarms, or exit maps. After you have made the tour, have a scavenger hunt. Divide children into groups led by an adult facilitator. Give each group a list of words or pictures of things they are to find that they saw on

their tour. Assign each group a color. Before you start the hunt, tape a piece of construction paper for each color at every destination. As children find each destination, they take their group's color ticket. When they have found all the spots and collected all their tickets, they return to the room. Have a special treat ready, such as red licorice ropes, red cherry jello, "Red Hots," or Dalmatian (chocolate chip) cookies.

Visit the nearest fire station or ask if the station will send a fire truck and some firefighters to your school for a presentation. Ask the firefighters to discuss "Stop, Drop, and Roll," what to do in case of a fire, demonstrate their gear, and show children features of the fire truck (especially the siren!)

Take pictures of the field trip and use them at circle time the next day as a review of what the children saw. Display the pictures in the writing center as a visual reminder and to encourage children to write and draw about the trip. Save the pictures to use as flashcards or as preparation for the field trip the next year.

Cut sheets of white paper in the shape of a fire truck. Staple together with red construction paper covers cut in the same shape and invite children to draw pictures and write about things they saw. Encourage children to use their own letters and invented spelling to express their thoughts in their journals.

After the children have seen the firefighters, ask children to draw pictures of something that they remember and dictate sentences for you to write about the pictures. Mail the pictures to the fire

station to say thank you. Include a photograph of all the children dressed in their fire hats.

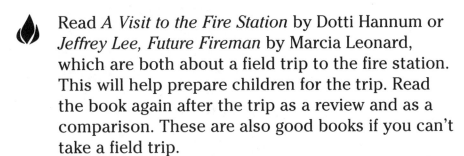 Read *A Visit to the Fire Station* by Dotti Hannum or *Jeffrey Lee, Future Fireman* by Marcia Leonard, which are both about a field trip to the fire station. This will help prepare children for the trip. Read the book again after the trip as a review and as a comparison. These are also good books if you can't take a field trip.

Substitute a good video for a field experience, if necessary. *Sesame Street Home Video Visits the Firehouse* is a 30-minute video of Big Bird's visit to the fire station. *There Goes a Fire Truck* is a 35-minute video showing real firefighters at work and comes with a "Hot Wheel"-sized fire truck that could be used in the sand table or block area. Another video showing real fire fighters at work is *Fire and Rescue* (1993, Focus Kids Video, 138 Main Street, Montpelier, VT 05602, 1-800-843-3686). All are good videos to show if a field trip is not possible, to prepare for a field trip, or as a review after a field trip.

"Smokey the Bear" is a nationwide program. To get information about having Smokey come to your school, contact your local U.S. or State Forestry Unit, listed in the telephone book under government agencies. You can also write for more information or to request materials and posters that can be used in your classroom.

Smokey Bear Headquarters
Washington, D. C. 20252

Parent Involvement

 Write to parents explaining that you are teaching about fire safety at school. Encourage them to discuss exit plans at home and to arrange a meeting place in case of a home fire. You might want to send home the parent letter and the certificate on the following page. Children who return the certificate might receive a small treat.

Dear Parents,

We are studying about fire safety this week. The children are learning about what firefighters do and what to do in case of a fire. They have learned:

- to stop, drop, and roll in case their clothes catch on fire.
- that smoke rises so they should crawl on the floor if they are in a smoke-filled room.
- to never return to a burning building.
- to check a door before opening it when they suspect a fire, leaving it closed if it feels hot and opening it if it feels cold.
- to call 911 to report a fire.
- to never play with matches or a cigarette lighter.

Please discuss and reinforce these concepts with your child. Below you will find a form for your child to return tomorrow. Discuss with your family at least two fire exit plans from your house (in case one is blocked) and decide on a place outside that you will meet. Children returning the completed form tomorrow will receive a small treat.

With safety in mind!

We talked about fire safety and discussed an exit plan from our home. In case of a fire, we will meet outside at

_____.

_____

(parent's signature)

Dentist's Office

Creative Play

If possible, set up your dentist's office near a sink. Supply the dentist area with materials such as a small syringe without needle, lab coats, plastic gloves, glasses without the lenses, bibs (or napkins and clothespins), small table or desk to hold tray of "instruments," hand-held unbreakable mirror, empty pump toothpaste containers, plastic gloves, empty mouthwash and dental floss containers, a large chair to use as the dentist's chair, small paper cups, small pads of white paper and pencils for the "dentists" to write prescriptions on, and whatever else you might wish to add.

Divide the area into the examination and waiting rooms. In the waiting room, add chairs, magazines, books, brochures and pamphlets (collected from your dentist's office) and a receptionist's desk with a window (puppet theater or a box with a window cut), appointment book and pens, sign-in sheet, and telephone.

Ask your dentist if he or she will keep trade magazines for you. Cut out appropriate pictures and mount on tagboard. Laminate and post around the dentist's office. Discuss with children what is happening in each of the pictures. Ask your dentist about old x-rays you might have to show the class. If your dentist's office is near a window, tape the x-rays to the window so the light shines through.

You might also inquire about molds of teeth for children to examine, free toothbrush/toothpaste sets, coloring books, and stickers that the dentist might be willing to give you.

Role-play with students the various jobs in the dentist's office, using appropriate vocabulary. For instance, the "patient" comes in and says, "My name is Shamika and I have an appointment with Dr. Hiroshi." The "receptionist" replies, "What time is your appointment?" and so on. You may have to role-play with the children several times before they take on the roles themselves.

Explain to children that putting your hands in someone else's mouth is unsanitary unless you take the extra precautions of a real dentist. The children may look in each other's mouths and use the mirror to look in their own mouths but they cannot put anything in another person's mouth. Look for stuffed animals to use as patients that have mouths that open and teeth.

Home Living

Put a baby bed with pillow and blanket in the home living area so baby dolls and stuffed animals can put their teeth under the pillow. Use an empty film canister for the tooth (a popcorn kernel) and then replace the tooth with pennies.

Have a pair of wings available (easy to find at Halloween or make a pair from tagboard, cloth, or stretch white nylon stockings over a bent wire clothes hanger) so students can pretend to be the

"Tooth Fairy." Decorate the wings using spray glue or tacky craft glue and glitter, sequins, and/or tinsel garlands. Look for other Tooth Fairy dress-up "stuff" (wand, crown, tu-tu).

Add a telephone book, pencil, and appointment calendar to the home living area. Encourage children to call and make dental appointments.

Circle Time

Many children will be able to share experiences about their visits to the dentist. Invite each child to tell the group about one experience. This information will give you an idea of what children already know so that you can build on their experiences.

Invite children make a list of things they would like to know about the dentist. Place yourself in the learner's role and share some things that you would like to learn. Decide on 3–5 things from the list that the class will research during this unit. Discuss with children how they can find out things they want to know (read a book, ask a dentist, and so on). Be sure to include these things in your unit.

Help children list things dentists do, such as clean teeth, fill cavities, put braces on teeth, make new teeth (false teeth), take X-rays of teeth, pull teeth, teach you how to keep your teeth clean, and so on.

With the children's help, make a list of reasons "Why we have teeth," such as so we can eat food;

to bite and chew before swallowing so we don't have to eat soft, mushy food; to help talk (try the 't' or 'th' sound as in *teeth*—where is your tongue?); an important part of your smile. See if children can decide why our teeth come in different shapes. The front, sharp teeth (eight incisors—four top and four bottom, and four canines or "eye teeth"—two top and two bottom) are for biting and tearing, cutting, and ripping your food. The back, flat teeth, called molars, are for chewing, grinding, and mashing food so that we can swallow it.

Invite children to make a list of other animals that have teeth, such as wolf, lion, horse, chimpanzee, hippopotamus, bear, alligator, dog, cat, dinosaur, beaver, bat, bottle-nosed dolphin, porpoise, whale, snake, and shark. Name animals with tusks, which are really teeth, such as an elephant and walrus. Name animals with fangs, which grow in pairs and are special teeth, such as snake, bear, sea lion, dog, and wolf. Look for an informational book about animal teeth, such as *What Big Teeth You Have!* by Patricia Lauber (Thomas Y. Crowell, 1986).

Share Shel Silverstein's poem "Tusk, Tusk" from *A Light in the Attic* (HarperCollins, 1981)—a short, humorous poem about a walrus who gets braces.

Look for picture cards of animals that show the teeth. Make a window for each card so that only the teeth show through the window. See if the children can guess whose teeth they are. Then slide out the animal card so they can see the whole face. Discuss how each of the animal's teeth look the same and how they look different. Be sure to include a smiling human. What great big teeth you have!

Ask children why they should keep their teeth clean and list their answers, such as so your teeth won't get yellow, so you won't get cavities, so your mom won't yell at you, so you won't have bad breath, so you'll have a nice smile.

Look for pictures (or take photographs in a dental office) to use as language cards while you work on this unit. Some words that you might want to illustrate include dentist, dental hygienist, syringe, tooth, lab coat, dental instruments (pick, drill), X-ray, toothbrush, dental floss, toothpaste, mouthwash, plastic gloves. After children have learned the names of the pictures, display them with the words written below in the writing center.

To illustrate what happens when children don't brush their teeth, bring in a hard-boiled egg. Explain to children that the eggshell is made of the same material as their teeth. Place the egg in a jar of vinegar for 24 hours. Explain that the vinegar is like the acid (food particles, sticky stuff) that gets on their teeth after they eat. After 24 hours, remove the egg from the vinegar and invite children to examine the shell, which will be very thin. Help children understand that acid on the teeth causes them to deteriorate. Children may also need to understand that their teeth are thicker and stronger than the eggshell and won't fall out or deteriorate after just one missed brushing!

Rhythm Time

Teach children this traditional fingerplay about a dentist.

> If I were a dentist
> I know what I would do. (Point to self.)
> I'd tell all the children, "Brush your teeth. (Imitate brushing teeth.)
> Keep a smile like new." (Make a big smile and point to lips.)
> And if a tiny hole should show, (Make circle with fingers.)
> I'd say, "Climb into my chair."
> I'd make my little drill go buzzzzzzzzzzz,
> And put a filling there!" (Point to teeth.)

Have children identify teeth, lips, tongue, and gums. Play this simple copycat game. Keep a steady beat by clapping as you say, "1-2-3. Do what I do." Then do one action exercising the mouth area, such as sticking out your tongue, making your tongue go side to side, trying to touch your nose/chin with your tongue, puckering for a kiss, smiling, making an "O" with your mouth, pretending to brush your teeth, "clicking" your tongue, or pretending to floss. Repeat the chant before each action.

Teach this song to the tune "Here We Go 'Round the Mulberry Bush."

> This is the way we brush our teeth, brush our teeth, brush our teeth.
> This is the way we brush our teeth
> After every meal.

To reinforce the link between oral and written language, write the verse on chart paper or a giant white tagboard tooth. Use a Tooth Fairy's "Magic Wand" as a pointer (a glittery star on the end of a wooden dowel works well). Point to each word as you sing it. Leave the pointer out beside the chart to encourage children to point to the words as they sing the song independently.

Teach the class this original poem.

I lost a tooth. Just look at me.
Now I'm missing 1-2-3!
It's under my pillow, I'm fast asleep.
A fairy arrives without a peep.
Up comes the sun and I awaken
To find my tooth was really taken.
Lift up my pillow and what do I see?
A special surprise just for me!

Write the poem on chart paper. Use a "Tooth Fairy's" magic wand as a pointer to reinforce left-to-right progression.

Invite two children (child and "Tooth Fairy") to act out the rhyme as the class reads it from the chart.

Encourage children to help you make up hand motions for each line of the rhyme.

Have each child illustrate the poem and place their illustrations on a bulletin board around a copy of the poem. If you like, use Carson-Dellosa's "Dental Health" CD-0122 bulletin board border.

Snack/Cooking Time

Many dentists will provide a toothbrush for each child in your class. If you can get a toothbrush for each child, review techniques of proper brushing and have children actually practice brushing one day after lunch. Children may use the following recipe to make their own toothpaste.

Toothpaste

2 Tablespoons salt
2.5 oz. water
2 cups baking soda
flavorings, such as lemon or mint

Invite small groups of children to mix batches of toothpaste. Encourage children to try each flavor and decide which one they like best. Keep each flavor in a clean, empty film canister.

Bring in at least three different flavors of toothpaste and offer children a taste of each on the end of a craft stick. Make a chart with the names of the toothpastes across the bottom or use the labels. Give children each a sticky note (or use Carson Dellosa's "Tooth" Self-Stick Notelets #CD-9143; Shapes Etc. "Mini-Happy Tooth" Note Pads #SE-778; Shapes, Etc. "Large Toothbrush and Happy Tooth"

#SE-91; or Ellison tooth-shaped die cut-outs) with his or her name to place above the column that indicates their favorite toothpaste. When all have decided, you will have a graph to discuss. Which toothpaste was the favorite, least favorite, how many children liked each toothpaste, and so on.

Favorite Toothpaste

Crest	Gleem	Topol
Jeff		
Aggie		
Roseanne	Cathy	
Ruth	Joe	Doug

Try to demonstrate the difference between clean and dirty teeth. First have each child eat a small piece of candy, such as a chocolate or caramel candy bar. Provide a mirror so that children may look inside their mouths immediately after they have eaten. Provide an apple for each child and have them check their teeth again after eating the apple.

Ask parents to send in healthy snacks that are low in sugar this week, such as apples, carrots, celery, strawberries or other fruit—these help prevent tooth decay. Keep a list of appropriate snacks. Children may draw pictures to illustrate the snacks or look for pictures from magazines. Send home the "Parent Connection" letter on page 199.

Discuss with children the role that milk plays in healthy teeth by providing calcium for strong bones and teeth. If possible, serve milk each day for snack. "Milk. It does a body good."

Cognitive Activities

Kindergartners are loosing teeth, so make a graph of teeth that have been lost. Write the children's names along the left side of a piece of tagboard (or use pictures of each child or a photocopy of the child's school picture). Use the pattern that follows to cut out teeth from white construction paper, use a sheet from a tooth mini-pad (see suggestions on page 181) or the Ellison die tooth cut from white construction paper. Children may add a tooth cut-out for each tooth they have lost. Title the graph, "How Many Teeth Have You Lost?" As children loose their teeth, they may add one to the graph. Discuss the graph periodically with the class. Who has lost the most teeth? How many students have lost two teeth? How many students haven't lost any teeth? Emphasize that everyone is different and children loose teeth at different rates. When introducing the graph, you might enjoy reading Marc Brown's *Arthur's Tooth*, which reinforces the idea that each child is different.

How many teeth have you lost?					
Courtney	🦷	🦷			
Maggie					
Ryan	🦷				
Wesley	🦷	🦷	🦷		
Matthew					

Be prepared for children who lose teeth during school. Small jewelry boxes, plastic zipper bags, envelopes, or empty film canisters can be used to take a tooth home safely. Attach a small tooth cut-out, tooth sticker, or mini-shaped tooth note to the container and have it on hand, ready and waiting. Add the child's name and date. It's wise to prepare several in advance.

Enlarge and use the toothbrush and tooth patterns below for matching colors with color words. Cut a toothbrush from tagboard in each of the basic colors. Cut tooth shapes from white tagboard and write one color word on each tooth shape. Children may match the appropriately colored toothbrush with the matching tooth color word.

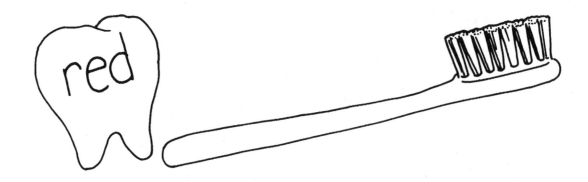

Use tooth-shaped cut-outs, Ellison tooth die-cuts, or sheets of tooth-shaped mini-pads to sequence numbers. Put one number on each tooth and invite children to order the numbers. This can also be done with upper or lowercase alphabet letters.

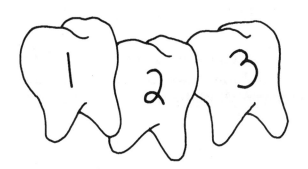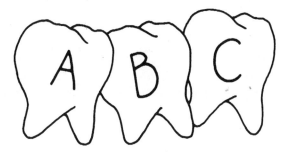

Cut five different sizes of teeth from tagboard. Encourage children to arrange them from largest to smallest or vice versa.

Look for a tooth rubber stamp or tooth-shaped stickers (such as Carson-Dellosa's "Fluorescent Happy Teeth" #CD-0436 in 5 colors). Write numerals from 1 to an appropriate number for your students down the left side of a piece of paper. Children may place the correct number of rubber stamps or stickers to match each numeral.

Enlarge and use the toothpaste and toothbrush patterns on page 186 on tagboard for matching numerals with number sets. On each tube write a number and on each toothbrush place the appropriate number of dots. Invite children to match each toothpaste with the correct toothbrush.

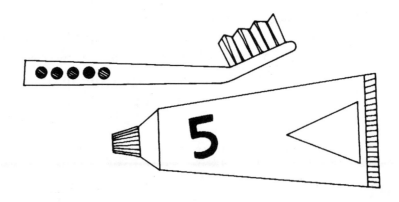

Use Tooth Fairy and magic wand patterns below for matching upper and lowercase letters (or letters to pictures representing initial consonant sounds).

Make some pillows using the patterns below. Write a money amount on each pillow. Children may use real or plastic money to count the appropriate amount onto each pillow.

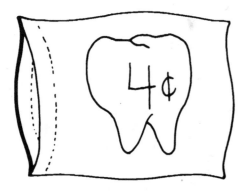

Draw simple pictures of children's smiling faces. Each child should have a different number of teeth, from 1 to 10. Invite children to identify the number of teeth and order the faces numerically.

Manipulative Center

Put out some puzzles such as these from Judy/Instructo: Dentist J6060024, 11 pieces; Dentist J066005, 12 pieces; Easy Fruit J120006, 4 pieces; Easy Vegetables J120007; Fruits with knobs J045002 and without knobs #J040002, 5 pieces; Vegetables with knobs J045003 and without knobs J040003, 5 pieces; and Fruits J506037, 7 pieces.

Play Dough Center

Use white play dough (see page 334) during this unit. Keep a tooth cookie cutter (such as the one by Wilton available at some Walmarts and craft stores) with the play dough.

Add tongue depressors and toothpicks to the play dough area. Children will think of many ways to use them.

Add strips of dental floss to the play dough area.
Show children how they can hold each end with
one hand and use the tightened dental floss to
"cut" the play dough. Roll white play dough into a
"snake." Show children how to use dental floss to
cut the "snake" into individual "teeth."

Water Table

Look for interesting dental things that can be added
to your water table this week, such as large
syringes without needles, small paper cups, old
toothbrushes, or empty mouthwash containers.

Use the white flat sponge available at craft stores
that expands when it gets wet into a tooth shape.
Float the "teeth" in the water table and encourage
children to count them; add tongs and/or clothespins for children to practice picking up the tooth-
shaped sponges from the water; add slotted
spoons, ladles, and aquarium fish nets for scooping
up the teeth; put the sponges in plastic buckets or
containers.

Art Center

Explain to children what dental floss is usually used
for. You can even demonstrate if you have a stuffed
animal with individual teeth. Tell children that
today you are going to use the floss in a novel way.
Cut the floss into different lengths and attach each

piece to a clothespin so the clothespin can be used as a handle. Give each child a piece of construction paper. Invite children to dip the floss into tempera paint (a craft stick or tongue depressor will help push the floss into the paint so it is well coated). Children may drag the paint-covered floss across the page to make designs. Use two or three different colors.

Put out old toothbrushes instead of paintbrushes (ask parents to save and send them in). Encourage children to try painting with toothbrushes.

Try fingerpainting with toothpaste. Use aluminum foil or finger-paint paper cut in the shape of a tooth. Try white pastes and colored or sparkle gels.

Make a collage of foods that are healthy vs. unhealthy for the teeth. Divide a sheet of construction paper (or a large paper plate) in half. On one side children may cut and glue drawings or pictures from magazines of healthy choices, such as fruits and vegetables. On the other side, they may glue unhealthy choices (foods with sugar), such as candy, cookies, and cake.

White is the color of the dentist. Put white paint at the easel that children may use on dark colored paper.

Cut several tooth and toothbrush shapes (or a Tooth Fairy shape) from tagboard. Give each child a sheet of white construction paper. Place a small piece of two-sided tape on each tooth shape and show children how to place them on the paper. Put out small bowls of tempera paint and large pieces of sponge. Children will sponge all over the paper with special attention to the edge of the tooth shapes. When the paint is dry, gently remove the tagboard teeth—children will discover white teeth underneath.

Invite children to design a new toothpaste. Begin by brainstorming all the names of toothpaste they can think of, such as Crest, Colgate, Gleem, Ipana, Stripe. Discuss the different names and how they think the toothpastes got their names. Then brainstorm names for a new toothpaste, such as Smile, Toothy, White Light, Pearl. Write all the names on a chart and give each child a large toothpaste shape. Children may choose names (from the list or create their own) and design new containers using paint, watercolors, markers, or crayons.

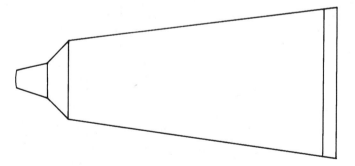

Invite children to draw pictures of what they think the Tooth Fairy looks like. Some students may dictate stories about the Tooth Fairy or write their own using temporary, invented spelling. Display each of these on a large tooth shape (or have them write final drafts on a sheet of Carson-Dellosa's "Tooth" Novel Notes CD-9244). To stimulate children's imaginations, read a book about the Tooth Fairy, such as one of the following.

Tooth Fairy by Audrey Wood
The Tooth Witch by Nurit Karlin
The Real Tooth Fairy by Marilyn Kaye
The Tooth Fairy by Anita Feagles
The Tooth Fairy by Sharon Peters

Help children make tooth fairies from sugarless lollipops and facial tissues. Place the tissue over the lollipop and tie a bow under the "chin." Use a gold or silver pipe cleaner for the "halo" and foil or clear plastic for wings.

Writing Center

Use a pocket chart and write on sentence strips some of the words that children may want to use in their writing, such as dentist, tooth, toothbrush, toothache, Tooth Fairy, money, pillow. Invite children to illustrate the words on small index cards. Glue the index card drawings beside each word. Or, write the words as they come up on a tooth-shaped chart, (Carson-Dellosa's "Tooth" Multi-Purpose Chart CD-0337).

Encourage children to design signs for the creative play center, such as Dentist Office, Receptionist, Waiting Room, Please ring bell for service, and so on.

Pair children with fourth or fifth grade volunteers for this project. Before older children come, discuss with your class some things they would like to know about the Tooth Fairy, such as where she lives, how she gets into their rooms, and what she looks like. When the older children arrive, younger children may dictate letters to the Tooth Fairy to older children. When letters are complete, put them in envelopes and pretend to mail them. Have the older students, either with you or with their own teacher, answer their younger partners' letters. (They will need to decide on some consistent answers. This is a great project for word-processing practice.) Make a big fuss on the day the letters from the Tooth Fairy arrive in your class! Place a little glitter in the envelope for "magic fairy dust" and a "stamp" with a tooth design.

Listening Center

This is a good unit in which to record yourself reading stories on tape. There are many good fiction selections, such as Marc Brown's *Arthur's Tooth*, Audrey Woods' *Tooth Fairy*, Nurit Karlin's

The Tooth Witch, David McPhail's *Bear's Toothache*, and William Steig's *Doctor DeSoto*. Check the book center list for more ideas.

Book Center

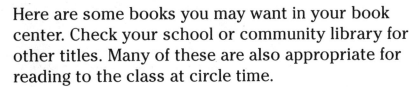

Here are some books you may want in your book center. Check your school or community library for other titles. Many of these are also appropriate for reading to the class at circle time.

(ps-K) Berry, Joy W. *Teach Me About the Dentist*. Childrens Press, 1988.
Typical visit to the dentist for cleaning and filling a cavity. Simple colored drawings.

(ps-K) Krementz, Jill. *Taryn Goes to the Dentist*. Crown Publishers, Inc., 1986.
Board book with photographs of 2 1/2 year-old Taryn's visit to the dentist.

(ps-K) Kuklin, Susan. *When I See My Dentist*. Bradbury Press, 1988.
Four-year-old Erica describes her visit to the dentist for a check-up. Color photographs of a real visit.

(ps-K) Linn, Margot. *A Trip to the Dentist*. Harper and Row, Publishers, 1988.
Questions with picture-answer options. Lift flap for answers.

(ps-1) Allen, Julia. *My First Dentist Visit*. Aro Publishing Company, 1987.
Simple storybook of a child's visit to the dentist's office.

(ps-1) Feagles, Anita. *The Tooth Fairy*. Young Scott Books, 1962.
Delightful book about all the things that the Tooth Fairy does with the teeth she collects.

(ps-1) Peters, Sharon. *The Tooth Fairy*. Troll Associates, 1981.
Speculates on what is and is not known about the Tooth Fairy. Lovely illustrations.

(ps-1) Scarry, Richard. *Nicky Goes to the Dentist*. Golden Press, 1978.
Nicky goes to the doctor for a check-up. Large rabbit illustrations, Richard Scarry-style.

(ps-1) Williams, Barbara. *Albert's Toothache*. Dutton Children's Books, 1988.
Nobody believes Albert when he complains of a toothache.

(ps-1) Wood, Audrey. *Tooth Fairy*. Child's Play, Ltd., 1985.
Delightful fiction about teeth that are chosen by the Tooth Fairy for the Hall of Perfect Teeth. Great for story time.

(ps-2) Karlin, Nurit. *The Tooth Witch*. Harper and Row, 1985.
A little witch decides to use teeth to put stars in the night sky and becomes the Tooth Fairy. Great for story time.

(ps-2) MacDonald, Maryann. *Rosie's Baby Tooth*. Macmillan Children's Group: Atheneum, 1991.
Rosie the Rabbit loses her tooth and has to write the Tooth Fairy a note. Later she finds the tooth, puts it under her pillow, and the Tooth Fairy leaves her a gold chain with her tooth attached so she can wear it around her neck always. Good for story time.

(ps-2) McPhail, David. *Bear's Toothache*. Little, Brown, and Co., 1972.
A little boy helps a bear pull out the bear's tooth.

(ps-2) Rogers, Fred. *Going to the Dentist*. Putnam Publishing Group, 1989.
Photographs prepare a child for his first visit to the dentist.

(ps-2) Steig, William. *Dr. DeSoto*. Farrar, Strauss and Giroux, 1982.
Newberry Honor Book about Dr. DeSoto, a mouse dentist, who copes with the toothaches of various animals except those with a taste for mice, until the day a fox comes in great pain. Available on a 35-minute video, *Doctor DeSoto and Other Stories* by Children's Circle. Great for story time.

(ps-3) Bate, Lucy. *Little Rabbit's Loose Tooth*. Crown, 1975.
When Little Rabbit's loose tooth finally comes out, she isn't convinced the Tooth Fairy will really come.

(ps-3) Berenstain, Stan and Jan. *Berenstain Bears Visit the Dentist*. Random House, 1981.
Sister and Brother get some needed dental attention. Good at story time.

(ps-3) Brown, Marc. *Arthur's Tooth*. Little, Brown and Company, 1986.
Arthur, tired of being the only one in his class who still has all his baby teeth, waits impatiently until Francine pushes him and the tooth falls out.

(ps-3) Luttrell, Ida. *Milo's Toothache*. Dial Books for Young Readers, 1992.
Milo Pig plans to visit the dentist about his toothache but his friends over-react and make the outing into a big problem. A Dial Easy-to-Read book.

(ps-3) Nerlove, Miriam. *Just One Tooth*. Margaret K. McElderry Books, 1989.
When a little bear named Ruth looses her beloved tooth, she doesn't believe the Tooth Fairy who says that a new tooth will grow in its place.

(ps-3) Rockwell, Harlow. *My Dentist*. Greenwillow Books, 1975.
Describes a visit to the dentist. Drawings. Easy reading with 1-2 lines per page.

(ps-3) Silverman, Martin. *My Tooth Is Loose*. Viking Children's Books, 1992.
Georgie has a loose tooth, but doesn't know how to pull it out. He doesn't want to tie it to a string or bite into a crunchy apple. Just when Georgie thinks his tooth will never come out, he gets a big surprise.

(ps-4) Noll, Sally. *I Have a Loose Tooth*. Greenwillow Books, 1992.
Molly can't get anyone to listen to her news about her loose tooth until she finds a special way to tell her grandmother. Good fiction.

(K-2) Carrick, Carol. *Norman Fools the Tooth Fairy*. Scholastic, Inc., 1992.
Norman tries to put a chip of soap under his pillow to fool the Tooth Fairy but has a scary dream about the Tooth Monster. The next day he really looses his tooth. Includes tips for proper brushing.

(K-2) Kroll, Steve. *Loose Tooth*. Holiday House Books, 1984.
Flapper and Fangs, twin bats, have a parting of the ways when Fang gets too much attention for a loose tooth.

(K-2) West, Colin. *The King's Toothache*. Lippincott, 1988.
Unable to find a dentist for the King's toothache, Nurse Mary tries a baker, a town crier, and a sailor before the poor man gets relief.

(K-3) Birdseye, Tom. *Airmail to the Moon*. Holiday House, 1988.
Delightfully humorous, Ora Mae Cotton of Crabapple Orchard has lost her tooth and when she catches 'em, she's gonna "open up a can of gotcha and send 'em airmail to the moon!"

(K-3) Chardiet, Bernice and Grace Maccarone. *Martin and the Tooth Fairy*. Scholastic Press, 1991.
Martin tries to go into business by buying teeth for three quarters and putting them under his pillow after he gets four quarters for one of his own.

(K-3) Cole, Joanna. *The Missing Tooth*. Random House, 1988.
A "Step 2 Book" from the "Step Into Reading Series." The story of best friends Aro and Robby who have a fight when one of them looses a tooth.

(K-3) Hoban, Lillian. *Arthur's Loose Tooth*. Harper and Row Publishers, 1985.
Arthur the chimp is a little worried about losing his loose tooth until his sister and babysitter show him the real meaning of bravery. An "I Can Read" book.

(K-3) Kaye, Marilyn. *The Real Tooth Fairy*. Harcourt, Brace and Jovanovich, 1990.
Delightful story for a child just beginning to doubt the Tooth Fairy myth.

(K-3) Mitra, Annie. *Tusk! Tusk!* Holiday, 1990.
Waking up on his birthday with a toothache, Elephant visits the dentist and learns about proper tooth care.

(K-3) Stamper, Judith. *What's It Like to be a Dentist*. Troll Associates, 1990.
Good watercolor pictures.

Outside

Have a Tooth Hunt. Write each child's name on three or four paper tooth-shaped cut-outs and hide them outside. Invite children to find the teeth with their own names on them. Children are not allowed to tell anyone else where their teeth are. The first to find all their teeth wins. Leave the teeth outside—children will enjoy hiding them for each other.

Field Study

Arrange a field trip to a dentist's office or ask a dentist or dental hygienist to come to the class, bring some tools, and explain the dentist's job. Ask the dentist to explain proper brushing and flossing, to bring a tooth model, some small dental instruments, such as a dental mirror and pick, discuss how teeth grow, and discuss foods children should eat to keep teeth and gums healthy.

Invite children to draw pictures of something they remember seeing on the field trip. Encourage them to use temporary, invented spelling and their own letters to label the pictures.

In a group, encourage children to tell you their favorite things about the field trip. Write the sentences on chart paper. Make a copy of the sentences with some of the children's pictures and send as a thank you to the dentist.

Ask an older child with braces to come and share with the class.

Parent Involvement

Use the letter on page 199 to let parents know you are studying about dentists and instructing children in the proper way to brush their teeth.

Dear Parents,

We are studying about the dentist. We are
encouraging children to remember to brush their
teeth two times every day. Enclosed you will find
a chart for each day of this week and 14 tooth
cut-outs. Have your child put a tooth cut-out next
to each day that he or she remembers to brush.
Each child that brings the chart to school next
Monday all filled in will get a special "good for your
teeth" treat.

Happy brushing!

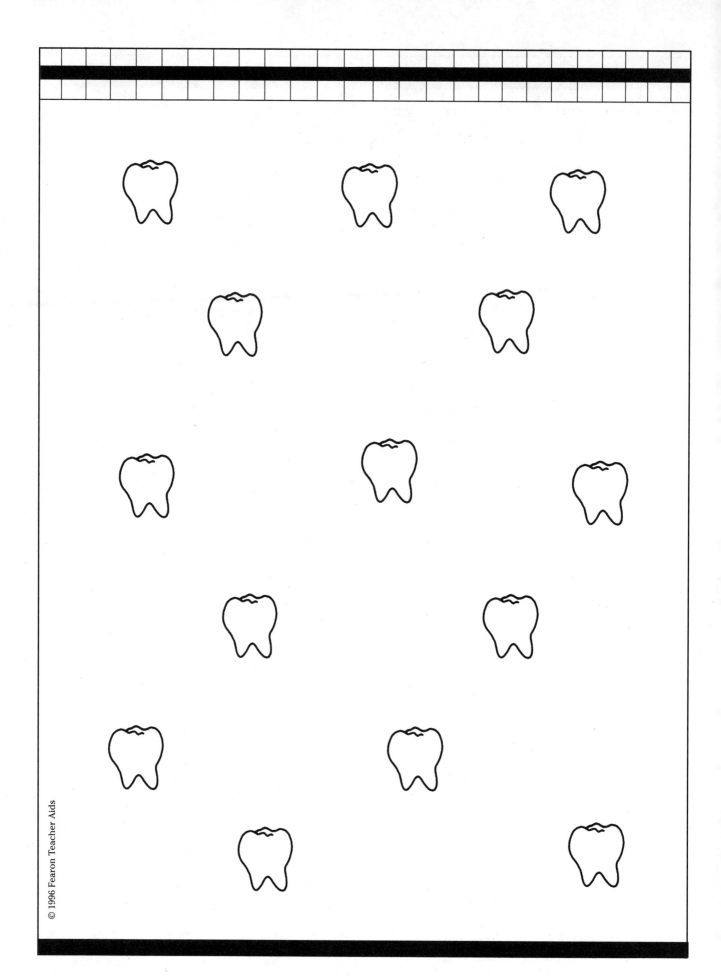

I Brush My Teeth!

Monday

Tuesday

Wednesday

Thursday

Friday

Saturday

Sunday

Police Station

Creative Play

🛡 Set up your police station in a corner of the room. Add a desk and chair for the reception area. On the desk, put a clipboard with paper and pencils and a telephone.

🛡 Put out items that will encourage children to pretend to be police officers, such as badges, paper and pencil, small pads of paper (for writing tickets), clipboard, walkie-talkies, handcuffs, flashlights, whistles (if you can stand the noise!), police hats, navy shirt, neon vests, and keys.

🛡 Add strips of black tagboard to turn a puppet theater into a jail. Or paint a refrigerator box black and add a door and window with bars. A self-sticking hook outside the door can hold a ring of keys.

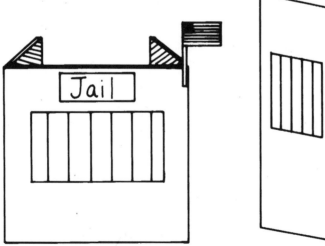

Contact your local police department or a retired police officer for "dress-up" items they might donate, such as a hat, shirt, badge stickers, patches that could be sewn on a navy shirt, and so on. Make some extra hats as well.

Manipulate play in the police station. Role-play a lost child and the police officer who helps the child. Be sure the child says he or she is lost. The police officer should reply by asking the child's first and last name, parent's name and address, and a telephone number. The officer may use the play telephone to call mom or dad. Role-play other situations as well, such as helping a child cross a busy street or taking the "bad guys" to jail.

Post "Most Wanted" posters on the wall (see page 220).

Hide a wallet or briefcase filled with play money in a dark closet or bathroom. Invite two children to dress up as police officers. Give each child a flashlight and encourage them to go into the closet and find the "loot."

Home Living

Place a play telephone (or a real, non-working telephone) in the home living center. Encourage children to practice making telephone calls by dialing their own phone numbers. You may need to use a very direct approach with some students— actually sit down with the child, call out the numbers one at a time, and be sure that the child identifies each number.

Let each child practice calling 911 and making emergency phone calls. Place a "911–Emergency" sticker on the play phone.

Place a "telephone directory" beside your play telephone. Use an index card for each child with a telephone number and name on each card (you may wish to add a picture of the child or a photocopy of a picture). Laminate the cards, punch a hole at the top, and bind together with a ring binder. For a fancier telephone book, use telephone-shaped pages. Children can look up friends' telephone numbers and practice calling them on the phone.

Circle Time

Discuss with children things they think a police officer does, such as help lost children, catch robbers, put bad people in jail, help people in trouble, direct traffic, give parking tickets, stop people that drive too fast and give them speeding tickets, put handcuffs on people, and so on. Much of their knowledge will probably be a result of what they have seen on television, but this will give you an idea of what the children already know so you can build on that information. Be sure to explain that police officers are hired to protect us and to enforce laws—they are the "good" guys.

Ask children what they would like to know about police officers. Place yourself in the learner situation and tell children something you would like to know. Decide with the class on 3–5 things to find out. Write these things on chart paper and discuss with children how they might find them out (look in books, ask a police officer). Be sure to include things they want to know as you plan your unit.

Keep an eye out for pictures you can use for vocabulary. Draw pictures, cut pictures from magazines, or go by the police station and ask to take photographs that can be mounted on tagboard and used as flashcards. Include words such as police officer, police car, police radio, baton, hand-cuffs, badge, whistle, speeding ticket, police officer's hat, uniform, motorcycle, and flashing light. When the children have learned to identify the pictures, ask them to tell you something about each picture. Or display all the pictures on a chalk ledge and give clues until children can identify which picture you are describing. Finally, display the pictures in the writing center with the words written underneath.

Use the picture flashcards to improve memory skills. Put out three picture cards and have a child identify each card. Pick up the cards, mix them up, and give them to the child to put down in the same order. Or have the child repeat to you verbally the order from memory. Vary the game by adding new cards.

 Make a police badge for each child (first name, last name optional on each badge), such as "Officer Ryan." Tape or hot glue a safety pin to the back of each badge. Or use a button machine if you are lucky enough to have one. Invite one child to be "officer of the day" and give out the badges (name recognition) or use them as flashcards and have the class say each of the names.

 Children should know their full names, their parents' names, addresses, and telephone numbers in case of an emergency. Work on teaching children to say their own telephone numbers during circle time. Send a note home with each child (see page 233) asking parents what number they would like their child to memorize in case of an emergency. Some children do not have a telephone and need to learn a neighbor's or parent's work number. When children have memorized their phone numbers, send home a little telephone shape (see diagram) that says "I know my phone number!" and invite them to post a telephone shape on a bulletin board with the same title.

I
know
my phone
number!

Careena

Use some of these activities with children having difficulty memorizing their telephone number:

Spread shaving cream over a cookie sheet. Have children write their telephone number in the shaving cream using their index finger.

As children watch, say and write each number of the telephone number on a card or white piece of paper with a crayon. Then have children say each number as they trace over it with an index finger several times (crayon will provide tactile reinforcement). Invite children to write the number in the air from memory several times, looking at the card as needed. Finally, turn the card over and encourage children to say the telephone number from memory. If a child stumbles, turn the card over for a peek until the child can say the entire number without looking.

Write the telephone number on a piece of white paper. Have children trace over each of the numbers with white glue. Sprinkle with blue glitter, allow to dry for a few minutes and shake off the excess. Later, children may trace an index finger over each number for tactile reinforcement as they say the telephone number.

Use two play telephones. Tell children you are going to call someone in the room. Choose a child's number and say numbers as you make the call (children who learn visually may also need a visual cue so have numbers printed out for those children to see. Less mature students may even need an index card with their phone number to hold in front of them so they can match the numbers). If the child recognizes his number, invite him or her to go to the other telephone and pick it up as you make "r-r-r-ring" sounds. Have a short conversation with the child and then call someone else. If children don't recognize their numbers, just say, "No one is at home" and go to another number.

Record each child's telephone number on a language master card. Then invite children to practice listening and recording their own numbers. For example, "Juan's telephone number is 241-6360." The language card also has a place to write the number for children that learn visually.

Discuss calling 911 with children. Many will have watched one of the television programs featuring emergency responses to a 911 call. Encourage children to tell these stories and to share any experiences they have had. Be sure children understand that you never play with the telephone and that calling 911 is serious business. In group, role-play an emergency such as the following and ask children to decide if they should call 911.

* There is a fire in the backyard and no one is at home.
    A friend fell off his bicycle and skinned his knee.
* Mom has fallen and you can't wake her up.
* You are alone at home and someone you don't know is
    trying to get in the house and won't go away.
    You can't find your cat.

* There was an automobile accident in front of your house.
* You smell smoke in your house.
  Your friend wants to play a trick and call 911.
* Someone on a bicycle is hit by a car.

It is inevitable that children will act out with guns and talk about guns as they discuss police officers. However, emphasize to children that there will be *no guns in school*. This is a good time to emphasize to children that guns are dangerous—children should never touch a gun, even if they are at home and believe the gun is not loaded.

Discuss the role of police dogs and how they aid the police. Record some segments of the television series "Canine Cops" or other appropriate police dog shows or specials. Choose some short segments for children to watch that illustrate the helpfulness of police dogs. Stories should have positive outcomes and not scare young children. Encourage children to write their own stories (dictated or using their own invented temporary spelling) with illustrations about dogs that help police.

Preview sections of the TV series *Top Cops* or other appropriate segments which show real-life police stories. Be selective as you record so as to emphasize characteristics of police officers that you want children to see. Choose sections with positive outcomes that will not scare young children.

Talk with children about "stranger danger." Read one of books on the subject, such as *Strangers* by Dorothy Chlad, *It's OK to say NO: A Book for Parents and Children to Read Together* by Amy Bahr, *Berenstain Bears Learn About Strangers* by Stan and

Jan Berenstain, or *Never Talk to Strangers: A Book About Personal Safety* by Irma Joyce.

 Read the story of "Little Red Riding Hood" to the class. Use this story to illustrate how dangerous strangers can be. Choose from the many versions of this story listed in the book section. You may wish to have children watch the animated videocassette version of the story from Learning Corporation of America or the more advanced and humorous "Fairie Tale Theatre" version by Platypus Productions.

Look for one of the commercial flannelboard versions of this popular folktale or make a set of your own.

For an interesting way to present the story, look for the commercially available magnetic wooden figures developed for this story by ChildWood, Inc. (8873 Woodbank Drive, Brainbridge Island, Washington 98110).

Children will enjoy acting out the story of Little Red Riding Hood. Simple props and masks will add to the excitement.

Invite children to help you re-write the story of Little Red Riding Hood so that she makes a better choice when the wolf (stranger) approaches her (she ignores the wolf and doesn't talk to him, she screams until an adult comes, she runs away from him, she runs to tell an adult)—and gets to grandmother's house safely where they enjoy their cookies and live happily ever after. Encourage children to role-play their new version.

Read Ed Young's Caldecott Medal winner, *Lon Po Po: A Red Riding Hood Story from China*. This story about three sisters endangered by a hungry wolf teaches the lesson not to open the door to strangers when parents are not home. Compare and contrast this story with the traditional Red Riding Hood story.

 Read the Caldecott Medal winner *Make Way for Ducklings* by Robert McCloskey—published in 1941 and still popular. It is the story of Mr. and Mrs. Mallard, proudly returning to their home in the Boston Public Gardens with their eight offspring, who are helped by a policeman named Michael. The book emphasizes safety, the need to live in a protective society, traffic control, and shows how a police officer uses his whistle.

This delightful story is one of five included in the Caldecott Video Library, Volume II produced by Weston Woods and can also be enjoyed by the class in video format. Discuss with children how the ducklings followed their mother very closely when they went places. Invite children to retell and illustrate the story using people—for example, going to the mall with mom.

 Read *The Story About Ping* by Marjorie Flack and Kurt Wiese to the class. The story can be used as a springboard to a discussion about why children should always stay with their parents in public places and the things that can happen should children get lost. Ping is a little duckling who lives on a boat in the Yangtze River with his extended family. He does not go home at the end of one day and the story chronicles his misadventures at the hands of strangers. The story has a happy-ever-after ending and Ping does find his family, none the worse.

 Teach children to play "Police Officer, Police Officer, Who Stole the Money?"—a variation on the game "Doggie, Doggie, Who Stole the Bone?" One child is the police officer and steps out of the room to the "police station." Another child hides an old wallet with some pennies or play money on his person (sits on it, holds it behind back, hides it under T-shirt). The police officer is invited back into the room. In unison, the class says, "Police officer, police officer, who stole the money?" Have the police officer choose three "witnesses." He or she can ask each witness one yes-no question, such as "Is the thief blond?" "Is the thief a girl?" "Is the thief wearing red?" After three questions, the police officer must guess. If correct, he or she has solved the case and gets another turn. If incorrect, the child with the wallet gets to be the police officer.

Rhythm Time

 Play "Police Officer Freeze." Have a whistle handy and play some music on the record player or cassette. Children may dance to the music but have to freeze when they hear the whistle and stay in that pose until they hear the whistle again. Invite some children to be police officers and blow the whistle (whistles can be cleaned between turns with alcohol or a disinfectant wipe).

Fingerplay (traditional)

Police officers are helpers wherever they may stand
(feet apart, hands on hips)
They tell us when to stop and go by holding up their hands.
(signal stop by holding up hand and go by pointing
index finger)

Write the fingerplay on chart paper, pointing to each word as you read to help children make the bridge between the spoken and written word.

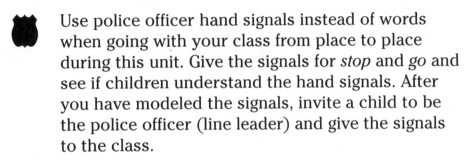

Use police officer hand signals instead of words when going with your class from place to place during this unit. Give the signals for *stop* and *go* and see if children understand the hand signals. After you have modeled the signals, invite a child to be the police officer (line leader) and give the signals to the class.

Use an extra police officer's badge cut from tagboard and hot glued to a dowel rod for a pointer during this unit. Pointing to each word as you say it will reinforce left-to-right progression. Leave the pointer out so children can "read the room" with the pointer in their spare time.

Teach the following original words to the tune "I'm a Little Teapot."

There's a police officer dressed in blue (hand from head
to toe)
He's (or she's) a friend to me (point to me) and you
(point to you).
See his (her) shiny badge (make a circle on chest with
both hands),
It's oh so bright.
He (she) keeps us safe both day (make large circle sun
over head)
and night (fold hands and go to sleep).

Write the rhyme on chart paper and have children identify the rhyming words.

Invite volunteers to illustrate each line of the poem. Place pictures in order on a bulletin board with words written underneath. Once children have enjoyed the pictures on the bulletin board, bind them together in book form, adding a title page.

 Teach this traditional fingerplay about crossing the street.

> *Stop, look, and listen when you cross the street.*
> *(stand tall, look both ways)*
> *First use your eyes, then use your ears,*
> *(point to the body part)*
> *And then you use your feet.*
> *(imitate walking)*

Discuss with children the rules for walking across the street using the fingerplay above. If you have a parking lot or back road that is not well-traveled, go outside and give each child a chance to say the rhyme and do the actions before crossing the street.

 Use this simple traditional fingerplay to teach children about the colors of traffic lights.

> *"Stop," says the red light. (hold up hand)*
> *"Go," says the green. (point index finger)*
> *"Wait," says the yellow light, (open and close hand)*
> *Blinking in-between.*

You may wish to make the traffic light in the Art Section (see page 221) and the "Stoplights" cookies in the Snack/Cooking Section (see page 215).

 Watch the delightful 25-minute video, *What I Want to Be!* by Kidsongs View-Master Video—a series of songs about occupations including "Mr. Policeman."

Snack/Cooking Time

 Use any round cookie or cracker. Invite children to design their own police officer badges with small tubes of frosting.

 Children may make their own stoplights using the following recipe.

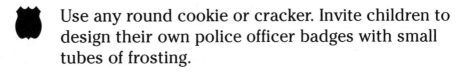

Stoplights

one-third of a large graham cracker
creamy peanut butter
red, yellow, and green candy pieces

Give children each a plastic knife, craft stick, or tongue depressor to spread cracker with peanut butter. Talk with children about what each color on the stoplight represents. Then invite children to choose a red, yellow, and green piece of candy to put on their stoplights.

 Try the following pasta salad.

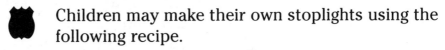

Police Officer's Pasta

wheel-shaped pasta (like a police car or badge)
shredded carrots
shredded cheddar cheese
sliced cherry or plum tomatoes
Italian dressing

Boil pasta according to package directions. Have children shred carrots and cheese and slice tomatoes. Add all to the pasta and sprinkle with a little Italian dressing.

Cognitive Activities

 Use Ellison lock and key dies for this alphabet match or cut your own from tagboard. On the locks, write uppercase letters of the alphabet. On the keys, write lowercase letters (or glue pictures representing initial sounds). Children may match the keys to appropriate locks.

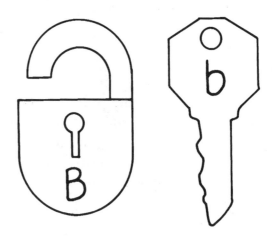

 Use the police car pattern below to cut 20–30 cars from tagboard. Cut two wheels for each car from tagboard as well. Put upper and lowercase letter matches on the wheels (or rhyming words/pictures). Children may locate matching pairs for each car.

Cut several badges from tagboard. Use different designs and colors to make a variety of pairs. Have children match badges that are alike. The badge format can also be used to match colors with color words.

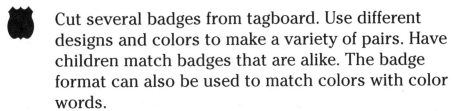

Cut some white rectangular pieces of tagboard and write a number from 5 to 10 or 20 on each card. Laminate strips of black tagboard. Invite children to put the number cards in order and then lay the appropriate number of jail bars (black laminated strips) on top of each card.

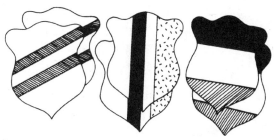

Manipulative Center

 Put out puzzles of police officers such as these available from Judy/Instructo: Police Officers J066053, 16 pieces; J606013, 14 pieces;

J606521,12 pieces; School Crossing Guard J606523, 13 pieces; Safety Signs without knobs J040026 and with knobs J045026, 5 pieces; Motorcycle J040111, 8 pieces; or foam rubber puzzle Police Car LR-2169, 24 pieces from Lauri.

Encourage children to pretend a pegboard is a jail. Tell children they have to put up bars (pegs around the perimeter) so the convicts won't escape. Add some small people for children to put inside the "jail." Another pegboard over the top makes a nice enclosure. Encourage students who are able to use colored pegs to make jail bars in a pattern, such as ABAB (red, green, red, green), AAB (yellow, yellow, blue).

Play Dough Center

Add some coffee stirrers, straws, toothpicks, tongue depressors, pegs, and craft sticks to the play dough and encourage children to design their own jails. A few pretend people to use as criminals and police officers will add to the role-playing.

Show children how to roll "snakes" and put them around each others' wrists to make handcuffs.

Look for police cars that have wheels with tire treads. Invite children to roll the police cars over flattened play dough "streets" to make tracks. Ride other cars through the play dough to see if children can tell the difference. Discuss with children how police officers might take prints of the tire tracks at a crime scene to help identify the car that was there.

Blocks

Add a few police cars (any cars will do—children will pretend they are police cars) and have children lay out block paths with roads, tunnels, and bridges for the police to chase cars that are speeding.

If you have a set of block traffic signs, this is a good time to bring them out. Or you can easily make some of your own. Make the signs from tagboard or cut some signs from a driver's manual and glue to tagboard. Attach craft sticks and add a mound of baker's clay or play dough so the signs will stand.

Put out a city floor mat (Drive Around Town Carpet LC1607, a washable carpet from Lakeshore Learning Materials, or Motor Map HOY-1 or Super Roadway Play Mat PT-500, both from Constructive Playthings) or draw one with the children using oilcloth and permanent markers. Tape the map to the floor and invite children to stage police car chases, journeys to crime scenes, and so on.

Sand/Water Table

Add some small cars and people to the sand table. Dampening the sand will make it easier to make mountains, valleys, tunnels, and roads. Encourage children to use some of the cars for police cars and some of the people as police officers.

Add coffee stirrers, tongue depressors, craft sticks, toothpicks, pegs, or straws to the sand so children can make a jail.

Art Center

Make police badges using patterns on page 206. Cover with aluminum foil and hot glue a safety pin to the back so it can be pinned on or use two-sided tape or masking tape.

Blue is usually the color of police officers. Put blue paint at the easel and encourage children to paint "police" pictures.

Invite children to draw head-and-shoulders pictures of "bad guys" on white drawing paper (or have children do self-portraits) and add "Most Wanted" in large black letters. Or try using a computer program such as Macintosh "Certificate Maker" (Springboard Software, Inc., 7808 Creekridge Circle, Minneapolis MN 55435) which provides a "Wanted" poster (option 16) with a place to add a photograph of the child's face over a convict's body. You can also use a digitizer or computer camera to make the posters. Hang the posters around your police station.

 Invite children to make police officers using the patterns below. Children may cut heads from pink or brown and bodies from blue construction paper. Encourage them to add facial features and hair with magic marker, crayons, or bits of scrap paper. Children may also wish to add buttons, belts, pockets, badges, keys, whistles, batons, or hats.

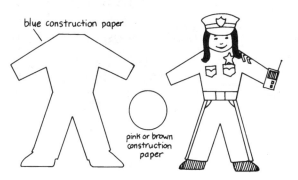

 Make traffic lights from one-quart milk cartons (ask parents to send them in well rinsed). Cut off the top and bottom of the carton and cover with construction or self-adhesive paper. Show children how to trace circles on red, yellow, and green construction paper and cut them out (make one set of lights or glue lights to all four sides). Hang the traffic lights around the room and try the fingerplay on page 214.

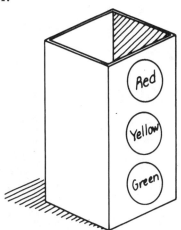

Invite children to design some "tickets" that can be given to children making bad choices or breaking rules, and some "awards" that can be given to children making good choices—"Good Citizen Awards." Invite a different child take on the role of "police officer" each day (that child may even wear the uniform for the day) and give out awards and tickets throughout the day.

Divide children into small groups and give each group a box large enough for children to pull up over their hips. Use boxes with the tops and bottoms cut off. Invite each group to design a car from the box. Children may decide what color to paint their car and take it outside to paint. At least one group should paint their car like the police cars in your town. Children may add small yellow paper plates for headlights and large black paper plates for wheels. Brake lights may be made by cutting the centers from two small paper plates and painting them red. Cut handles on each side so children can step into the cars and pull them up.

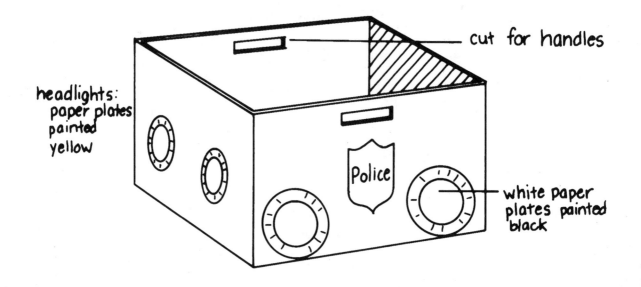

cut for handles

headlights: paper plates painted yellow

Police

white paper plates painted black

When groups have painted their boxes, invite some children to pretend they are driving in traffic. One child may be a police officer and use stop and go signals (with their hands or actual signs) to help direct traffic. Give the police office a pad of paper and pencil so he or she can give tickets to cars that speed. This is a great activity for outdoors.

 Make each child a driver's license. Children may draw self-portraits or you may use school pictures. Use your photocopier to make the pictures smaller. Have children write their names beside the pictures and laminate. Or use a computer program such as Macintosh "Certificate Maker" (Springboard Software, Inc., 7808 Creekridge Circle, Minneapolis, MN 55435).

My Drivers License
PO461272

Rosa Iglésias
135 34th Avenue
Miami, Florida

Rosa Iglésias

 Bring in a walkie-talkie for children to experience or see if your school has one you can borrow for the demonstration. Compare the walkie-talkie with telephones and police car radios. Then make walkie-talkies from small candy boxes. Wrap each box in brown or gray construction paper or have children paint their boxes. Add details with marker or construction paper cut-outs. Add pipe-cleaner antennas. Encourage children to use the play walkie-talkies both indoors and out.

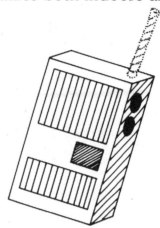

Writing Center

Use a pocket chart and write some of the words on sentence strips that children might want to use in their writing, such as police officer, badge, crook, criminal, knife, jail, whistle, robber, ticket. Add to the list as children ask you to spell words or as you see words appear in their writing. Invite individuals to illustrate some of the words on small index cards and place the pictures beside the words.

Practice writing the numbers 911. Children may also practice writing their telephone numbers and the numbers of friends.

Use permanent marker on a plastic laminate table to draw some simple pictures from this unit, such as badge, whistle, stoplight. Write the word under each picture. Provide tracing paper, drawing paper, markers, and crayons so children can trace the pictures and words or draw them from the model.

Permanent marker can be removed with alcohol or hair spray.

Listening Center

- Record yourself reading the story of Little Red Riding Hood or select a pre-recorded version (Scholastic or Confetti Enterprises). Both come with cassette and book.

- Record yourself reading *Berenstain Bears Learn About Strangers* or use the prerecorded cassette from Random House, which comes with a copy of the book.

- Record yourself reading *Make Way for Ducklings* or use the book/cassette sets from Viking Press or Puffin Books.

- Record yourself reading *The Story About Ping* or use the book and cassette from Puffin Books.

- Look for other stories to record in the book center list. Keep a copy of the book with the tape so children can follow along.

Book Center

- Make an ABC book about police officers. Encourage children to think of a word for each letter of the alphabet. Here are some suggestions if you get stuck.

attack, arrest
badge, baton
car (police), criminal, caution
dog (police)
emergency
fast (running), flashlight
green means go
handcuffs, (police) helicopter
ink (fingerprints), injury
jail
keys
lights (on police cars), lock
"Most Wanted"

night patrol, 911
officer
police officer
red light, rescue, radio
speed limit, stoplight
ticket
uniform
vest (neon)
whistle, walkie-talkie
X marks the spot
yellow means caution, yell
zip to the crime scene!

Write each alphabet letter on a single page of construction paper and invite volunteers to illustrate each word. These make a nice bulletin board when put up in order. After enjoying the bulletin board, put the pictures in alphabetical order, add a title page, and bind together as a class book for the writing center. Once the class book has been "published," read *Police Officers: A to Z* by Jean Johnson to the class.

 Here are some books you might want in your book center. Check your school or community library for other titles. Many of these are appropriate for reading to the class at circle time.

(ps-K) Mayer, Mercer. *Police Critter.* Paperwing Press, 1986. Board book cut in the shape of a police officer with Mercer Mayer's delightful drawings. Tells about activities of a police officer.

(ps-1) Berenstain, Jan and Stan. *The Berenstain Bears Learn About Strangers.*
Papa tells the bears they should never talk to strangers. Sister views all strangers as ominous until Mama offers some common sense. Available on 30-minute video along with The *Berenstain Bears and the Missing Honey* (Random House Home Video). Also available on audio cassette from Random House with a copy of the book.

(ps-1) Chlad, Dorothy. *Strangers*. Childrens Press, 1982.
Presents some rules for safe behavior around people you don't know. Simple and straightforward.

(ps-1) Fox, Naomi. *Little Red Riding Hood*. Confetti Enterprises, 1993.
Traditional story. Set comes with book and cassette.

(ps-1) Joyce, Irma. *Never Talk to Strangers: A Book About Personal Safety*. Golden Press, 1985.
Large book with bright illustrations. Rhyming text always ends with the phrase "Never talk to strangers."

(ps-1) Schmidt, Karen. *Little Red Riding Hood*. Scholastic, Inc., 1986.
Traditional story. Comes with 15-minute cassette.

(ps-2) McCloskey, Robert. *Make Way for Ducklings*. Puffin Books, 1993.
Set includes Caldecott book and cassette. Also available on videocassette from The Caldecott Video Library, Volume II by Weston Woods, 1992. Series includes four other Caldecott winners: *Owl Moon* by Jane Yolen, *In the Night Kitchen* by Maurice Sendak, *Strega Nonna* by Tomie de Paola and *Crow Boy* by Taro Yashima.

(ps-2) McCloskey, Robert. *Make Way for Ducklings*. Viking Press, 1941/ 1969.
Caldecott Medal book with beautiful brown and white drawings. Mr. and Mrs. Mallard and their offspring proudly return to their home in the Boston Public Gardens with the help of a policeman named Michael.

(K-1) Kincaid, Lucy. *Little Red Riding Hood*. Rourke Corporation, 1983.
"Now You Can Read" book with large type for first readers.

(K-1) Morris, Anna. *Little Red Riding Hood Rebus Book*. Orchard Books, 1987.
Rebus version of the traditional folktale with tiny pictures replacing some words. Bright, detailed illustrations.

(K-2) Bahr, Amy. *It's OK to say NO: A Book for Parents and Children to Read Together*. Grossett and Dunlap, 1986.
What to do if you are approached by a stranger and if someone touches you in an uncomfortable way. Well done.

(K-2) Baker, Donna. *I Want to be a Police Officer.* Childrens Press, 1978.
Ramon's uncle explains the work of a police officer to Ramon and his friends. Realistic color drawings.

(K-2) Flack, Marjorie and Kurt Wiese. *The Story About Ping.* Puffin Books, 1977.
Ping is a duckling who lives with his extended family on the Yangtze river. The story chronicles his misadventures at the hands of strangers and end happily.

(K-2) Galdone, Paul. *Little Red Riding Hood.* McGraw-Hill, 1974.
Retelling of the folktale about a little girl in a red cloak who finds a wolf in her grandmother's clothing.

(K-2) Heller, Rebecca. *Little Red Riding Hood.* Western Publishing Company, Inc., 1985.
Little Golden Book Special Edition of the traditional folktale.

(K-2) Hillert, Margaret. *Little Red Riding Hood.* Follett Publishing Company, 1982.
Retells in primer words the tale of the little girl who meets a wolf in the forest on her way to visit grandmother.

(K-2) Lenski, Lois. *Policeman Small.* H. Z. Walck, 1962.
Story of Policeman Small's day directing traffic.

(K-2) *Little Red Riding Hood.* Learning Corporation of America, 1979.
13-minute animated video of the Brothers Grimm tale.

(K-2) Marshall, James. *Red Riding Hood.* Dial Books, 1987.
Traditional version of the story in James Marshall's pictures and style.

(K-3) Hannum, Dotti. *A Visit to the Police Station.* Childrens Press, 1985.
Field trip book that describes activities at a police station and various duties of policemen and women.

(K-3) Hyman, Trina. *Little Red Riding Hood.* Holiday Books, 1983.
This Caldecott Honor Book has romantic, detailed pictures of the traditional folktale, including wonderfully illustrated borders and small vignettes. Watch the cat.

(K-3) *Little Red Riding Hood*. Platypus Productions, Inc., 1983. Video from the "Fairie Tale Theatre" series directed by Shelley Duvall. Humorous retelling of traditional folk tale.

(K-3) Johnson, Jean. *Police Officers: A to Z.* Walker and Company, 1986.
Photographs in an alphabet format. Lots of words but good for children learning the alphabet.

(K-3) Kelley, Iran. *Benjamin Rabbit and the Stranger Danger.* Ideals Publishing Company, 1985.
Police Officer Strong visits Benjamin Bunny's school and discusses do's and don'ts about strangers.

(K-3) Matthias, Catherine. *I Can Be a Police Officer.* Childrens Press, 1984.
Photographs of life as a police officer.

(K-3) Rey, Margaret. *Curious George Visits the Police Station.* Houghton Mifflin, 1985.
A book in the Curious George series in which the delightful monkey visits the police station.

(K-3) Young, Ed. *Lon Po Po: A Red Riding Hood Story from China*. Philomel Books, 1989.
Caldecott-winning story of three sisters home alone who are endangered by a hungry fox disguised as their grandmother. The sisters outwit the sly fox before their mother gets home. Beautiful watercolors with an Oriental flare.

Outside

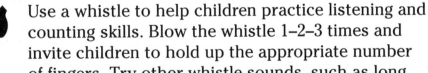

 Use a whistle to help children practice listening and counting skills. Blow the whistle 1–2–3 times and invite children to hold up the appropriate number of fingers. Try other whistle sounds, such as long or short, soft or loud. This is great activity to do right before going inside.

Buy a small, inexpensive plastic whistle for each child, such as the ones available as party favors. Put children's names or initials on whistles and invite them to blow to their heart's content . . . outside! This will encourage children to play police officer outside where there is plenty of room to chase the criminal.

Teach children to play "Red Light, Green Light." The "police officer" turns away from the group and says "green light." After a short wait, he or she turns quickly toward the group and says "red light!" Children freeze when they hear "red light." If the police officer sees anyone move, that child returns to start. The object of the game is to touch and replace the police officer first. Everyone else returns to the beginning to start again. Start by being the police officer yourself.

Teach children to play "Cops and Robbers" like "Chase" or "Hide and Seek." Pick a spot to designate as "jail," such as a tree. Children who are "caught" go to "jail." You may also want to designate a spot "home free"—a safe spot where children may rest.

Use tricycles and other riding toys as cars on the street. Have one child pretend be the police officer and direct traffic or pretend to give out tickets. Children may practice crossing the street with one child acting as the crossing guard.

Field Study

Many counties have "Officer Friendly" programs in which a police officer comes to school to talk to young children. They usually have a pre-planned agenda for each age group. Contact your local police for more information.

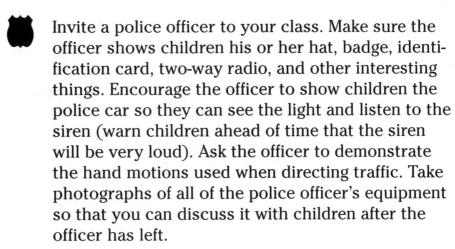 Invite a police officer to your class. Make sure the officer shows children his or her hat, badge, identification card, two-way radio, and other interesting things. Encourage the officer to show children the police car so they can see the light and listen to the siren (warn children ahead of time that the siren will be very loud). Ask the officer to demonstrate the hand motions used when directing traffic. Take photographs of all of the police officer's equipment so that you can discuss it with children after the officer has left.

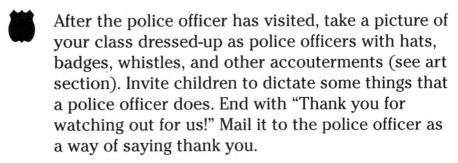 After the police officer has visited, take a picture of your class dressed-up as police officers with hats, badges, whistles, and other accouterments (see art section). Invite children to dictate some things that a police officer does. End with "Thank you for watching out for us!" Mail it to the police officer as a way of saying thank you.

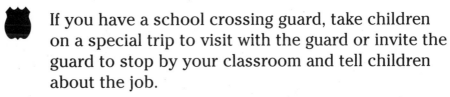 If you have a school crossing guard, take children on a special trip to visit with the guard or invite the guard to stop by your classroom and tell children about the job.

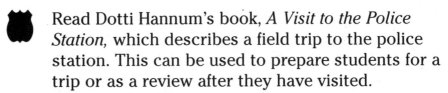 Read Dotti Hannum's book, *A Visit to the Police Station,* which describes a field trip to the police station. This can be used to prepare students for a trip or as a review after they have visited.

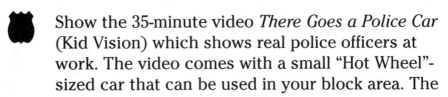 Show the 35-minute video *There Goes a Police Car* (Kid Vision) which shows real police officers at work. The video comes with a small "Hot Wheel"-sized car that can be used in your block area. The

video makes a great substitute if a field experience cannot be arranged.

 After children have visited the police station or the police officer has visited your class, have children each complete a sentence strip, "The police officer _____" by dictating something they have learned, such as the police officer wears a blue uniform, takes criminals to jail, or rides in a police car. Children may illustrate their sentences on small index cards and glue them to the sentence strips. Put the sentence strips together in book form by punching a hole in each strip, adding a title strip, and binding with a ring binder.

Parent Involvement

 Use the letter on page 233 to let parents know how they can help with what you are teaching at school.

Dear Parents,

We are learning about police officers and how they are our friends. I am encouraging children to memorize their home telephone numbers or the number of a neighbor or family member that they can give to a police officer if they should get lost. Please write the number below that you would like your child to memorize. Help your child to learn the number at home and to practice calling that number on your telephone. I will ask children to say their telephone numbers each morning. When they have said it for me successfully, I will send you a note. Mission accomplished!

You are the best!

- -

Child's name _____

Please have my child memorize the following number in case of an emergency.

_____

When asked, "What are your parents' names?" I want my child to answer,

_____

When asked, "Where do you live?" I want my child to answer,

_____

Italian Restaurant

In this time of multicultural awareness, the Italian restaurant is offered as only one example of a multicultural dining experience. Feel free to adapt the ideas for other types of restaurants, such as Chinese, Thai, Greek, Japanese, American fast food, French, or Mexican. What a wonderful way to teach cultural diversity—through food! You may wish to consider leaving the restaurant area in place all year and changing the area each month to feature a different cultural experience.

Creative Play

 Set up your dramatic play area beside the home living center so you can make use of the dishes, stove, refrigerator, table, and chairs. Use the home living space to prepare food. Add a serving area beside the kitchen with table and chairs, red-and-white checked tablecloth, and flowers or a candle dripping down a straw-encased bottle as a centerpiece.

 Add a tray, plates, cups, glasses, forks, spoons, knives, bowls (plastic, paper, or "play"), salt and pepper shakers, napkins, placemats, water pitchers, and menus.

 Add a white hat and apron for the chef.

Visit an Italian restaurant or pizzeria, tell them what you are doing, and ask if they will give you some spare items, such as pizza boxes, "doggie" bags, signs, menus, placemats, brochures, a waitress apron, or a t-shirt.

You will also need "pretend" Italian foods (laminated foods cut from magazines, pictures from magazines glued or taped to small wooden blocks, foods made from hardened baker's clay, purchased sets of "play" food (such as Pizza Party from Little Tikes), pots and pans, mixing bowls, empty spice containers, measuring spoons and cups, serving trays, and so on. Try using pieces of white string or yarn as spaghetti. Tongs make good servers.

Add a pad and pencil to encourage children to take orders.

Put out an erasable board with chalk or markers or a magnetic board with magnetic letters to post the "Specials of the Day."

Look for a tape of Italian opera music to play in the restaurant area (or borrow one from a parent). Try to find a tape of spoken Italian (ask at the local high school if Italian is taught).

Ask your art teacher for prints of some works by famous Italian sculptors and painters, such as Raphael, Michelangelo, and Leonardo daVinci, to hang on the wall of the restaurant.

Add a box of dress-up clothes so customers may dress for dinner. Pocketbooks, wallets, and play money will encourage customers to pay for their dinner. Hats, shawls, jewelry, coats, blazers, and ties make nice, easy accessories.

Use a small desk (table, rocking boat turned on its side, or cardboard box) as the check-out area. Add a small cash register and play money so that customers can pay for their food and leave tips! Add a basket of mints with a small spoon.

Invite children to help you make some signs (painted, drawn and colored, computer-generated) for the restaurant, such as "Please wait to be seated," "No Smoking," the restaurant's name, nametags for waiters and waitresses, Open/Closed, and others you and the children may think of.

Role-play with the children. Practice waiting to be seated. Have the waitress seat the customers, give out menus, take orders, deliver the food, and clear the table. Customers may practice giving orders from the menu, putting napkins in laps, pretending to eat, leaving a tip, and paying the bill.

Circle Time

Find out what children know. Ask who cooks in their homes, what their favorite meals are, and about any cooking experiences they have had. Build on this knowledge to explain roles in a restaurant.

Ask the class what they would like to know about an Italian restaurant. Put yourself in the learner situation and share with children something that you would like to know. Write down 3–5 questions you can all agree on and discuss with children how they can find the answers to their questions (ask someone who works at an Italian restaurant, look in books, ask the librarian, ask someone born in Italy). Begin with these ideas to plan the contents of your unit.

 Explain to children that Italian recipes came from a country in Europe called Italy. Bring out a globe or world map and have children first locate the country and state where they live. Then help them find Italy. Read *It Looked Like Spilt Milk* by Charles B. Shaw to the children and have them decide what they think Italy looks like (a high-heeled boot kicking a ball (Sicily).

 Explain to children that like every country in the world, Italy has its own flag. The Italian flag was designed by Napoleon. He liked the French flag and used a similar design, changing the color blue on the French flag to green because green was his favorite color. Children may make an Italian flag on white construction paper. Discuss with children the difference between the Italian and American flag.

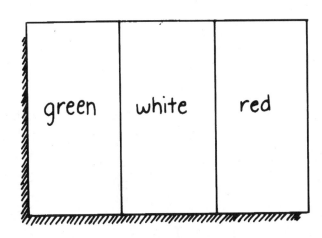

Depending on the maturity and interest of the group, use books from the library to learn some basic facts about Italy.

Our Country Italy by Jillian Powell, Bookwright Press, 1992.

Take a Trip to Italy by Chris Fairclough, Franklin Watts, 1983.

Italy by Barbara Walsh Angelillo, Steck-Vaughn, 1991.

Countries of the World: Italy by Jillian Powell, Bookwright, 1989.

Italy by Anna Sproule, Silver, 1987.

Italy by Kathryn Bonomi, Chelsea House, 1988.

Italy by R. Conrad Stein, Childrens Press, 1989.

Italy Is My County by Benice and Cliff Moon, Bookwright, 1989.

Passport to Italy by Cinzia Mariella, Franklin Watts, 1986.

A Family in Italy by Penny and John Hubley, Lerner Publications Company, 1986.

Here are some interesting facts about Italy.

Major cities: Rome (capital), Vatican City (home of the Pope), Milan, Florence, Venice, Naples

Famous sites: Coliseum (sports stadium), St. Peter's Cathedral (the largest church in the world), La Scala (famous opera house), Leaning Tower of Pisa (a tower that actually leans)

Schools: children start elementary school at age 6. The day starts at 8 a.m. and finishes at lunch time but they have classes on Saturday.

Favorite sports: soccer, bicycling, boxing, automobile racing

Favorite music: opera

Transportation: motor scooters, cars, buses, trains, gondolas (slender boats pushed by gondoliers with long poles)

 Find a video, film, or film strip about Italy to show the class. Look for simple travelogues that give

basic information about the people and their culture.

 Learn some Italian words and phrases.

> *Buon giorno.* (Hello)
> *Ciao.* (pronounced *chow*) (Good-by)
> *Magnifico!* (Magnificent)
> *Grazie.* (Thank you)

Add some basic Italian language books to the book center, such as Dennis Sheheen's *A Child's Picture English-Italian Dictionary* (Modan Adama Books, 1986), Berlitz's *Italian: Parlo Italiana* (Macmillan Children's Group, 1992) or Angela Wilkes' *Italian for Beginners* (NTC Publishing Books, 1988). Encourage children to look up simple words and phrases and to use them in the restaurant.

 Teach students to count to 5 or 10 in Italian:

1	uno	(OO-no)
2	due	(DOO-ay)
3	tre	(tray)
4	quattro	(KWAHT-troh)
5	cinque	(CHEEN-kway)
6	sei	(say)
7	sette	(SEHT-tay)
8	otto	(OHT-to)
9	nove	(NO-vay)
10	dieci	(DYAY-chee)

Read *Count Your Way through Italy* by Jim Haskins, which has terrific illustrations and includes a page and an interesting fact about Italy for each number.

 Look in your library for some good Italian cookbooks with pictures of Italy and Italian foods. With the children's help, make a list of some Italian foods, such as spaghetti, lasagna, pizza, pasta, mozzarella cheese, Parmesan cheese, minestrone soup, linguine, rigatoni, ravioli, cannelloni, prosciutto (dry-cured ham), marinara (tomato sauce), salami. Children may start with a very limited list but keep adding to it throughout the unit. Have children bring labels from home of frozen foods, jars, and cans of Italian food. Glue these to the list, collage-style, as they come in. In Italy, many people shop each day for fresh food instead of using canned and frozen foods. Eating together is very important to the Italian family. Their main meal is at lunch time, when stores are closed for two hours.

 Before children come in one day, cook up a pot of spaghetti noodles, letting them cool in the cooking water. Be sure not to overcook or the spaghetti will be gummy. Bring the noodles to the circle in a pot with the lid on. Blindfold the children or have them close their eyes. Invite them to put their hand in the pot and feel the "mystery food." Make a list with children of words that describe how the mystery food feels. Do not have children guess what it is until you have a good list of describing words. When you are finished with the spaghetti at circle time, pour it, water and all, into the sand/water table or a large tub with some tongs, scoops, measuring cups, and bowls, just for fun!

 Use a large cooking pot with a top as a "mystery box." Put items in the pot that are used in cooking, such as an apron, measuring spoon, measuring cup, spatula, can opener, egg beater, garlic press, or strainer. Go through your own kitchen drawers and choose items that you use often yourself to add to the pot. Add new items as children learn to identify the ones you start with and know what they are used for.

Use the previous items and the large cooking pot to reinforce memory skills. Start with three items that children have learned to identify and play "Memory." Show the three items to the children and then have them close their eyes while you remove one. Children may then open their eyes and guess which item is missing. You can make the game more difficult by adding more items or by hiding two items instead of one.

Help children make a list of all the pizza toppings they can think of. Make a class book by cutting circles, inviting children to each choose one topping, and draw a pizza with that topping. Add the topping word, "Pizza with _____ on top" at the bottom of the pizza picture. The pages can be bound together with a ring binder.

Make a graph of "Favorite Pizza Toppings" (see page 242). Use hand-made pizza slices with each child's name on one or Carson Dellosa's "Pizza Slice" self-sticking notelets (CD-9150).

Favorite Pizza Toppings

Look for pictures in magazines, draw pictures, or take photographs at an Italian restaurant of vocabulary you would like to teach in this unit, such as bowl, plate, fork, knife, spoon, glass, check, dessert, waitress, host, hostess, chef, menu, restaurant, restroom, tip, waiter, waitress, spaghetti, lasagna, and pizza. Use the pictures as flashcards for children to identify.

As children learn to identify the pictures, line the cards up on a ledge and ask "w" questions.

> *Who shows you where to sit when you come in to a*
> *restaurant?* (host/hostess)
> *What do you use to order?* (menu)
> *Where do you go if you need to wash your hands* (restroom)

Children may volunteer to choose the card that answers each question. As children become better at this, encourage them to pose their own questions to their classmates.

Here are some stories based on Italian folklore. Choose one or more to read to the class.

> *Jingle the Christmas Clown* by Tomie de Paola
> *Looking for Daniela* by Steven Kroll
> *Tony's Bread* by Tomie de Paola
> *Strega Nona* by Tomie de Paola and the sequel,
> *Strega Nona Meets Her Match*
> *The Gondolier of Venice* by Robert Kraus
> *The Prince of the Dolomites* by Tomie de Paola

Uncle Alfredo's Zoo by Judith Vigna
Any of *The Adventures of Pinocchio*, including the Disney version.

After reading one of the stories, encourage children to study the pictures and words and decide what things help them to know the story takes place in Italy, such as buildings or Italian phrases. Make a list of all the Italian phrases from the story and their English counterparts. Practice saying the words.

Rhythm Time

 Teach children to sing the humorous "On Top of Spaghetti" from *Eye Winker Tom Tinker Chin Chopper* by Tom Glazer (Doubleday, 1973) or in its own book. Children may make a reproduction of the song in book form. Invite volunteers to illustrate each line of the song on white paper. Add the lyrics and put the pages in order to make a class book.

> On top of spaghetti, all covered with cheese,
> I lost my poor meatball when somebody sneezed.
> It rolled off the table and onto the floor,
> And then my poor meatball rolled out of the door.
> It rolled in the garden, and under a bush,
> And then my poor meatball was nothing but mush.
> The mush was as tasty, as tasty can be,
> And early next summer, it grew into a tree.
> The tree was all covered with beautiful moss,
> It grew great big meatballs, and tomato sauce.
> So if you eat spaghetti, all covered with cheese,
> Hold on to your meatball, and don't ever sneeze.

Help children identify the rhyming words in the song. Underline pairs of rhyming words with the same color marker.

Share with children Shel Silverstein's humorous poem "Spaghetti" from *Where the Sidewalk Ends* (Harper and Row, 1974). Write the poem on chart paper and point to each word as you read to reinforce left-to-right progression. Use cloze for nouns and have children supply the words. They will quickly memorize the poem.

Have children make their own spaghetti and meatballs by cutting a piece of construction paper into a round plate (or use small colored paper plates). Help children dip cream-colored yarn or string in white glue and arrange on the plate like spaghetti. Add brown pompoms for meatballs.

 Sing these original words to the tune of "Bingo."

There is a meal I love to eat and pizza is its name-o.
P-I-Z-Z-A, P-I-Z-Z-A, P-I-Z-Z-A and pizza is its name-o.

Cut the letters P-I-Z-Z-A from felt and place each letter on the flannelboard as you sing the song.

Make simple flashcards of the letters to hold up (or have a child do it).

 Try this new version of the song, "I Like to Eat Apples and Bananas."

I like to eat, eat, eat, pizza and spaghetti.

 Teach these original words to the tune "For He's a Jolly Good Fellow."

Oh how I love pizza.
Oh how I love pizza.
Oh how I love pizza.
Thank you for pizza. Hooray!

Snack/Cooking Time

 This is a great unit for cooking. Have children don their chef hats (see page 259) and aprons and try some of the recipes that follow.

 Provide recipe cards (or make rebus task cards—a sequence of pictures with words under each picture to demonstrate steps in the cooking project). Or write the recipe on chart paper if appropriate for your students. An attractive cooking chartlet for recipes is available from Carson-Dellosa (CD-6066).

 Consider taking pictures as children follow each step of a recipe. After the cooking is done, glue each picture to a larger card and encourage children to decide on captions for each picture. Children may also sequence the pictures.

Pizza Man Pies

half a hamburger bun or English muffin per child
spaghetti or pizza sauce
grated cheese—cheddar or mozzarella
pepperoni, sausage, or other pizza topping (optional)

Have children spread spaghetti sauce on an English muffin or half a hamburger bun and sprinkle grated cheese over the top. Encourage children to make faces on their pizzas by using cheese for eyes, nose, and mouth. Place under the broiler (in the microwave or toaster oven) until the cheese bubbles for delicious individual pizzas.

Or make pizza with the class from any of the boxed or ready-to-make pizza kits. Ask children to bring one topping for the pizza from home.

Antipasto
(before the meal)

lettuce
sliced onions rings, shredded carrots, chopped tomatoes
or cherry tomatoes, sliced cucumbers, spinach leaves,
sliced fresh mushrooms, croutons (optional)
for the Italian flair—diced provolone, pitted black olives,
chopped yellow peppers, artichoke hearts, chunks
of salami

Ask each student to bring in one ingredient for the
antipasto. Just before serving, add salt (sparingly), a
coating of olive oil, a bit of red wine vinegar, pepper
(optional), or your favorite Italian dressing from the supermarket. Sprinkle with Parmesan cheese. Serve with slices
of Italian bread (can be spread with garlic butter and
warmed in the oven) or bread sticks.

Easy Spaghetti

jar or can of spaghetti sauce
browned ground beef, browned Italian sausage, meatballs,
sliced fresh mushrooms, sautéed chopped onions, or
sautéed chopped celery (optional)

Add ingredients to a large pot and let simmer all morning,
covered, over low heat. Cook spaghetti according to
package directions. Spoon sauce over pasta and sprinkle
with a little Parmesan cheese (use canned or have children
grate the real thing).

You might ask parents if they have a favorite
spaghetti sauce recipe they would like to come in
and make from scratch with the class. Parents may
work in a corner of your room—children will come
help with preparations as interest dictates.

Pasta e Fagioli
(Noodles and Beans)

small pasta in any fancy shape
1 onion, chopped
2 cloves garlic, minced
1 stalk celery, chopped
4 slices bacon
1 large can Italian plum tomatoes
1 can kidney beans
1/3 cup parsley
1/2 tsp. salt
1 tsp. basil

Fry bacon and drain on paper towels. In remaining bacon grease, sauté chopped onions, garlic, and celery for about 5 minutes. Break bacon into small pieces and add to vegetable mixture along with 1 large can of tomatoes. Cook 5 minutes and add drained kidney beans. Add herbs and salt and cook over low heat, covered, for about an hour. Then add 1 cup uncooked pasta and some water if the mix seems too thick. Cook 10 more minutes and add grated Parmesan. Serves 6–8 little people.

 Gelato is ice cream that was invented in Italy. Gelato shops and stands, called *gelateria,* are found all over Italy. Make (or have a parent help make) some homemade ice cream with the class.

 Ask a parent to bring in some Italian ices from the supermarket for the class to try. Make a "T" graph, asking the question "Do you like Italian ice?"

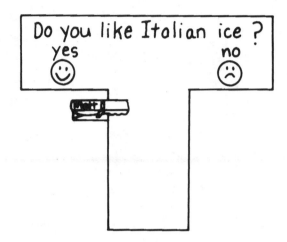

 Read Tomie de Paola's *Jingle the Christmas Clown*. Then make Italian star-shaped cookies, called *Donna Chiara's Stelline d'Oro*, with your class. The recipe is provided at the end of the book. Or try the "Quick Macaroni Salad" at the end of Melinda Corey's *Let's Visit a Spaghetti Factory*.

 If you have a parent who makes pasta from scratch, invite him or her to come in and demonstrate how it's done. Set the cook up in a corner of the room and encourage children to come and go as their interest dictates to help with the preparations.

 Consider a special Parent Night or Parent Luncheon. Have children design invitations and placemats for their parent(s). Serve spaghetti, Italian salad, and bread, or any combination of Italian foods. Serve the dinner on red-checked tablecloths (paper, cloth, or pieces of red-and-white checked fabric) and play Italian music in the background. Children may want to perform the humorous song, "On Top of Spaghetti." This is great way to share with parents some of what children have learned.

Cognitive Activities

 Ask each child to bring in one bag of pasta. Use what comes in for the activities and art projects that follow. Put out a large bowl of mixed pasta and invite children to sort the noodles into "like" kinds.

 Color some pasta by soaking it in rubbing alcohol with several drops of food coloring added. Remove pasta from the alcohol with a slotted spoon, letting most of the alcohol drip off, before placing on waxed paper to dry overnight. Make red, green, blue, and orange pasta and mix it all in a large bowl. Children can sort the pasta by color. Colored pasta can also be used in other projects.

 Try pasta patterning. Glue some beginning patterns on sentence strips or strips of tagboard. Set out a large bowl of mixed noodles and invite children to extend the pattern.

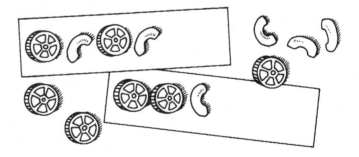

 Write a number from 1 to 10 or 20 on small colored plates or bowls with permanent marker. Put out a bowl of mixed medium-sized pasta shapes and/or "meatballs" (brown pompoms) and invite children to count the appropriate number of pasta shapes and meatballs onto each plate or bowl.

Make a "Pasta Alphabet." Give each child one letter written on colored tagboard with marker. Help children put white glue over the marker line and then place pasta shapes in the glue to outline the letter.

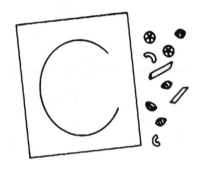

 Choose any of the pasta shapes. Write the numbers 1 to 10 or 20 down the left side of a piece of drawing paper or have children write the numbers. Put out the small pasta shapes and white glue in a plastic lid or Styrofoam tray. Children may dip the pasta shapes into the glue and place the appropriate number of shapes next to each numeral.

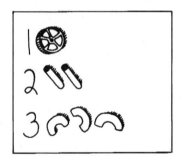

 Write each child's name in large letters on a piece of colored tagboard. Children may put glue on one letter at a time and use one type of pasta noodle to place on the letter. Explain that they will then glue another letter, choose another type noodle, and so on until they have "noodled" their names.

 Using pizza pans (for large puzzles) or colored plastic plates, cut a circle from tagboard the same size as the inside of the pan or plate. Cut the "pizza" into slices and program the pieces so they fit back together by matching uppercase letters to lowercase letters. You can also use Carson Dellosa's Pizza Novelty Notes (CD-9261) mounted on tagboard and cut into slices for this activity.

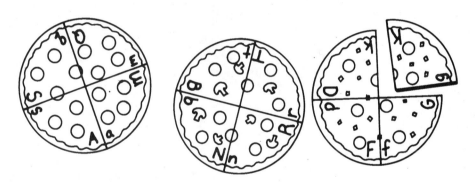

Play Dough Center

 Invite children to help you make play dough. Follow the recipe on page 334.

 Make some play dough spaghetti and meatballs. Put out some small paper plates and a garlic press with your white play dough. Use the play dough in the garlic press to press out long strands of spaghetti.

Add some red or brown play dough to make meatballs.

 On another day, put out plates, spoons, forks, knives, napkins, and plastic glasses. Plastic placemats with the outline for the place setting will encourage children to set the table correctly before "eating" (use a permanent marker to outline utensils on a plastic placemat—marker can be removed with hair spray later). Encourage children to hold their forks correctly, as this is the same grasp used in writing. Children may add play dough food to the place setting.

 Make play dough pizzas. Ask at a pizza parlor for a few cardboard rounds to lay pizzas on and some small pizza boxes or bring in round pizza pans from home. Put these in the play dough center to encourage children to make "pizzas." Provide a rolling pin, pizza cutter, server, and some small plates with which to serve the play dough "pizza."

 Introduce children to some famous Italian artists, such as Michelangelo, Raphael, and Leonardo da Vinci. Look in encyclopedias and books for pictures of paintings and sculpture by these artists.

Hang some of the pictures around the play dough area so children can pretend to be famous Italian sculptors.

Manipulative Center

 Provide napkins (paper or cloth), forks, spoons, and knives (plastic will be fine). Show children how to take one of each utensil, lay the napkin out, place the utensils together at one corner of the napkin, and roll the utensils inside the napkin. Place the "ready-to-use" utensils on a tray or in a shoe box for the restaurant.

 Cut pieces of white string or yarn into three different lengths and place several of each length on a large paper or plastic plate. Invite child to divide the "spaghetti" by lengths, putting all the pieces that are the same length together. As an option, challenge children to do it with tongs.

 Put out puzzles, such as Table Setting J066008, 10 pieces, from Judy/Instructo.

Water/Sand Table

 If you have a real sink in your room, add a sponge, wash cloth, drying rack, liquid dish soap (add a little soap and a lot of water to a squirt bottle—children are likely to use an entire bottle washing one sink of dishes). Encourage children to wash all the dishes from the restaurant and home living area. Review vocabulary as they wash with phrases such as, "First, wash all the plates," "What do you want to wash next?" and so on. Make sure to provide water shirts. If you don't have a sink area that you can turn over to the children, put a tub in your water table and have children wash dishes in the tub. Place the drying rack beside the tub of water inside the water table.

 Fill your water table with cooked spaghetti and some water (actually any of the cooked pasta will do) for a day. Do not overcook the pasta. Add a strainer/colander, tongs, pasta server, spoons, and forks. Show children how to twirl the spaghetti onto a fork using the spoon as a base.

 Add some dry pasta to the sand. Children will use their imaginations to make "Italian" dishes. Add some pots and pans, spoons, slotted spoons, strainers, colander, and other containers from your kitchen.

 Put a sheet over the sand in your sand table and add a pan or bowl of flour with a flour sifter to provide hours of fun. The sheet will keep the sand undisturbed and keep you from having to empty it to enjoy another filler. Flour can be somewhat messy and can be enjoyed outside as well.

Art Center

 Put green, white, and red tempera paint at the easel and invite children to paint an Italian flag on a large sheet of white paint paper folded into thirds and reopened. On the Italian flag, the panel on the left is green, the middle white, and the last red.

Use large sheets of construction paper for place-mats. Children may make place settings for an Italian meal. Use plastic silverware (or Ellison dies of spoon, knife, fork) and paper plates, napkins, and cups. Have children glue these onto the "place-mats" in the appropriate places. They may cut Italian food from magazines, draw the foods on the plates, make foods from scraps of construction paper, or use white yarn and brown pompoms to make spaghetti and meatballs to glue to the plates. Children should create their own designs.

 Collect placemats from several Italian restaurants or pizzerias to show students. Then invite children to design their own placemats on construction paper (have them choose their own color). Children may make up a name for the restaurant, you may assign a name, or children can choose from a list of names that the class has brain-stormed before the activity. Laminate and use the placemats in the Italian restaurant.

 Collect examples of menus from several Italian restaurants and pizzerias. Encourage children to design their own menus. Children may decide on the name of the restaurant and design pictures for the front of the menus. Inside the menus, children may draw or find pictures in a magazine for the food in their restaurant. About four pictures, such as spaghetti, salad, pizza, and soda, will do. Write the words under each picture and have children decide on prices to write beside each picture. Laminate for durability and use in the restaurant.

 Invite children to dictate to you how their mothers or fathers make their favorite foods. Write their instructions word for word. At the bottom of each paper, have children draw a picture of how the food looks. Bind all of these together to make a "Recipe Book" to photocopy for each child to take home. (An all-time favorite was the child who said the best thing his mother made was spaghetti and meatballs and then described how she opened the can, put it in a bowl, and into the microwave. "Delicious!")

 Try a little "spaghetti art." Cook some pasta (adding a little vegetable oil to the boiling water so it will not stick together) with a little food coloring in the cooking water. Do not overcook. Pour the pasta into a colander to drain and cool. Keep it moist as you work. Or dip cooked spaghetti into tempera paint and lay on construction paper for great abstract art.

 Invite children to make paper pizzas. Start with a large sheet of tan construction paper cut into a circle. Show children how to sponge-paint the red tempera "sauce." They will sponge-paint the ingredients after the "sauce" has dried or use construction paper cut-outs. Use real mushrooms, cut lengthwise, to print mushrooms, a round sponge or cork to print brown slices of pepperoni. Paint with glue and sprinkle a little cornmeal "cheese" over the top.

Pre-cut pictures from magazines (or have children cut pictures at home) of things that might be served in an Italian restaurant. Children may use these to make "theme" collages, such as desserts, main dishes or entrees, vegetables or salads. Children should each choose one theme, write the category name, and glue the pictures collage-style to a paper plate.

 Make an Italian pasta wreath. Collect different types of pasta (have each child bring in one small bag) such as macaroni, rigatoni, bow ties, spirals, shells, rotelli, wheels. Cut a heavy cardboard circle about 10-inches (25 cm) in diameter with a 2-inch (5 cm) circular hole in the middle for each child. Have the children place the pasta around the cardboard using plenty of white glue. Children can use a pattern or just place the pasta randomly. Give the wreaths plenty of time to dry, add a pretty bow, and hang around the Italian restaurant. Or spray-paint the wreaths with green or gold paint and add a bow or use colored pasta (color by soaking in rubbing alcohol and food coloring). Wreaths can be hung or laid flat with a candle in the middle. They make wonderful gifts, especially at Christmas time.

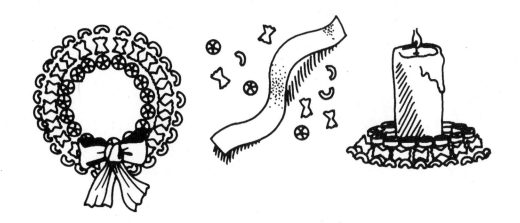

Use the assorted pasta you collect for children to make a picture using different types of pasta. Some children will be able to think of a picture they would like to make—some children will need suggestions. Hang the pasta pictures on the bulletin board with the title "Pasta-bilities."

 Some uncooked pastas are wonderful for stringing. The pasta can be used plain or can be colored by soaking it in rubbing alcohol and food coloring. The longer the pasta sits in the alcohol, the darker the color will be. Pasta will not get soggy. Remove with a slotted spoon or strainer and let the pasta dry on waxed paper. Choose pastas that will be easy for your class to string. Children can string randomly or you can teach patterning. Shoe laces, yarn with one end dipped in white glue and dried, or individual colored wires from telephone cable make nice strings for necklaces.

 Invite children to make pictures using the different types of pasta. More mature children may be able to think of pictures they would like to make. Less mature children can make simple pictures such as faces.

 Help children make white chef's hats using the following directions. Discuss with children why the chef wears a hat (to keep hair from falling in the food).

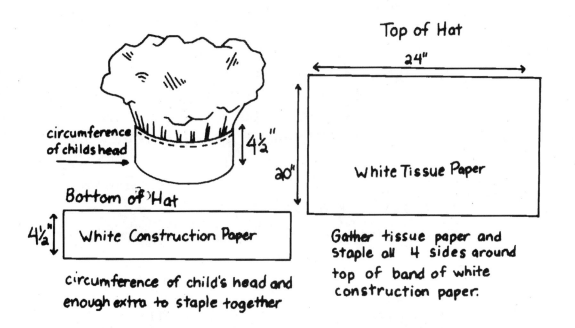

Top of Hat

24"

White Tissue Paper

20"

circumference
of child's head

4½"

Bottom of Hat

4½"

White Construction Paper

circumference of child's head and
enough extra to staple together

Gather tissue paper and
staple all 4 sides around
top of band of white
construction paper.

Writing Center

 Use a permanent marker to draw simple pictures
from this unit, such as a bowl, chef's hat, spoon,
fork, knife, pizza, on a plastic laminate table. Draw
the picture and write the word underneath. Provide
tracing paper so children can trace over the picture
and the word or provide drawing paper so children
can copy the picture and word using the model.

Provide a dark outline drawing of Italy. Put out tracing paper so children can make their own maps of Italy.

Cut pictures of Italian foods from magazines and glue to index cards. Write the name of the food on each card. Display these in the writing center so children can see the words as they practice writing.

Listening Center

Tape yourself reading *More Spaghetti, I Say!* or *Cloudy With a Chance of Meatballs*.

Tape the children singing "On Top of Spaghetti." Provide a copy of the book or a class reproduction of the book for children at the listening center.

Tape yourself reading some of the stories set in Italy, such as *Looking for Daniela* by Steven Kroll, or some of Tomie de Paola's books, such as *Tony's Bread, Jingle the Christmas Clown, Strega Nona*, or *Strega Nona Meets Her Match*.

Book Center

Make a class ABC Book with things from the Italian Restaurant. Have children brainstorm something for each letter of the alphabet. If you get stuck, use some of these.

anchovies, antipasto, apron
bake, bill, breadsticks
calzones, colander, candle
dough
eat
fork, flag
gondolas, gelato, garlic, grapes
hot, host/hostess
Italy, Italian ice
jewelry, just delicious
knife
lasagna, Leaning Tower of Pisa
meatballs, menu, macaroni
noodles, napkin
olive, "Open"
pizza, pizzeria, pasta,
   pepperoni
quattro (four in Italian)
ravioli, recipe, Rome
spoon, spaghetti, spaghetti
   sauce
tip, toppings (pizza)
uno (one in Italian)
Venice, Vatican City
waiter/waitress
Xtra pasta, please!
yellow peppers, yummy
"z-z-z-z," a hard day's work

 Here are some books you may want in your book center. Check your school or community library for other titles. Many of these are also appropriate for reading to the class at circle time.

(ps-K) Fann, Charlie. *Lots on Top*. The Wright Group, 1989. From a group of four "Food Theme Story Books"—the sentences follow a predictable pattern—"I eat____with____on top." Starts with "jam on bread" but quickly moves to the ridiculous—"chips on fish." After reading this book, children might enjoy making up their own ridiculous sentences and illustrating them.

(ps-1) Cocca-Leffler, Maryann. *Wednesday Is Spaghetti Day*. Scholastic Hardcover, 1990.
Fictional story of a group of cats who make and enjoy Italian spaghetti on Wednesday while the children are away at school.

(ps-1) Doyle, Charlotte. *Freddie's Spaghetti*. Random House, 1991.
The story of little Freddie as he waits for mom to cook spaghetti.

(ps-1) Hines, Anna Grossnickle. *Daddy Makes the Best Spaghetti*. Clarion Books, 1986.
This sparkling picture book depicts family life at its best as everyday routines are transformed into joyful games.

(ps-1) Marzollo, Claudio. *Fat and Thin*. Macmillan Publishing, 1975.
Few words but children will enjoy explaining the action. The illustrations tell the story of a man in a restaurant who runs his waiter ragged getting him the things he wants.

(ps-1) Swayne, Dick and Peter Savage. *I am a Chef*. J.B. Lippincott Company, 1978.
Text and photographs follow a chef as he selects the ingredients for and prepares his creations. The chef in this case is a young boy doing adult activities. Easy text, super photographs.

(ps-2) Coplans, Peta. *Spaghetti for Suzy*. Houghton Mifflin, 1993.
Suzy loves spaghetti for breakfast, lunch, and dinner. She goes to the park and meets three animals who show her another world and introduce her to fruits.

(ps-2) Florian, Douglas. *A Chef*. Greenwillow Books, 1992.
Demonstrates how different types of chefs work with food and describes some of the utensils they use. Excellent overview of different types of chefs.

(ps-2) Gelman, Rita Golden. *More Spaghetti, I Say!* Scholastic, Inc., 1987.
A delightful, humorous, easy-to-read book about the eating antics of Minnie and Freddie. What they can do with spaghetti! Also available in big book format from Scholastic, Inc., 1987.

(K-2) Calmenson, Stephanie. *Dinner at the Panda Palace.* HarperCollins Publishers, 1991.
Starting with one hungry elephant, two carsick lions, three pigs running from a wolf, other playful animals come to the Panda Palace restaurant for a hearty meal. The food is superb and there is always room for one more. Delightful illustrations. Story told in rhyme.

(K-2) Greene, Carol. *I Want to be a Chef.* Childrens Press, 1956.
Older book which is an easy reader. Bobby visits a baker as he makes goodies.

(K-2) Kraus, Robert. *The Gondolier of Venice.* Windmill Books, Inc./ E. P. Dutton and Co., Inc., 1976.
Gregory, the Gondolier of Venice, is worried because Venice is sinking. Even the great thinkers cannot help him save his beloved city. Finally he finds an ingenious solution. Black and white pictures provide exquisite details of Venice.

(K-2) Quackenbush, Robert. *Henry's Awful Mistake.* Parent's Magazine Press, 1980.
The story of Henry, who invites Clara for dinner—as he is preparing the meal, he sees an ant. One mistake leads to another until the meal and house are destroyed. Delightful story.

(K-2) Rey, Margaret and Alan J. Shalleck. *Curious George and the Pizza.* Houghton Mifflin, 1985.
Curious George creates havoc in a pizza shop but redeems himself by making an unusual delivery.

(K-2) Slepian, Jand and Ann Seidler. *The Hungry Thing.* Scholastic, Inc., 1967.
Delightful fiction about the Hungry Thing who comes to town and eats and eats and eats. Children will delight is figuring out just what he wants to eat.

(K-3) Barrett, Judi. *Cloudy With a Chance of Meatballs.* Houghton Mifflin Company, 1978.
Delightful bedtime story of the town of Chewand Swallow where all the food falls from the sky. After reading this book, have children draw pictures of their favorite food falling from the sky,

(K-3) Bourne, Miriam Ann. *A Day in the Life of a Chef.* Troll Associates, 1988.
Follows the head chef of a hotel restaurant through his day as he plans the amounts and varieties of dishes to be made and oversees their preparation and service.

(K-3) Corey, Melinda. *Let's Visit a Spaghetti Factory.* Troll Associates, 1990.
Story of making pasta, beginning with the durum wheat growing in the fields and ending with the pasta in the super-markets. Includes a recipe for "Quick Macaroni Salad." After reading the book, see if the class can list the steps from wheat to spaghetti.

(K-3) de Paola, Tomie. *Jingle the Christmas Clown.* G. P. Putnam's Sons, 1992.
When Jingle, the young clown, and Il Circo Piccolo, the Little Circus, arrive at the Italian village ready to perform on Christmas Eve, only the older villagers are left and they are too poor to pay the circus or to celebrate Christmas. The circus decides to go on to the big city but leaves Jingle and the baby animals behind to rest. When Jingle sees how sad the villagers are, he decides to give the village a special Christmas Eve circus, bringing joy to the village. After the performance, the Christmas angel appears with golden stars. At the end of the book is a recipe for star-shaped Italian cookies.

(K-3) de Paola, Tomie. *The Prince of the Dolomites.* Harcourt Brace and Jovanovich, 1980.
Uncle Storyteller comes to the small Italian village and tells the children the old Italian tale of the Prince of the Dolomites.

(K-3) de Paola, Tomie. *Strega Nona.* Prentice-Hall, Inc., 1975.
A Caldecott Honor Book and winner of several other literary prizes, this delightful old tale is about wise old Strega Nona "Grandmother Witch." Everyone in the Italian village comes to her for potions and cures, magic and comfort. When she hires Big Anthony to take care of her house and garden, he thinks he uncovers her secrets. Full of humor and warmth.

(K-3) de Paola, Tomie. *Strega Nona Meets Her Match*. G. P. Putnam's Sons, 1993.
Sequel to *Strega Nona*. Strega Nona (Grandma Witch) has old-fashioned cures for headaches and warts. Soon her friend, Strega Amelia, comes over the mountain and offers modern gadgets, sweets and cappuccino. Big Anthony unwittingly helps Strega Nona prove that sometimes the old ways are best. Uses many Italian words in context with the English equivalent.

(K-3) de Paola, Tomie. *Tony's Bread*. Whitebird Books, 1989.
Story of Tony the baker, who makes the best bread in all of northern Italy and marries off his daughter Serafina in the bargain.

(K-3) Glazer, Tom. *On Top of Spaghetti*. Doubleday and Company, Inc., 1963.
Includes words to the song, musical score, and pictures.

(K-3) Haskins, Jim. *Count Your Way through Italy*. Carolrhoda Books, Inc., 1990.
Includes pronunciation for numbers one to ten in Italian. Each number has a corresponding page of a fact about Italy. Excellent!

(K-3) Kroll, Steven. *Looking for Daniela*. Holiday House, 1988.
Antonio, a street performer, who admires a rich merchant's daughter, must use his talents juggling, tightrope walking, and guitar playing when he rescues her from bandits and tries to get her home again.

(K-3) Machotka, Hana. *Pasta Factory*. Houghton Mifflin Company, 1992.
Tour of the Tutta Pasta Factory in words and photos describing the pasta-making process.

(K-3) Poskanzer, Susan C. *What's It Like to be a Chef*. Troll Associates, 1990.
Describes work of a chef as he goes about his job cooking a variety of meals in a big restaurant.

(K-3) Tomchek, Ann. *I Can Be a Chef*. Childrens Press, 1985.
Explores the world of those who want to cook for a living, examining where they work and what they do in preparing meals for others. Good pictures of tall white hats worn by chefs—includes both male and female chefs.

(K-3) Vigna, Judith. *Uncle Alfredo's Zoo*. Albert Whitman and Company, 1994.
Anna and her Grandmother visit a small Italian village where "nonna" grew up. Anna is anxious to visit Uncle Alfredo's stone zoo but is heartbroken to learn that after he died, the stones mysteriously disappeared. On St. Antuono Day, the day the priest blesses the animals, a miracle happens. Beautiful warm watercolors.

(1-4) Sobol, H. L. *Cosmo's Restaurant*. Macmillan Children's Group, 1978.
Black and white photographs follow a family through a typical day as they participate in a variety of activities involved in running their small Italian restaurant in New York City.

Outside

 Take your water table outside on a warm day. Put pitchers, plastic glasses and plastic serving trays in the water table and encourage children to put glasses on the trays, fill them with water, and practice carrying them as if they were waiters and waitresses. Any spills (and there will be many!) will dry quickly.

 Use your tricycles and wagons as pizza delivery cars. Have children write some signs, such as "Pizza Presto," or draw some pictures of pizza that can be taped to the sides of the tricycles and wagons. A few small, empty cardboard pizza boxes will add to the fun. Consider making pizzas with play dough or cardboard early in the day and placing them in boxes to "deliver."

Field Study

 Consider going on a field trip to a pizzeria for lunch. Or invite someone to come to the classroom to make pizza. Be sure to talk about good manners before you go. Ask if the class can be placed where they can watch as the pizza is made or select a pizzeria where hand-tossed pizza is always demonstrated.

 After the field trip, have children each draw something they remember seeing. Encourage children to tell you about their pictures. Write down what they tell you. Send the pictures with dictation to the restaurant as a thank you.

 After the field trip, take a picture of the class dressed in their white chef hats. Make a banner that says "_____ Pizza is the Best!" (painted and/or computer generated) for children to hold in the picture. Write a language experience story of the trip to add to the picture and send it to the restaurant.

 Take photographs during the field trip. Display the pictures in a pocket chart to remind students of what they saw. Encourage students to create captions. These same pictures can be used next year to illustrate words or as preparation for the same field trip. Later have children bind the pictures and captions together for a class big book.

 For a "stay at school" field trip, find a pizzeria that delivers. Ask parents to send pizza money to school with their children. Children should figure out how much money they have, what type of pizza they want to order, and how much pizza they think they will need. Take children with you to order the pizza and be sure it is delivered directly to your room. Pre-arrange for the delivery person to stay a few minutes for a brief "Show and Tell." Offer a small tip and send a thank you note for the extra service.

 Read to the class *Pasta Factory* by Hana Machotka and/or *Let's Visit a Spaghetti Factory* by Melinda Corey. After reading the book, have children work together to write a list of the steps involved in making pasta.

Parent Involvement

 Encourage parents to help with the cooking experience by sharing some ways they can reinforce at home what you are doing in school. Consider the following letter.

Dear Parents,

We are studying about jobs in an Italian restaurant. To help your children experience what they might have to do in jobs like these, try cooking with your children this week. Encourage their help with the family supper or, if you like, have them help make something for the class snack. Don't try anything too difficult. Simple is fine! Be sure to talk about all the things that you use, such as the recipe, measuring cups, spoons, cookie sheet, oven, or whatever, and be sure to enjoy the time together!

If you have a favorite family recipe for spaghetti sauce, make pasta from scratch, or have any other favorite Italian dish that you would like to come fix in the classroom, please let me know and we will arrange for you to come in and share the experience with the kids!

Happy cooking!

School

Dramatic Play

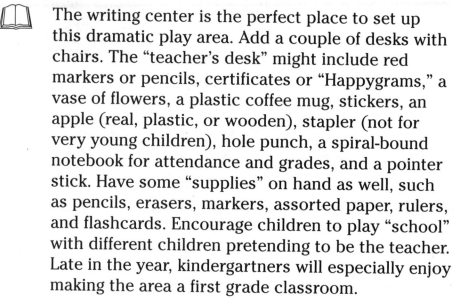

The writing center is the perfect place to set up this dramatic play area. Add a couple of desks with chairs. The "teacher's desk" might include red markers or pencils, certificates or "Happygrams," a vase of flowers, a plastic coffee mug, stickers, an apple (real, plastic, or wooden), stapler (not for very young children), hole punch, a spiral-bound notebook for attendance and grades, and a pointer stick. Have some "supplies" on hand as well, such as pencils, erasers, markers, assorted paper, rulers, and flashcards. Encourage children to play "school" with different children pretending to be the teacher. Late in the year, kindergartners will especially enjoy making the area a first grade classroom.

If this center is near the chalkboard, be sure to put out chalk. All teachers write on the chalkboard!

Use a clothes tree or a simple box for teacher "dress-up" clothes. Go through your own closet. You might include a tie, suit jacket, briefcase, dress, purse, wallet, wigs, eye glasses, and a teacher's tote bag.

Use dolls or stuffed animals as "students" in some of the desks.

Put lots of books on a shelf in the "school" or set up a "library" in the book center where children can check-out books. Add a small table or desk for check-out and a rubber date stamp.

 Change the housekeeping area into the kitchen and cafeteria. Place a longer table with chairs in the area, adding some extra plates, silverware, paper bags, cafeteria trays, play food, empty lunch boxes, and other things that the cafeteria will give you. Look at your school cafeteria for ways to make your own area more "authentic."

Circle Time

 Encourage children to list reasons why they go to school, such as to learn to read, because my mom makes me, to listen to stories, to do puzzles, to eat lunch, because my friends go, or for recess.

 Make flashcards for the numbers 1–10 or 20. Use school shapes. Precut notepads make great flash-cards (Novel Notes with 50 sheets each: School Bus, Pencil, Computer, Notebook Paper, by Carson-Dellosa, Shapes, Etc., and other companies). Use a different set of flashcards each day. Flash the number cards in order and then mix them up. "Round and round the school we go—where we stop nobody knows!" and flash the cards in random order. Leave the cards in the cognitive activities area for students to put in order or leave them in "school" for students to use when they are the "teacher." Flashcards can also be used for learning the letters of the alphabet and learning the names of students in the class.

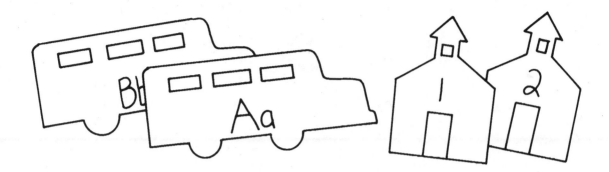

Make a list of all the school workers. Name each job and the person who does that job in your school.

Principal	Ms. Kellam
P.E. Teacher	Mrs. Tipton
Art Teachers	Mrs. Trkula, Mrs. Hubbard
Custodian	Mr. "C"
Media Specialist	Ms. Ford
Secretary	Mrs. Price
Office Helpers	Mrs. Barr, Mrs. Jensen
Bus Driver	Ms. Joni

Talk about each school worker. Go around the school and take a picture of each one (or photo-copy their pictures from previous yearbooks). Use these as flashcards at circle time. Help children learn each person's name, the titles of the jobs they do, and what types of things they do in their jobs.

Have children select a school worker to come to the room to be interviewed. Before the interview, invite children to brainstorm a list of questions they would like to ask. Children may practice by interviewing you about your job. After the school worker comes, encourage children to draw pictures of one of the things that worker does.

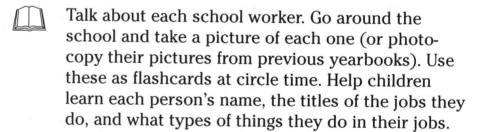

Make a list of things the class could do to help the custodian who cleans the room, such as pick up the big trash, put chairs up on tables—talk to your custodian for some additional ideas. Plan a special day when children do all the things on the list (they should be encouraged to do these things every day) and even bake some cookies or another treat to leave for the custodian as a way to say thank you. Notes or pictures to the custodian saying thank you will also be appreciated.

Whisper the name of one of the school workers to one of the children. Invite that child to pretend to be that worker by acting out things that person does in his or her job. Other children may try to guess the identity of the worker. In some cases, you may have to do the acting yourself.

Make a list with children of things you find in school, such as chalk, chalkboard, television, VCR, record player, records, cassettes, tape recorders, books, pencils, pens, markers, crayons, rulers, yard or meter stick, map, globe, scissors, glue, construction paper, writing paper, cubbies, desk, table, plants, paint, paintbrush, rubber bands, paper clips, stapler, hole punch, bookshelves, bulletin board, and flannelboard. Write each word on a sentence strip and have each child take a word to illustrate on a small index card. Glue each picture card by the appropriate word and place in the writing center.

Invite children to go around the room and count each of the things you listed. Use a graph similar to the one on page 274 to record each item counted.

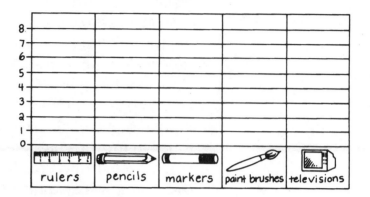

Look for picture cards of supplies from your list (available with language vocabulary sets) or take photographs in your room. Use these cards as flashcards. When children are able to identify each picture, line the cards across a chalkboard ledge and ask children questions such as the following.

What do you write with? Color with?
What do you paint with?
What do you cut with?
Where do you sit when you are writing?

Use the cards to play memory games. Use a teacher's tote bag as a "mystery box." Put several of the cards (or the actual items) in the bag. Pull out each one for children to identify. Then place all the items back in the bag. Remove all but one and ask children to guess which one is missing. Vary the difficulty of the game by having more items in the tote bag or leaving more items in the bag.

Use the cards to practice sequential memory. Lay 3–5 cards in front of the students and identify each picture. Mix up the cards and then give them to a volunteer to put out in the same order you did.

Estimate. Each day, fill a small transparent plastic container with one of the items you are identifying, such as paper clips, rubber bands, or pencils. Each child may take a turn estimating how many are in the container. Have children write the numerals on sticky notes along with their names and stick their estimates to a designated spot, or record their names and guesses on an erasable marker board. At the end of the day, pull all the children together, count the items, and discuss the results.

Have children help you make a list of school rules. Keep the list simple and short (3 or 4 rules), such as these:

> Walk quietly in the halls.
> Put on a water shirt at the water table.
> Use your "inside voice" in the classroom.

Write the rules on chart paper and display them in the room. You might want to add simple illustrations for each rule, have children illustrate the rules, or take photographs of children illustrating the rules to add to the chart.

Read *The Teacher Who Could Not Count* by Craig McKee and Margaret Holland. This delightful story ends with children forming the numbers 1–9 with their bodies. Even without the book, encourage children to try making each number with their bodies.

Divide children into "teacher" and "student" pairs. The teacher traces a number or letter on the student's back using a finger. The student may respond verbally or by tracing the number or letter (a guess) in the air. Children may exchange roles if you wish.

Give each child an individual chalkboard and piece of chalk or a marker board with an erasable marker. Play a different game each day, such as calling out a number for children to write; showing a number set and having children write the numeral; calling out a letter of the alphabet and having children write the upper or lowercase letter (or both); or holding up a picture that illustrates an initial consonant sound and having children write the letter. Each child may have a chance to be "teacher."

Each day, invite a different child to be teacher by leading the morning exercises (checking attendance, leading the pledge, putting the number on the calendar), and other things you would do. Give the "teacher" a special apple pointer, teacher apron, or other symbol that would identify the child to the class as "teacher."

Prepare children for *The Day the Teacher Went Bananas* by James Howe by giving each child a banana (whole, cut into halves or fourths) and telling them that this story is about a teacher who really liked bananas. Invite children to predict what the story will be about from the book cover. After the children have enjoyed the story, have them "change it up" by imagining the teacher's day at the zoo. Invite each child to illustrate the teacher with one of the animals and use temporary, invented spelling to write about the picture. Children may also dictate sentences about the story to you. Display the pictures on bulletin board and later bind them into a class book.

Encourage children to help you make a graph of the way they go home from school. Cut some simple shapes representing a yellow school bus, a car (to represent parent pick-up), a bicycle, a shoe (to represent walking home), a van (to represent day care pick-up). Draw your own shapes or use Ellison dies. Have children choose the appropriate shapes and add their names. Make the graph from the bottom up and discuss the results with the children. How many children walk home? Ride the bus? How do most children get home?

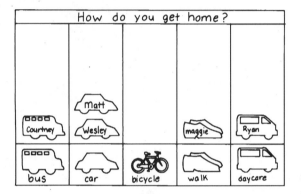

Rhythm Time

 Teach children the traditional song, "The Wheels on the Bus."

The wheels on the bus go round and round,
Round and round, round and round.
The wheels on the bus go round and round,
All through the town.
(Roll hands round and round each other)

Children may enjoy making up additional verses after you have taught them the original ones. The following are verses used by a Pre-K class, some traditional and some written by the class.

The wipers on the bus go swish, swish, swish . . .
(Swish with forearms back and forth, like windshield wipers)
The horn on the bus goes beep, beep, beep . . .
(Pretend to beep horn)

The doors on the bus go open and shut . . .
(Cross forearms one across the other, fingers touching
elbows for closed, raise arms for open)
The lights on the bus go blinkity, blinkity, blink . . .
(Open and close fingers)
The stop sign on the bus goes out and in . . .
(Stick one arm out and bend at the elbow, toward the body
and away)
The children on the bus go bumpity-bumpity-bump . . .
(Pretend to go up and down while sitting, as if on a
bumpy ride)
The babies on the bus go wah-wah-wah . . .
(Wipe eyes with both fists)
The teacher on the bus goes sh-sh-sh . . .
(Put index finger up to lips)

Write the verses on chart paper. Use simple pictures above key words to help children "read" the chart. Point to each word as you read the chart with the class, using a ruler or yardstick as a pointer.

Invite children to illustrate the verses they like best. Underneath each picture, write the words to that particular verse. Display the verses on a bulletin board and later, bind them together into a class big book.

Help children place a small, bus-shaped sticky note each time they see the word *bus* on the chart. When learning this song, sticky notes can be used as rebus symbols instead of the word. Count the number of sticky notes.

Different children may take turns being "teacher" by pointing to the words of the song with a ruler or yardstick as the class sings. The real teacher takes a student role.

Role-play the bus driver. Have one student pretend to be bus driver and stop the bus. "Pick up" each student by having them join a train-like line of kids. Walk around the room picking up more kids and singing "The Wheels on the Bus."

 Teach children the nursery rhyme "Mary Had a Little Lamb."

Mary had a little lamb.
It's fleece was white as snow.
And everywhere that Mary went
The lamb was sure to go.

It followed her to school one day
Which was against the rules.
It made the children laugh and play
To see a lamb at school.

And so the teacher turned it out,
But still it lingered near.
And waited patiently about
'Til Mary did appear.

"Why does the lamb love Mary so?"
The eager children cried.
"Why, Mary loves the lamb you know!"
The teacher did reply.

This rhyme can be taught by using the traditional tune. Look for the tune and additional verses in *Wee Sing Nursery Rhymes and Lullabies.*

Copy the rhyme on chart paper with small pictures above key words. Point to each word as you read the rhyme with the class. Put a large white pom-pom or large fluffy cotton ball on the end of a dowel to use as a pointer.

Children love acting out this rhyme. Have one child play Mary, one the teacher, one the lamb, and the rest of the children "the children who laughed and played."

"Change up" the rhyme by inviting children to think of a pet they would like to have. Have each child complete the sentence, "(Name) had a little (pet animal)" at the bottom of a piece of white drawing paper. Children may draw self-portraits with the pets of their choice at the top of the paper. Display these on a bulletin board and later, add a title page and bind them into a class big book.

Estimate. Cut a lamb shape from tagboard and add one cotton ball. Children may estimate how many cotton balls they think it will take to cover the lamb. Have children write their names and estimates on sticky notes (look for lamb-shaped sticky notes!) and graph on a chart. Later in the day, when all the children have had a chance to guess, gather the children together, take out the glue, and fill the lamb shape with cotton balls. Count the actual number of cotton balls used to cover the lamb. Compare the actual number with children's estimates. For younger students, use a shape that can be covered with less than 20 cotton balls.)

Read *Rhyme Readers: Mary Had a Little Lamb*, published by the Wright Group, or the delightful photo-illustrated *Mary Had a Little Lamb* by Sarah Josepha Hale to the children.

 Teach children the following original words to the tune of "Here We Go 'Round the Mulberry Bush."

This is the way we read a book,
Read a book, read a book.
This is the way we read book
At our school each day.
(act out reading a book and turning the pages)

Try some of these verses, acting out each verse.

This is the way we paint at the easel . . .
This is the way we eat our lunch . . .
This is the way we write with a pencil . . .
This is the way we color with crayons . . .
This is the way we play with play dough . . .
This is the way we build with blocks . . .
This is the way we hang up our coats . . .
This is the way we learn at the computer . . .

Go around the circle and invite each child to make up a verse.

Invite children to decide on verses they would like to illustrate. Write the words at the bottom of sheets of white drawing paper and have children draw their pictures at the top. Hold up each picture as you sing the corresponding verse. Later these can be displayed on a bulletin board or bound into a big book with a title page added.

 Try chanting and using a steady beat with these original verses.

This is what the teacher does,
teacher does, teacher does.
This is what the teacher does,
She reads us stories.

Adapt this last line for your particular class—she teaches ABC's, or he teaches reading and math.

This is what the custodian does . . .
He cleans the room.

This is what the art teacher does . . .
She draws and paints .

This is what the music teacher does . . .
She sings the songs.

Add as many verses as you like. Children will think up some things different workers do in the school (principal, coach, P.E. teacher, bus driver, lunch lady, secretary, assistant, librarian, office helper), and help you make up additional verses. Encourage their participation. You might want to substitute workers' names for their job titles.

Write these verses on chart paper and invite volunteers to illustrate the verses. These can be displayed in the hall outside the room, on a bulletin board, or bound together with a title page for a big book.

 Try these new words to the tune "Mary Wore a Red Dress."

> *Guess who works at my school,*
> *My school, my school.*
> *Guess who works at my school*
> *All day long?*
>
> *Mrs. Tipton works at my school,*
> *My school, my school.*
> *Mrs. Tipton works at my school.*
> *She teaches P.E.*
>
> *Mrs. Kellam works at my school,*
> *My school, my school.*
> *Mrs. Kellam works at my school.*
> *She's the principal.*

Use names of the workers at your school and their occupations. Hold up pictures of the workers, their photographs, or pictures drawn by the children, as you sing each new verse.

 Try this adaptation of a traditional fingerplay.

> *Way up high in the apple tree (cup hand over eyes and*
> *   look up)*
> *I (point to self) wanted an apple for teacher and me.*
> *I shook that tree as hard as I could (pretend to shake tree)*
> *Down came the apples (wiggle fingers of both hands down)*
> *M-m-m, M-m-m good. (rub tummy)*

To the tune of the Campbell's Soup jingle:

That's what Campbell's Soup is,
M-m-m, M-m-m good!
That's what apples are,
M-m-m, M-m-m good! (rub tummy)

 Bring in different kinds and colors of apples. Invite students to try each type and decide which they like the best. Graph the results with apple shapes. Label the graph "Apples A-Peel to Me."

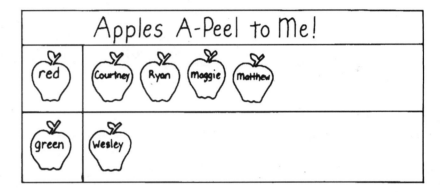

Use apples to make a counting book. On large sheets of paper, write or have children write the numbers from 1 to 10 or 20. Cut apples in half and have children print the apple shape using tempera paint and the flat side of the apple to represent the appropriate number set.

Bulletin Board

 Read to the children *My Teacher Sleeps in School* by Leatie Weiss. If you are comfortable with the idea, share things about your life at home with children (pictures are great). Put photographs, such as pictures of husband or wife, children, parents, picture of your house, picture of you doing things you like to do, your baby picture, and a picture of you the same age as the children, on the bulletin board. Label each picture and title it "About Your Teacher." This is a good bulletin board to have up for the first parent visit.

 Make a number line for the class. Cut 10 or 20 schoolhouse shapes from red tagboard (or school bus shapes from yellow tagboard). Write a number on each school house. Take photographs of the children around the room and attach a photograph showing the appropriate number of children to each card. (This can also be made into a game. Laminate the photographs and have children match the photograph with the correct numeral flash-card.)

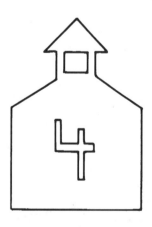

Snack/Cooking Time

This is a good time to talk about cafeteria workers and what they do. Prepare some cookies that you can bake in the cafeteria oven, make jello to put in their refrigerator, or plan to tour the cafeteria kitchen and have the workers give children each a cookie and some milk for snack. Get them involved in your learning!

Invite one of the cafeteria workers to come to your classroom and make a snack of his or her choice with the class, such as biscuits or cookies.

Invite children to plan a "bag lunch" day. Help children brainstorm possibilities on chart paper and guide them into selecting a "balanced" lunch, such as a peanut butter and jelly sandwich, apple, and a box drink. Ask parents to send in the supplies. Children may decorate their bags and then make their own lunch (actually making the sandwich and putting it into a plastic zipper bag and so on). Children may take their special lunches to the cafeteria or eat them on a blanket in the room or outside for a special picnic.

Cognitive Activities

Cut pictures of school bus shapes (use Ellison dies or bus-shaped note pads) from yellow tagboard. Make up to 20 cards (depending on the group of children). Write one number on each bus. Use lima beans for counters. On each bean, draw two eyes, a nose, and a mouth with permanent marker. Each bean represents a child on the bus. Count the appropriate number of "children" onto each bus card.

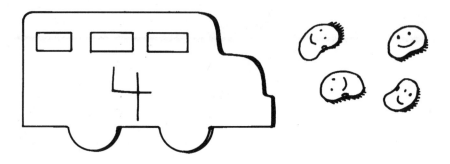

 Use sturdy colored plastic cups, empty individual milk cartons, or juice cans covered with solid-colored self-adhesive paper. Put a number from 1 to 10 or 20 on each cup. Supply a box of unsharpened pencils and have children count the appropriate number of pencils into each cup.

Write uppercase alphabet letters on red school-house shapes (or Ellison dies). Print the matching lowercase letters (or pictures symbolizing the initial consonant sounds) on paper dolls to represent children.

 Give each child a box of crayons that opens so all of the crayons are exposed. Inside the box, write the color words so that each time children use and replace a crayon, they have to match the word with the appropriate color crayon.

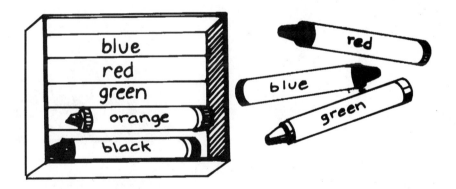

Or make a large "crayon box" from a piece of tagboard. Write the color words on the tagboard and have children put on either real, chubby crayons, matching the color crayon with the color word, or crayon-shaped tagboard (using an Ellison die).

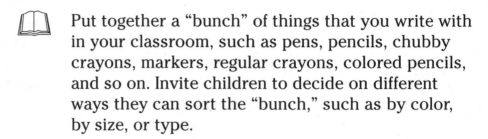 Put together a "bunch" of things that you write with in your classroom, such as pens, pencils, chubby crayons, markers, regular crayons, colored pencils, and so on. Invite children to decide on different ways they can sort the "bunch," such as by color, by size, or type.

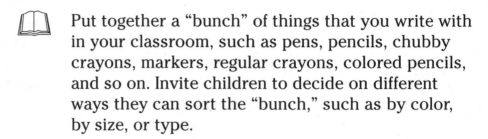 This same "bunch" of writing items can be used as counters. Put out number flashcards and have children count the appropriate number set of "writing things" onto each numeral.

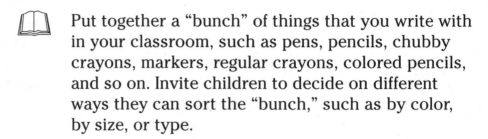 Glue real school items, such as 1 pen, 2 pencils, 3 crayons, 4 paper clips, 5 erasers, 6 rubber bands, on heavy tagboard or the inside lids of shoe boxes. Children may sequence the number cards.

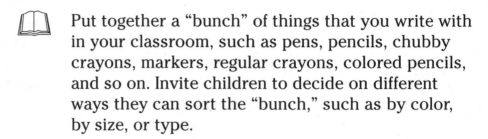 Place a schoolhouse or bus shape on small boxes or individual milk cartons. Write a number on each shape. Make "kid counters" from craft sticks or tongue depressors. At the tip of each stick, attach a circle face drawn on a sticky dot or draw the face directly on the stick. Count the appropriate number of "children" onto each bus or into each school.

Write the numbers 1 to 10 or 20 down the left side of a long piece of white drawing paper. Children may stamp the appropriate number of school-related items beside each number. Look for rubber stamps such as Shapes Etc. Apple SE-420, School Bus SE-459, Flag SE-447.

Manipulative Center

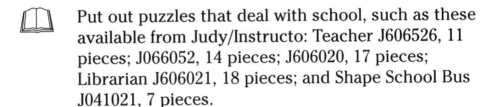 Put out puzzles that deal with school, such as these available from Judy/Instructo: Teacher J606526, 11 pieces; J066052, 14 pieces; J606020, 17 pieces; Librarian J606021, 18 pieces; and Shape School Bus J041021, 7 pieces.

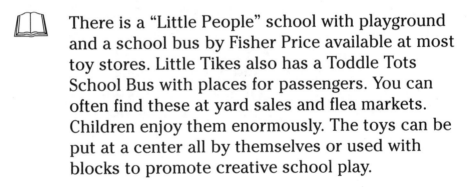 There is a "Little People" school with playground and a school bus by Fisher Price available at most toy stores. Little Tikes also has a Toddle Tots School Bus with places for passengers. You can often find these at yard sales and flea markets. Children enjoy them enormously. The toys can be put at a center all by themselves or used with blocks to promote creative school play.

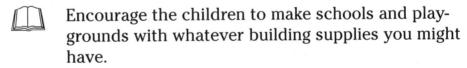 Encourage the children to make schools and playgrounds with whatever building supplies you might have.

Play Dough Center

There are many school-related cookie cutters available, such as an apple, pencil, computer, bus, and a schoolhouse. Collect different cookie cutters to add to the play dough this week. Red is a good "school" color for the play dough.

 Add alphabet cookie cutters to the play dough. Encourage children to use the cookie cutters to write their names. Offer a little guidance by using the cookie cutters as stencils and posting the children's names around the play dough area.

 Add number cookie cutters to the play dough. Encourage children to make play dough numbers from 1 to 10 to sequence, telephone numbers, or to match to the appropriate number of play dough cutouts (apples, buses, schoolhouses).

Blocks

 Encourage children to use big cardboard brick blocks to make a schoolhouse.

 Put a bus in the block area. Children may build roads, tunnels, bridges and houses where the bus makes its stops.

Sand/Water Table

 Use school supplies for a sink or float activity at your water table. Try paper clips, pencils, pens, crayons, markers, rulers (plastic and wooden), rubber bands or other items listed in the vocabulary section of circle time. After you have introduced this activity, children will find many other things around the room to try.

Art Center

 Make school collages. Go through all of your "stuff" and choose some things that can be used in a collage, such as paper clips, rubber bands, sticky notes, pencils too short to keep, empty glue bottles, broken crayons, markers and pens that have run out of ink, sheets of notebook paper cut into smaller pieces and just about anything else you find that you probably won't ever use. Go through an old supply closet and pull out some of those things that are faded and gathering dust! Give children each a piece of heavy paper and invite them to glue whatever they want in any design they like.

 Take children to the front of the school building. Point out details such as the shape of the building, color and building material used, flag, trees, flowers, shrubbery, sidewalks, shape and color of the front door, shape of the windows and how many, name of the school, and other words or signs. Give children drawing paper and crayons and encourage them to draw the school building while looking at it or from memory back in the classroom.

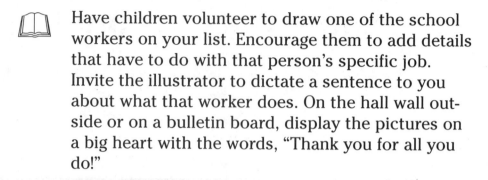 Have children volunteer to draw one of the school workers on your list. Encourage them to add details that have to do with that person's specific job. Invite the illustrator to dictate a sentence to you about what that worker does. On the hall wall outside or on a bulletin board, display the pictures on a big heart with the words, "Thank you for all you do!"

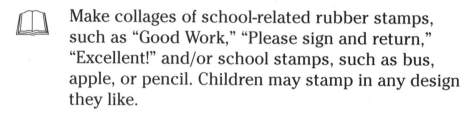 Make collages of school-related rubber stamps, such as "Good Work," "Please sign and return," "Excellent!" and/or school stamps, such as bus, apple, or pencil. Children may stamp in any design they like.

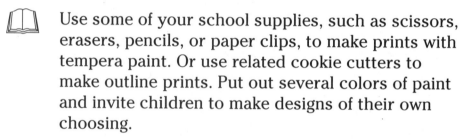 Use some of your school supplies, such as scissors, erasers, pencils, or paper clips, to make prints with tempera paint. Or use related cookie cutters to make outline prints. Put out several colors of paint and invite children to make designs of their own choosing.

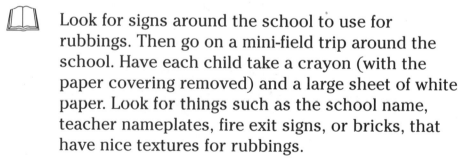 Look for signs around the school to use for rubbings. Then go on a mini-field trip around the school. Have each child take a crayon (with the paper covering removed) and a large sheet of white paper. Look for things such as the school name, teacher nameplates, fire exit signs, or bricks, that have nice textures for rubbings.

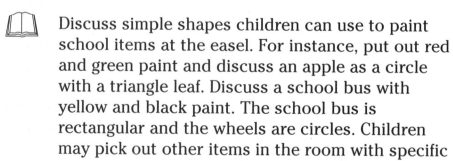 Discuss simple shapes children can use to paint school items at the easel. For instance, put out red and green paint and discuss an apple as a circle with a triangle leaf. Discuss a school bus with yellow and black paint. The school bus is rectangular and the wheels are circles. Children may pick out other items in the room with specific

shapes to practice drawing and painting using their new information about shapes.

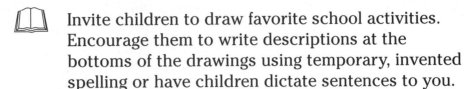 Invite children to draw favorite school activities. Encourage them to write descriptions at the bottoms of the drawings using temporary, invented spelling or have children dictate sentences to you.

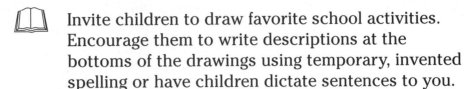 Turn a large refrigerator box into a school bus that the children can climb into. Turn the box on its side. Cut lots of windows and add a door on one side. Glue a small box to the front of the larger box for the hood. Take the boxes outside and have children paint the bus yellow. After it is dry, add headlights, wheels, and other details with paint, painted paper plates, or colored paper. A Frisbee makes a good steering wheel.

Take a photograph of each child in the school bus. Glue the photographs to yellow construction paper cut in bus shapes. At the bottom of each photograph, write "(Name) rides the school bus." On the last page, have a picture of the teacher, and write "And (teacher's name) rides the school bus too!" Display on a bulletin board and later add a title page and bind into a book.

Turn a large refrigerator box into a schoolhouse. Take the box outside and cut a door and windows. Have children paint the box red. Add a sign with the school's name, other identifying features, and even a flag outside or on top. Children will enjoy using the school as a cozy individual reading nook during this unit.

Writing Center

 Go around the school and take photographs of school signs, such as Office, Exit, school name, Clinic, teacher's names, and put them up in the writing center so children can identify this environmental print and use the words in their writing. Be sure children know that this is reading! Give each child one picture and take a walk around the school—see if children can match the photographs with the actual signs.

 Use a permanent marker to draw simple school shapes, such as bus, schoolhouse, bell, pencil, apple, on a plastic laminate table. Write the appropriate word under each drawing. Provide tracing paper so children can trace the drawing and the word. Marker can be erased with hair spray or alcohol.

Listening Center

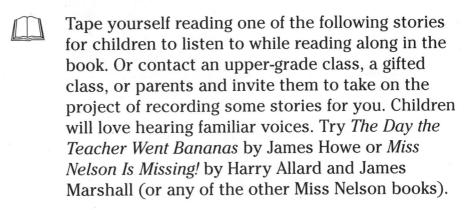 Tape yourself reading one of the following stories for children to listen to while reading along in the book. Or contact an upper-grade class, a gifted class, or parents and invite them to take on the project of recording some stories for you. Children will love hearing familiar voices. Try *The Day the Teacher Went Bananas* by James Howe or *Miss Nelson Is Missing!* by Harry Allard and James Marshall (or any of the other Miss Nelson books).

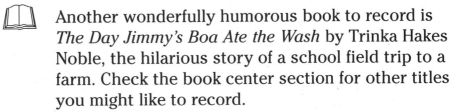 Another wonderfully humorous book to record is *The Day Jimmy's Boa Ate the Wash* by Trinka Hakes Noble, the hilarious story of a school field trip to a farm. Check the book center section for other titles you might like to record.

Book Center

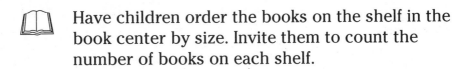 Have children order the books on the shelf in the book center by size. Invite them to count the number of books on each shelf.

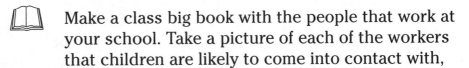 Make a class big book with the people that work at your school. Take a picture of each of the workers that children are likely to come into contact with,

such as principal, assistants, special area teachers, media specialist, custodian, bus drivers, you, and any other people in the school. Use the format of Bill Martin, Jr.'s *Brown Bear, Brown Bear.* Cut out the pages in the shape of a school (see diagram). Start the book with a picture of the school and the text: " (School), (school), what do you see inside of me?" On the next page at the top, "I see the principal looking at me." Under the picture at the bottom of the page, "(principal's name), (principal's name), what do you see?" and so on. On the next-to-the last page, have your picture and at the bottom "(teacher's name), (teacher's name), what do you see?" and on the final page, a picture of the children in the class. "I see beautiful children! That's what I see!"

Make an ABC book of school things. Help children make a list of words for each of the letter of the alphabet. If you get stuck, try some of the following.

apple, art, Assistants/Aides
books, bus, bell, bulletin board
crayons, custodian, computer
desk, door
eraser, easel
friends, flashcards, flag
guidance office, glue, globe
hole punch, halls
instruments (musical), ink pen
jump rope
kitchen, kickball
lunch, library, lunch box
music, media center, markers
notebook

office
P.E., principal, pencils, paint
Quiet!
rulers, record player, recess
stapler, scissors, snacks,
     school
teacher, television, tacks
United States map
VCR, Vice-Principal
writing paper, write
Xtra special children
yardstick
"Z-z-z-z-z" (rest time)

Consider things particular to your school to add to each letter of the alphabet, such as the school name, names of special teachers, school mascot, school colors, or other distinguishing things about your own school. Put each letter of the alphabet on a single sheet of white drawing paper. Invite volunteers to illustrate each letter. Alphabetize the pictures and add a title.

Make a bulletin board display by putting the pictures in order and pointing to each letter as you sing the "ABC Song" with the class. Leave out the pointing so the children will pick it up and sing the song independently. Bind the pages in alphabetical order for an ABC book when you take them down.

 Encourage children to be the teacher or librarian who "reads" a story to other children for story time. Some students may be more comfortable if you gather the stuffed animals and dolls in a circle to listen to their story.

 Here are some books you may want in your book center. Check your school or community library for other titles. Many of these are also appropriate for reading at circle time.

(ps) Gobatz, Norman (illustrator). *School Bus*. Grosset and Dunlap, Inc., 1993.
Board book with real moving wheels.

(ps-K) Ahlberg, Janet and Allan. *Starting School*. Viking Children's Books, 1988.
This humorous book will put any preschooler's jitters to rest by showing what going to school is like.

(ps-K) Bracken, Carolyn. *The Busy School Bus*. Grosset and Dunlap, 1986.
Board book shaped like a school bus with real moving wheels.

(ps-K) Chlad, Dorothy. *Riding on a Bus*. Childrens Press, 1985.
Rules for riding on a bus.

(ps-K) Ewers, Joe. *Little Yellow School Bus*. Random House, 1992.
Board book shaped like a school bus with real moving wheels.

(ps-1) Hale, Sarah Josepha. *Mary Had a Little Lamb*. Scholastic, Inc. 1990.
Beautiful photo-illustrations telling the traditional nursery rhyme with contemporary style. Sarah Josepha Hale (1788-1879) first published "Mary Had a Little Lamb" as a poem in 1830.

(ps-1) Marshall, Val and Bronwyn Tester. *Scat! Scat!* The Wright Group, 1987.
Big book about insects and animals that invade Mrs. Mountain's class. This predictable book is great for shared reading. Many excellent whole language activities to help integrate the book into the curriculum.

(ps-1) Muntean, Michaela. *I Like School*. Western Publishing Company, Inc., 1980.
Sesame Street gang goes to kindergarten for the first time. Labels all the items in the school.

(ps-1) Berenstain, Stan and Jan. *The Berenstain Bears Go to School*. Random House, 1978.
Sister Bear, nervous about entering kindergarten, overcomes her fears when she discovers that school is really great.

(ps-1) Cohen, Miriam. *The New Teacher*. Macmillan Children's Corporation, 1989.
The first grade doesn't understand why their new teacher had to have a baby. They wonder what the new teacher will be like. This insightful book takes a look at children's fears.

(ps-1) McKee, Craig and Margaret Holland. *The Teacher Who Could Not Count*. School Book Fairs, Inc., 1981.
Delightful story about a teacher who could not count. Her students, who liked her very much, found a way to make their bodies into numbers to help her.

(ps-1) Noble, Trinka Hakes. *The Day Jimmy's Boa Ate the Wash*. Dial Press, 1980.
Jimmy's boa constrictor creates havoc on the class field trip to the farm. Delightful pictures by Steven Kellogg.

(ps-1) Rockwell, Anne. *I Like the Library*. E.P. Dutton, 1977.
Good overview of the public library.

(ps-1) *Rhyme Readers: Mary had a Little Lamb*. The Wright Group, 1991.
Traditional rhyme in big book form with beautiful illustrations.

(ps-1) Weiss, Leatie. *My Teacher Sleeps in School*. Frederick Warne and Company, Inc.
When a group of children start thinking about it, they are sure that their teacher sleeps at school. The teacher soon clues them in.

(ps-2) Bridwell, Norman. *The Witch Goes to School*. Scholastic, Inc., 1992.
A normal day at school becomes special when the Witch comes for a visit and uses her magic.

(ps-2) Howe, James (illustrated by Lillian Hoban). *The Day the Teacher Went Bananas*. Dutton Children's Books, 1984.
A class's new teacher, who leads the children in a number of very popular activities, turns out to be a gorilla.

(ps-3) Allard, Harry and Marshall, James. *Miss Nelson Is Missing!* Houghton Mifflin Co., 1985.
Good-natured Miss Nelson's rowdy children take advantage of her until she disappears and returns disguised as the poisonous Viola Swamp. Others in this series about Miss Nelson and her class are *Miss Nelson Is Back* and *Miss Nelson Has a Field Day*.

(K-2) Bunting, E. *Our Teacher is Having a Baby*. Clarion Books, 1992.
The children are excited about their teacher having a baby, but when it comes, they worry if the teacher will come back.

(K-2) de Paola, Tomie. *The Art Lesson*. Trumpet Club, 1989.
Tommy has experiences at school with the kindergarten teacher and an art teacher.

(K-2) Giff, Patricia Reilly. *Today Was a Terrible Day*. Puffin Books, 1980.
Ronald's day goes from bad to worse until the end of the day, when his teacher writes him a note.

(K-2) Wiseman, B. *Morris Goes to School*. Parents Magazine Book Clubs, Inc., 1970.
An "I Can Read" Book. Morris the Moose goes to school to learn to count.

(K-3) Beckman, Beatrice. *I Can Be a Teacher*. Childrens Press, 1985.
Describes in simple terms the training and duties of a teacher. Great color photographs of teachers at work.

(K-3) Brown, Marc. *Arthur's Teacher Trouble*. Joy Street Books/Little, Brown and Company, 1989.
Third-grader Arthur gets the "strictest teacher in the whole world" and then is amazed when he is chosen to be in the school spell-a-thon. Also the basis for a computer program (Macintosh CD-ROM from Random House/Broderbund), winner of five awards including Computer's Choice Award for Best Early Childhood Program.

(K-3) Calmenson, Stephanie. *The Principal's New Clothes*. Scholastic, Inc., 1989.
The famous Hans Christian Anderson tale about a vain emperor's invisible clothing gets an updated twist in this humorous tale. Although this story tells very little about the job of a principal, the children will delight to see the principal parading in his underwear.

(K-3) Daniel, Kira. *What's It Like to Be a . . . Teacher.* Troll Associates, 1989.
Describes the many educational, supportive, and fun things one teacher does with and for the students in his class.

(K-3) Gibbons, Gail. *Check It Out! The Book About Libraries.* Harcourt Brace and Jovanovich, 1985.
Discusses what is found in libraries and how different libraries serve the community. Excellent. This book also comes with a 7-minute cassette from the Listening Library.

(K-3) Greene, Carol. *I Can Be a Librarian.* Childrens Press, 1988.
Describes the work of librarians, the many different kinds of libraries they work in, and how to become a librarian. A good information book.

Outside

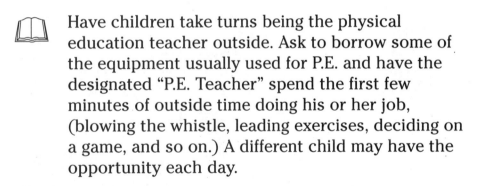 Have children take turns being the physical education teacher outside. Ask to borrow some of the equipment usually used for P.E. and have the designated "P.E. Teacher" spend the first few minutes of outside time doing his or her job, (blowing the whistle, leading exercises, deciding on a game, and so on.) A different child may have the opportunity each day.

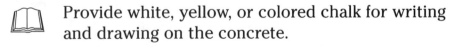 Provide white, yellow, or colored chalk for writing and drawing on the concrete.

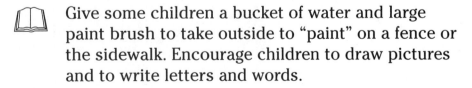 Give some children a bucket of water and large paint brush to take outside to "paint" on a fence or the sidewalk. Encourage children to draw pictures and to write letters and words.

Field Study

 Read to the class *The Day Jimmy's Boa Ate the Wash* by Trinka Hakes Noble—the story of a class field trip to the farm that is wrecked by Jimmy's boa constrictor. Invite children to make a list of field trips they think they would like to take. Make a "Yes or No" graph with each child using a clothespin to answer the question, "Would you like to have been on the field trip with Jimmy's class and his boa constrictor?" Follow this story by teaching the class the silly song, "I'm Being Swallowed by a Boa Constrictor!" or by sharing the poem "Boa Constrictor" from Shel Silverstein's *Where the Sidewalk Ends* (Harper and Row, 1974).

Take some mini-field trips. Arrange for the class to go to the school library. The media specialist may talk about what he or she does and read a story to the class. Or you might go to the principal/director's office, guidance counselor's office, to visit the custodian's closet, to the clinic to visit the nurse, or to the lunchroom to tour the school's kitchen. If you are a church school, be sure to visit the sanctuary/minister's office and let him or her talk about the job. Pre-arrange for each visitor to give children a little "souvenir," such as a band-aide from the nurse, a pencil from the secretary, a smiley sticker from the guidance counselor, a cookie from the cafeteria staff, a bookmark from the media specialist, or something to help children remember the trip.

After each mini-trip to visit a school worker, have children come back and draw pictures of the worker and use temporary, invented spelling and their own letters to write about their pictures. Or write a class language experience story. Give the pictures or story to the person as a way to say thank you. They will delight in the children's pictures and words.

Have an in-the-room field study by planning a scavenger hunt. Divide children into smaller groups and give them a prepared picture-list of things in the room, such as a pencil, crayon, piece of blue paper, ruler, and so on. The first group to find all their items gets to serve the others a special snack.

Watch the 30-minute video *Barney Goes to School* (recommended for ages 2-8) from The Lyons Group:

Barney Home Videos (300 E. Bethany Rd., P.O. Box 8000, Allen, Texas 75002-1306). The video includes instruction in the basic skills—numbers, letters, colors and shapes—and helps explain why children love to go to school. Children may compare the classroom in the video with their own. Make two lists—things that are alike and things that are different.

Parent Involvement

 Parents really are the key to a successful school program. Parents are a child's first teachers and while teachers come and go, parents stay forever. No matter how much we influence a child in the year they are with us, it is a small amount of time when compared to a parent's influence. Not all parents are available or feel comfortable coming into the school but all parents believe they are sending you their most treasured possession. We, as educators, have a responsibility to continue to communicate with parents on a regular basis throughout the year, even when we hear no response from them. Often the communication is making a difference that we can't even see. The poem that follows in the Parent Connection by an unknown writer shares with parents the view that we are all in this together, each making a contribution to the life and growth of their child.

Dear Parents,

I believe that children do their best when the home and the school work together. This lovely poem expresses some of my own feelings about what can be accomplished when we accept the education of your children as a joint venture.

Unity

I dreamed I stood in a studio
And watched two sculptors there.
The clay they used was a young child's mind
And they fashioned it with care.

One was a teacher—the tools he used
Were music, books, and art.
The other, a parent, worked with a guiding hand,
And a gentle, loving heart.

Day after day, the teacher toiled with touch
That was careful, deft and sure.
While the parent labored by his side
And polished and smoothed it o'er.

And when at last, their task was done,
They were proud of what they had wrought.
For the things they had molded into the child
Could neither be sold nor bought.

And each agreed they would have failed
If each had worked alone.
For behind the parent stood the school
And behind the teacher, the home.

—Author Unknown

The Community

There are many commercial materials included in this chapter, which speaks to its popularity among early childhood educators. However, feel free to use what you have on hand. Imagination is a powerful tool!

Getting Started

 Start by learning about parents' employment. Ask each of the children what their parents do. Most children will at least know their parents' job titles. When you are faced with, "My mom doesn't work. She just stays home and takes care of my little brother," discuss what kind of work mom does at home, paid versus unpaid work, and ask children if they think being a homemaker is a job! You may also have a child whose parent is unemployed. Take that opportunity to read *Matthew and His Dad* by A. Alda, which is about unemployment.

After the discussion, have each child draw a picture of the kind of work their dad or mom does (this can be inside or outside the home). After they have drawn their pictures, have children describe them to you and write a few sentences about the kind of work their parents do. Many parents will be surprised at what their children think they do! Read *Mommies at Work and Daddies at Work* by Eve Merriam or other books that talk about work

parents do. Bind the drawings to make class book entitled "Mommies at Work and Daddies at Work."

Gather the children in a circle and ask what they would like to know about their parents' jobs. Some of the children may have visited their parents' workplaces and may want to tell the group about it. Generate a list of questions that children would like to ask their parents. From their questions, create an interesting questionnaire to send home to each parent (see page 308). Discuss the questionnaires with children before you send them home so children will be familiar with all the questions. Allow each child to ask another specific question which you can write on the back of the home interview.

Parent Survey

To begin our study of the community, we will be talking about jobs that our parents do. Please spend a few minutes with your child talking about the questions on the survey. We would appreciate it if you would take the time to write the answers so that we may use them in class. Thank you!

My child's name is _____

My name is _____

My job is _____

I work at _____

Some "tools" that I use in my job are _____
_____

Some things I do each day at my job are _____
_____

This is how I get to work each morning _____
_____

For lunch I usually _____
_____

Something interesting about my work is _____

Unfortunately, we do not have time for every parent to come in. If you think children would enjoy hearing about your job and you would like to come in and talk about it, please check. _____ yes

I think my job site would be a fun place for little children to come for a field trip and I would be willing to set one up for the class. _____ yes

© 1996 Fearon Teacher Aids

Parent Survey

To begin our study of the community, we will be talking about jobs that our parents do. Please spend a few minutes with your child talking about the questions on the survey. We would appreciate it if you would take the time to write the answers so that we may use them in class. Thank you!

My child's name is _____

My name is _____

My job is _____

I work at _____

Some "tools" that I use in my job are _____

_____

Some things I do each day at my job are _____

_____

This is how I get to work each morning _____

_____

For lunch I usually _____

_____

Something interesting about my work is _____

_____

Unfortunately, we do not have time for every parent to come in. If you think children would enjoy hearing about your job and you would like to come in and talk about it, please check. _____ yes

I think my job site would be a fun place for little children to come for a field trip and I would be willing to set one up for the class. _____ yes

After the interview questionnaires come back, children may generate lists of questions, such as how do parents get to work, what kind of tools do parents use at work, where do parents eat lunch, and so on. Many of the answers can be graphed.

Arrange to have some of your parents come in for interviews. Select parents whose jobs can be easily described and who will feel comfortable with the interview. Encourage them to bring tools of their trade so that the interview will be "hands-on" and ask that they keep their presentations short. Children may make up a list of questions before-hand that they would like to ask the parent—remind children of their questions right before the parent comes in. Before the first interview, children may practice by interviewing you about your job. After each parent interview, invite children to draw or write some of the things they learned about that job.

Find out which parents would like to have the class make a site visit to their workplace. Encourage parents to think about what would be interesting to young children and to show them things that offers hands-on experiences. Have children draw pictures or write about the things they remember seeing on the field trip. The pictures can be bound together and sent as a thank you.

 Introduce children to the words *career* and *occupation*. Discuss what they think these words mean. Help them make a list of all the different kinds of jobs they can think of. Write the list on chart paper. This will give you an idea of what foundation children have. Add to the list through-out the week.

 Put up pictures around the room and on the bulletin board showing different occupations (commercially available bulletin board aids from Frank Schaffer: Bulletin Board Set "Careers" FS-9470, 20 pictures with occupation names, or "Career Pictures" MTC-1004, a set of full-color language cards, or Carson-Dellosa's "Community Helpers" CD-1708, 12 16" characters and a 6-page resource guide). A novel way to present different occupations is to buy the Barney and Baby Bop Coloring Book, "When I Grow Up" (Western Publishing Co.) which depicts Barney and Baby Bop dressed for many different occupations. The pictures can be colored, mounted, and laminated to put around the room or on a bulletin board.

 If your school is in an area surrounded by buildings, take a walk around the neighborhood. Be sure to note any workers you see and what they are doing. When you come back, write down the children's observations of who and what they saw. Encourage childrens to draw pictures of the things they saw and use their own temporary, invented spelling to label their pictures.

 Consider a "Job Board" for jobs outside the class-room. Put hats on hooks with a child's name beside each hat, such as a mail carrier's hat to deliver attendance to the office or to take messages to other teachers, a chef's hat to take money to the cafeteria, and a nurse's hat to escort sick children to the clinic.

 Assign work jobs in the classroom to show children that a community is much like the classroom, with different people doing different jobs to make everything work. Include jobs such as the following.

Watering the plants (a spray bottle will keep children from over-watering)
Feeding the fish
Setting table for snacks
Line leader
Door holder
Calendar helper (put the number on the calendar each day)

Add other jobs appropriate for your class. Put an envelope or library card pocket by each job and put the appropriate child's name in each envelope or pocket on a daily or weekly basis. Or have each child provide a handprint (printed with paint or traced and cut from construction paper). Children put their names on the hands and use them to identify their jobs. For younger children, use photographs, (school pictures, photocopies of school picture, snapshots), in addition to the names.

Creative Play

 Put an assortment of hats on a hat rack in a corner of the room. Ask for donations from friends and

parents. Collect hats everywhere you go. Hats can be ordered commercially, of course, from companies such as Lakeshore Learning Materials (Career Hat Box LC491, 8 kid-sized hats), but you'll get just as good an assortment on your own. Halloween sales provide a variety of choices. Yard sales, rummage sales, and thrift shops are great sources for hats. A good sturdy child-proof mirror adds greatly to this area.

Community-helper uniforms can also be purchased (Costume Sets LC858X, 7 uniforms, from Lakeshore Learning Materials or individual uniforms from Constructive Playthings) but children will be encouraged to use their own creativity if you simply provide an assortment of shirts, pocket-books, shawls, and what-have-you.

Home Living

This is a good time to talk about jobs that moms and dads do at home, whether they work outside the home or not, such as wash clothes and dishes, mop, vacuum, change bed sheets, cook, take care of children, sweep, mow the grass, fix things, and all the rest. Make a list of all the jobs children can think of that parents do at home.

Take snapshots of children in the home living area doing some of the jobs their moms and dads do. Post the pictures around the area with the action word underneath or bind the pictures into a big book for the class.

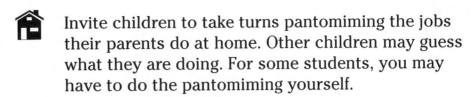

Invite children to take turns pantomiming the jobs their parents do at home. Other children may guess what they are doing. For some students, you may have to do the pantomiming yourself.

Make materials and props available for role-playing, such as dishes, drying rack, dishcloth, dish towel, fake food, broom, dustpan, cot, sheets/blanket, baby dolls, diapers, clothes, telephone, paper, pencil, ironing board, tools, books, newspaper, mailbox, and a first aid kit.

Circle Time

Start circle time by coming to group wearing a special career hat. Pretend nothing is out of the ordinary. Children will quickly notice the hat. When they ask about it, pretend you have no idea what they are talking about until finally they "coax" you into telling them about the hat. Or have children guess how the hat might have gotten in the classroom and what type work the person normally wearing such a hat might do.

Another way to start circle time each day is to put a career hat in a "Surprise Box." Cover a cardboard box with colorful self-adhesive paper. You will need a box with a lid that comes off easily. (There are hat boxes available for purchase also.) Give the children clues and have them guess what is inside. Or have them play "Twenty Questions" by asking any question you can answer with a "yes" or "no." When children make the correct guess, take out the hat and invite children to take turns telling you

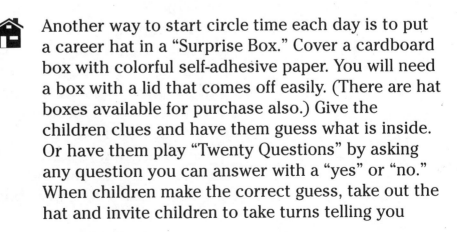

something they think the person who wears that hat might do on the job.

 Put on a career hat and pantomime what that person would be doing on the job. For example, put on a police officer's hat and pretend to direct traffic. Have children guess who you are and what you are doing. More mature children can take turns wearing the hats and pantomiming themselves.

 Collect language pictures cut from magazines of different workers to use as flashcards (or the following available from Trend Enterprises: "Community Helpers Fun to Know" T-1654, 26 picture cards with facts about each occupation on the back). Have children divide the cards into people that work inside or outside, people that wear uniforms or don't, or any other way children can think to sort the cards.

 If you have a "story mitt," consider ordering the "Helpers/911" characters to tell a story about emergencies from Constructive Playthings, WZ-107.

 Have a "Hat Day." Invite each child to bring a hat from home to wear for the day (have extras for those who forget). A variation on this activity could be to make hats in class (patterns in art sections of each thematic unit of this book). Have a parade around the room and through the halls with children wearing the hats they brought. During circle time, have each child stand and let the other children decide if the hat would be worn for a particular job and what that job might be (some hats will be just for fun and may not suggest a job). Read some of the following books about hats.

Hats, Hats, Hats by Ann Morris
Caps for Sale by Esphyr Slobodkina
Jennie's Hat by Ezra Jack Keats
Martin's Hats by Joan W. Blos
Barney's Hats by Mary Ann Dudko and Margie Larsen
The 500 Hats of Bartholomew Cubbins by Dr. Seuss
A Three Hat Day by Laura Geringer

Rhythm Time

 Adapt these original verses to the traditional tune "Here We Go 'Round the Mulberry Bush."

The firefighter puts out fires,
Puts out fires, puts out fires.
The firefighter puts out fires when he goes to work.
   (Pretend to put out fires)

Try these other verses.

Police officer directs the traffic . . .
   (Pretend to direct traffic)
The mail carrier delivers the mail . . .
   (Pretend to deliver mail)
The bus driver drives the bus . . .
   (Pretend to drive)
The baker bakes the cookies and bread . . .
   (Pretend to knead bread)
The teacher reads books to kids . . .
   (Pretend to read)

Encourage children to make up other verses to the same tune. Write the verses on chart paper. Draw simple pictures over key words to help children "read" the words. Be sure to point to each word as you read the chart with the children.

Invite volunteers to illustrate favorite verses with crayons, markers, or tempera paint. Write the words to each verse under the pictures and display on a bulletin board. Later bind the pictures into a

class big book. Show or point to the page as you sing each verse.

Help children memorize the nursery rhyme "Rub-a-dub-dub." A tune can be found on page 26 of *Wee Sing Nursery Rhymes and Lullabies.*

> *Rub-a-dub-dub three men in a tub,*
> *And who do they think they be?*
> *The butcher, the baker, the candlestick maker*
> *And all of them gone to sea.*

Discuss with the class what kind of work each of these community helpers does. For example, the butcher cuts meat, the baker bakes breads and goodies, the candlestick maker makes candles. Have children "change up" the rhyme by using other workers: ". . . the policeman, the grocer, the mail carrier, all of them workers, all three."

Have children keep a steady beat by clapping their hands on their knees. Say the following rhyme to their beat:

> *This is what the firefighters do*
> *The firefighters do, the firefighters do.*
> *This is what the firefighters do.*
> *They fight the fires.*

Try some of these other verses:

> *This is what the butchers do . . .*
> *They cut the meat.*

> *This is what the teachers do . . .*
> *They teach the kids.*

> *This is what the doctors do . . .*
> *They make us well.*

> *This is what the nurses do . . .*
> *They give the shots.*

> *This is what the dentists do . . .*
> *They fix our teeth.*

This is what the mail carriers do . . .
They deliver the mail.

This is what the bakers do . . .
They bake the sweets.

Children may make up other verses as well. Write each of the verses on chart paper. Point to the words as you say each verse.

Invite volunteers to illustrate each of the verses on white paper. Glue the pictures on a larger sheet of paper and write the words to each verse under the picture. Place the pictures first on a bulletin board. Give the children a pointer so they can go over and "read" the bulletin board by pointing to each word. Once children have enjoyed the pictures on the bulletin board, take them down and bind the pages together into a big book for the book center.

Puppet Center

 This is a great time to put out your puppet stage. You can make a puppet stage by using a large refrigerator box or by simply turning a table or rocking boat on its side. Career Puppets can be ordered commercially to use with this unit (Learning Resources: Set 1 LER511: fireman, doctor, chef, business man, farmer; and Set 2 LER512: nurse, business woman, construction worker, police officer; or a set of six machine-washable puppets available from Lakeshore Learning Materials: Career Puppets AF807).

 Have each child make a career puppet using the basic patterns on the following page—a rectangle for the body and accordion-folded arms and legs. Children may choose appropriate construction paper colors and add details to help distinguish particular occupations. Staple or hot glue a tongue depressor handle and encourage children to make up little skits with their puppets. This is a good final review project when children have studied each community helper.

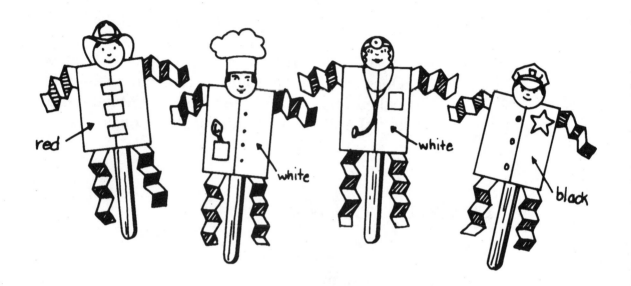

 Purchase or make one of the life-size cardboard puppet sets ("What Am I?" Careers CD-644 from Carson-Dellosa, 12 characters). Children place their heads through a pattern that has the community helper's head and body. Or consider the patterns available from Teacher Created Materials, "Grocery Bag Art: Careers." This teacher resource provides patterns for turning simple grocery bags into costumes and masks.

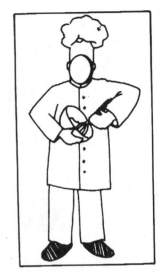

Invite children to act out poems, songs, or fingerplays while playing the parts of the different community workers.

Take each child's picture in the puppet costume of his or her choice and use the pictures to make a class big book. Glue each photograph on a page with the sentence: (Child's name) wants to be a (career choice). For example, Ari wants to be a firefighter. Bind them all together and put the title "When We Grow Up" by (teacher's name's) class on the cover. Children will learn to "read" this book in no time.

Cognitive Activities

 Make your own lotto game using community helper stickers or buy a commercially available career lotto game, ("Community Helpers Lotto" T-1533 by Trend Enterprises, 2-8 players).

 Career stickers can also be used to make a concentration game. Put two of the same stickers on individual pieces of tagboard or index cards. Laminate for durability. Place all the cards face down. Each child in turn flips over two (or three) cards. If there is a match, the child keeps the matching pair and gets another turn. If there is no match, the child turns the cards back over and the turn ends. The child with the most matches wins.

 The same career stickers can be used to make a domino-type game. Cut rectangular pieces of tagboard and put a career sticker on each end. Match "like" career pictures and play like traditional dominoes.

 Career stickers can be used to graph students' favorite occupations. Place the stickers across the bottom of a posterboard and draw lines to separate the columns. Have each child place their name or their school picture (which can be photocopied for numerous projects) in the career column of their choice.

Lisa			
Chris		Megan	Brent

Commercially-purchased career cards or self-made photocopied ones can also be used to match the career to a tool used on that job, such as a mail carrier to an envelope.

Manipulative Center

 Put out career figures and vehicles, such as Duplo Family Workers 244830, 18 figures, 8 family members and 10 community helpers, or Duplo Community Vehicles 281527, 25 pieces, 8 community vehicles, 8 figures, 3 commodity bricks, or from Lakeshore Learning Materials, Community Action Figures BE3126, 31 figures. If specific career figures and vehicles are not available, simply make available a variety of vehicles and figures—children will pretend they are who and what they need.

 Put out career-oriented puzzles, such as "City Floor Puzzle" FS-3717, 2' x 3' (60 cm x 90 cm) floor puzzle from Frank Schaffer, which includes building workers and vehicles for the hospital, fire station, post office, grocery store, and library); "Community

Workers" CD-9806, 2' x 3' (60 cm x 90 cm) floor puzzle from Carson-Dellosa which includes 12 workers with a work mat.

 Make available Judy/Instructo puzzle J106021, "Rub-a-dub-dub," 9 pieces, and any individual career puzzles you might have.

Blocks

 Small toy cars, vans, and buses make great additions to the block area during this unit. Look also for miniature road signs (or make your own with craft sticks or straws, a wad of self-hardening clay for a base and homemade signs or signs cut from a driver's manual). These added pieces will encourage the children to build roads, tunnels, and bridges.

 Look for community vehicles, such as a fire truck, police car, ambulance, or mail truck, to add to your blocks. Or encourage children to use their imagination. You may also make traditional trucks and cars into community vehicles. Put down a community road map (Drive Around Town Carpet LC1607, a washable carpet from Lakeshore Learning Materials, or Motor Map HOY-1 or Super Roadway Play Mat PT-500, both from Constructive Playthings) which shows community buildings and streets for the vehicles to travel through. Even more fun is to have children help you make your own map on a large sheet of tagboard or oil cloth. Cut pieces of construction paper to represent roads and buildings or have children paint or draw buildings with permanent marker, cut them out, and glue them to appropriate places on the floor map. Laminate the tagboard. Sit with the students in the block center and help them create a variety of situations. For example, "Two children were playing over here in the park and one fell down and broke her leg. Get the ambulance from the hospital to go get her and take her to the emergency room."

 Add community workers, such as wooden stand-up characters (Community Career Figures GC-116, set of 12 hardwood wedgie figures from Constructive Playthings) or flexible rubber people (Playmobile Community Service People PLM-3126, 21 assorted community workers from Constructive Playthings) to the block area. If you can't find them commercially, make your own. Draw, trace, or photocopy community helpers from magazines. Color the workers, back with cardboard, cut out, and laminate. Place figures in a mound of self-hardening clay so they will stand or attach each to an empty cardboard tissue tube so it will stand (cut a 1.5" (3.75 cm) slice to form a ring and glue figure to front flush with base).

 Build a community in your block center. Lay out a large sheet of green tagboard (or several sheets taped together on the underside) as the base for

your community. Children may draw the fronts of their homes using construction paper of their choice, apartment buildings, houses, and community buildings (post office, school, library, grocery store, police station). Tape these pictures to different-sized blocks from your block center (or tape them to shoe boxes, gift boxes or empty cardboard tissue tubes). Add streets by cutting strips of black tagboard. Have children paint white dotted lines down the middle of the strips. Make railroad tracks by cutting strips of white tagboard and having children draw tracks with a black marker. Trees can be added by cutting green tree tops and gluing to craft sticks. Use a mound of self-hardening clay as a base for the trees. Traffic signs can be added in the same way. Add community vehicles and people to the scene.

Art Center

 Make a class collage of community helpers. Invite children to cut pictures from magazines and glue them to a large sheet of paper. Write the title of the helper under each picture. Hang the collage in the writing center to encourage children to write some of the names of the community helpers.

 Have children draw or paint pictures of what they would like to do when they grow up. Write the child's name and occupation on the picture and anything the child says about it. Frame with construction paper and display with the title "When I Grow Up . . ."

 Another way to use pictures children draw is to make a class big book. On the right-hand page, place the child's picture. On the left, complete the sentence: (Child's name) wants to be a (occupation) and (describe what he does). For example, Ryan wants to be a firefighter and fight fires.

Make hats for the various community helpers and props used on the job (see art sections of each unit within this book). If you have chosen an occupation that is not highlighted in this book, adapt what you see in this text. For example, to make a carpenter's hat, you might use the postal worker design and design a tool belt out of tagboard with a wrench, screwdriver, and hammer attached.

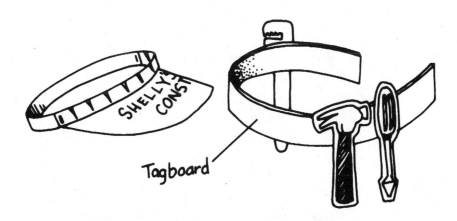

Tagboard

 Make the community helpers found in the puppet center (see page 317) and hang them from the ceiling instead of mounting them.

 Instead of traditional drawing and painting media, give each child a sheet of clear acetate used for overhead slides. Children may draw pictures of what they want to be using wipe-off markers. At the end of the unit, project each of the pictures on a screen and invite children to comment on their illustrations.

Flannelboard

 Use one of the commercial flannelboard sets ("When I Grow Up I Want to Be" IN171 from Judy/Instructo, or Constructive Playthings' 66 flannel pieces representing 36 occupations). Use the pieces during circle time the same way you do flashcards. Leave the pieces out for children to manipulate individually.

 You can make your own flannelboard characters with pylon (available in fabric shops). Find a picture and trace it onto the pylon (just as you would use tracing paper). Color the pylon with crayons, markers, or colored pencils. Place on the flannelboard and invite children to manipulate the pieces themselves. Use the pieces at circle time.

 Also available are "Career Character Dress-up Dolls" from Lakeshore Learning Materials. These are free-standing wooden "paper" dolls covered with felt. The kit comes with 29 felt career uniforms, LC1578.

Book Center

  Make an ABC Career Book with the class. Write the letters of the alphabet down the left side of a piece of chart paper and have children suggest an occupation for each letter. If you get stuck, use some of the following.

astronaut, athlete, ambulance driver, acrobat
baker, butcher, banker, barber
carpenter, cashier, custodian, coach
diver, doctor, dentist, dad, dancer
engineer, environmentalist
firefighter, farmer, factory worker
grocer, gymnast
helicopter pilot, host, hostess
ice skater, ice hockey player
janitor, jet pilot
kindergarten teacher
librarian, lifeguard, lawyer
mom, mail carrier, media specialist,
movie star, mechanic
nurse
official, ophthalmologist, office manager
pilot, principal, police officer, plumber, president
queen, quiz show host
receptionist, reporter, researcher
secretary, surgeon, sanitation engineer
teacher, truck driver, trainer
usher, umpire, urologist
Vice President, veterinarian
waiter, waitress
Xtra special _____, x-ray technician
yachtsman, yard man
zoo keeper, zoologist

Invite volunteers to draw pictures of one community worker each. Write the alphabet letter with dark marker on a sheet of white paper and have children add the illustrations. Display the pictures in order on a clothesline across your room or on a bulletin board. After children have enjoyed the display, make a title page for a big book. On the title page, invite children to draw small pictures of what they would like to be when they grow up. Cut around each picture and glue them, collage-style, on the title page. Bind the alphabet pictures together into a book for children to enjoy in the book center.

 Here are some books you may want in your book center. Check with your school or community library for other titles. Many of these are also appropriate for reading to the class at circle time.

(ps-K) Butterworth, Nick. *Busy People*. Candlewick Press, 1992.
Introduces people who work around town and the equipment they use with simple colorful drawings.

(ps-K) D'Andrea, Deborah Bennett. *If I Were a Firefighter, or a Doctor, or an Astronaut, or. . .* Picture Me Books, Inc., 1991.
Creative book with a die-cut in the center to place an individual child's picture so as the pages are turned, the child's face appears in each occupation. This is a good book to recommend to parents or you can have children make individual books. Jean Warren's 123 Books has patterns for children to make a book entitled "What Will I Be?"

(ps-K) McCue, Lisa (illustrator). *Corduroy's Busy Street.* Viking Penguin Inc., 1987.
Board book features Don Freeman's Corduroy as he goes through the neighborhood meeting different workers.

(ps-1) Blackner, Terence. *If I Could Work.* J.B. Lippincott, 1988.
A child fantasizes in rhyme about the different kinds of work he would do if he weren't so young. Bold, colorful illustrations.

(ps-1) Brown, Richard (illustrator). *100 Words About Working.* Gulliver Books, 1988.
100 different jobs illustrated with clear color drawings. Great reference book.

(ps-1) Hudson, Wade. *I'm Gonna Be*. Just Us Books, 1992.
The Afro-Bets Kids ponder what they would like to be when they grow up. Real-life African-American role models are presented along with a description of their occupations.

(ps-1) Lasker, Joe. *Mothers Can Do Anything*. A. Whitman, 1972.
Text and illustrations demonstrate many occupations of mothers.

(ps-2) Florian, Douglas. *People Working*. Thomas Y. Crowell, 1983.
Simple pictures and one-line text describes where people work and how they work.

(ps-2) Merriam, Eve. *Daddies at Work*. Simon and Schuster Books for Young Readers, 1991.
Portrays daddies in different jobs.

(ps-2) Merriam, Eve. *Mommies at Work*. Simon and Schuster Books for Young Readers, 1991.
Examines many different jobs performed by working mothers.

(ps-2) Scarry, Richard. *Richard Scarry's Busiest People Ever*. Random House Books for Young Readers, 1976.
Highly detailed panoramic views of Busytown. Explores jobs people have and what they do to keep things running smoothly.

(ps-2) Scarry, Richard. *Richard Scarry's Postman Pig and His Busy Neighbors*. Random House, 1978.
Reviews different workers in the neighborhood as Postman Pig makes his daily deliveries in detailed Richard Scarry-style pictures..

(ps-2) Wandro, Mark. *My Daddy Is a Nurse*. Addison-Wesley, 1981.
Describes the work of men with 10 occupations traditionally identified with women.

(ps-3) Grossman, Patricia. *The Night Ones*. Harcourt Brace Jovanavich, 1991.
The night bus carries people who work at night to their jobs in offices buildings, a bakery, a hotel, an airport, a dockyard. The morning bus takes them home again.

(ps-3) Komaiko, Leah. *My Perfect Neighborhood*. HarperCollins Children's Books, 1990.
A little girl takes a walk in her urban neighborhood and delights in its quirky personality. Shows workers in the community.

(K-2) Arnold, Caroline. *Who Works Here?* Franklin Watts, 1982.
Text and photographs describe how diverse jobs add to the vitality of a community.

(K-2) Berson, Harold. *The Boy, the Baker, the Miller and More*. Crown Publishers, 1974.
Circle story based on a French folktale. In return for a piece of bread he requests from the baker's wife, a little boy is sent on an errand that goes on and on.

(K-2) Miller, Margaret. *Who Uses This?* Greenwillow, 1990.
Colorful photographs of tools of various trades are preceded by the question, "Who uses this?" Double-page spreads show both professionals and children using the tools.

(K-2) Moncure, Jane. *Jobs People Do*. Childrens Press, 1972.
Introduction to various occupations done walking, talking, and standing; indoors and out; day and night.

(K-2) Perham, Molly. *People at Work*. Dillon Press, 1986.
Text and photographs describe various jobs performed by people around the world, including nursing, fishing, sheep farming, film-making, and fire fighting.

((K-2) Rice, Melanie. *All About Things People Do*. Doubleday, 1990.
Colorful big book describing workers by categories, such as sports, at the theater, in the hospital, at the restaurant. A good "information" book.

(K-2) Rockwell, Anne. *When We Grow Up*. Dutton, 1981.
Children demonstrating jobs they want when they grow up.

(K-2) Sesame Street. *People in Your Neighborhood*. Western Publishing Company, 1976.
A variety of occupations using riddles to heighten interest.

(K-2) *Sesame Street. Trucks in Your Neighborhood.* Random House/ Children's Television Workshop, 1988.
Book has actual wheels and shows seven trucks representing different occupations.

(K-2) Van Laan, Nancy. *People, People Everywhere!* Knopf, 1992.
Lively rhyming text and colorful illustrations depict a busy city and the people who live and work there.

(K-3) Civardi, Anne. *Things People Do.* Usborne Publishing Ltd., 1985.
A good "information" book. Colorful cartoon characters with much detail show the work of several different types of workers in a community on the island of Banilla.

(K-3) Mitchell, Joyce Slayton. *My Mommy Makes Money.* Little Brown and Co., 1984.
Introduces moms doing various jobs such as architect, artist, salesperson.

(K-4) Ancona, George. *And What Do You Do? A Book About People and Their Jobs.* E. P. Dutton and Co. Inc., 1976.
Good "information" book. Black and white photographs illustrate the work of 21 people involved in careers that do not require a college degree.

Videos

 Videos are a wonderful way to present material to children. Try one of the following. Play the video many times during the unit. Children will learn the songs and enjoy it over and over.

Richard Scarry's Best Busy People Video Ever, Random House Home Video, 1993.
Characters in the Busytown Playground answer the question "What do you want to be when you grow up?" Investigates jobs such as teacher, firefighter, farmer, truck driver.

What I Want to Be. Kidsongs View-Master Video, Warner Brothers Records Inc., 1987.
25-minute music video about different occupations.

Barney Goes to School. 30-minute video that includes many different aspects of school life but one especially good segment on "What I Want to Be."

Parent Involvement

 Consider the letter on page 333 to let parents know what you will be studying and how they can help at home.

Dear Parents,

We are studying about the people that work in our community. Please talk with your child about the kind of work that you do. Show him or her some of your "tools" and talk about the kind of things that you do in a typical day. If possible, take your child to your workplace. Each of the children will have a chance to draw and tell about the kind of work that their parents do, whether it is at home or at a particular place of business. I hope this will be the foundation of your child's understanding that we all contribute to the welfare of the community.

Keep on workin'!

Baker's Dough

2 cups flour
1/2 cup salt
3/4 cup water
food coloring

Mix all ingredients and knead until smooth. This dough will harden in 2–3 days or sooner in a warm oven.

Homemade Play Dough

2 cups flour
1 cup salt
2 cups water
2 Tbsp. vegetable oil
4 tsp. cream of tartar
food coloring

Mix all ingredients. Cook over medium heat. Play dough is done when it pulls easily away from the sides of the pot.

Homemade Fingerpaint

2 cups cold water
1 cup dry starch
3 cups soap flakes
food coloring/paste

Pour water, food coloring, and starch into bowl. Add soap flakes. Beat until fluffy with an egg beater, electric mixer, or food processor.

School supplies and manipulatives mentioned throughout *When I Grow Up . . .* may be ordered through your local retail school-supply dealer, who may be able to suggest other relevant products as well. The following list of specialty manufacturers may also be useful.

Focus Video Productions, Inc.
138 Main St.
Montpelier, VT 05602

Kid Vision
A & V Vision
75 Rockefeller Plaza
New York, NY 10019

The Little Tikes Company
2180 Barlow Road
P.O. Box 2277
Hudson, OH 44236-0877

Magnetic Way
Division of Creative Edge, Inc.
2495 N. Forest Rd.
Amherst, NY 14069

Oriental Trading Company, Inc.
P.O. Box 3407
Omaha, NE 68103-0407

Shapes Etc.
8840 Route 36
P.O. Box 400
Dansville, NY 14437